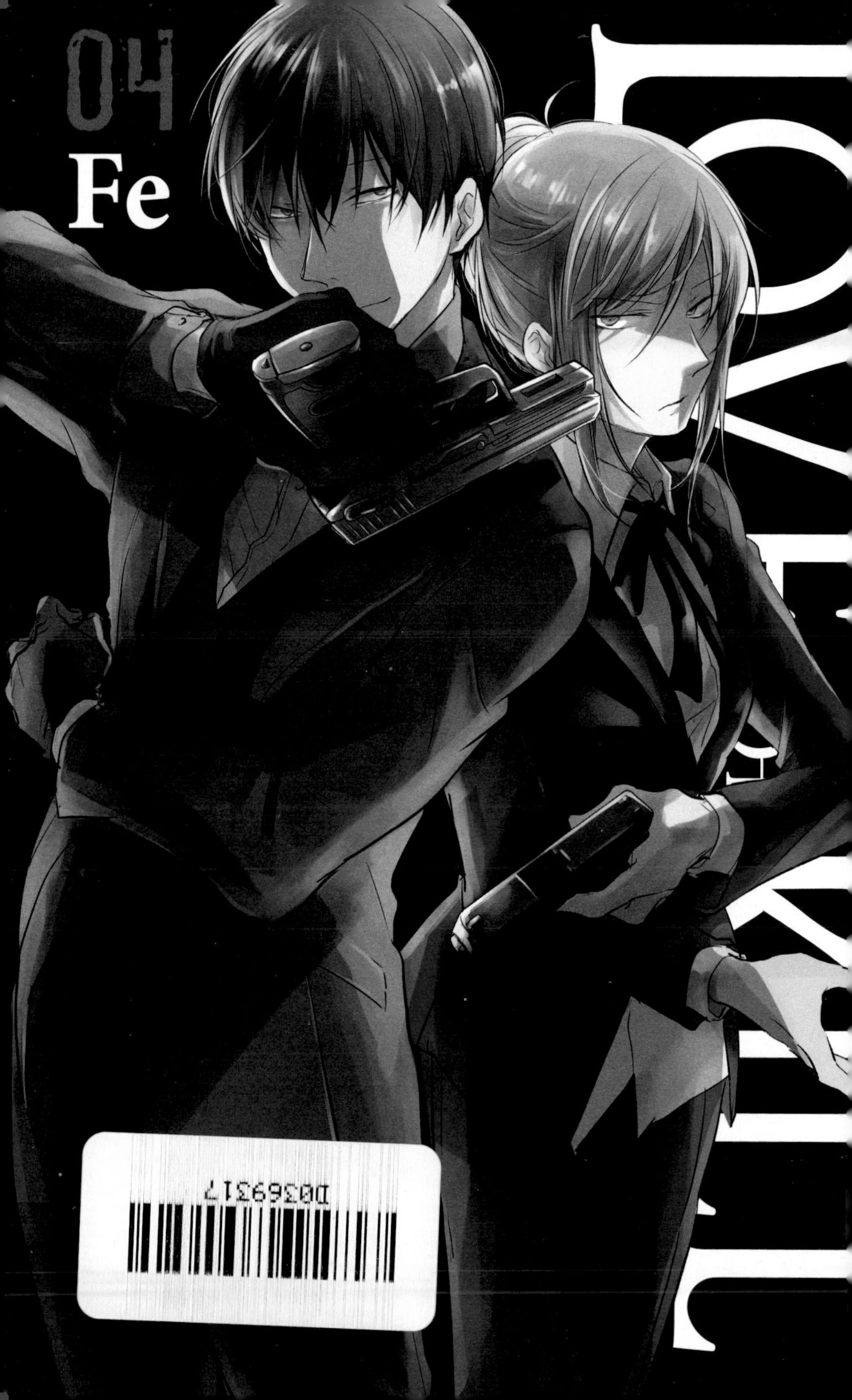
04
Fe

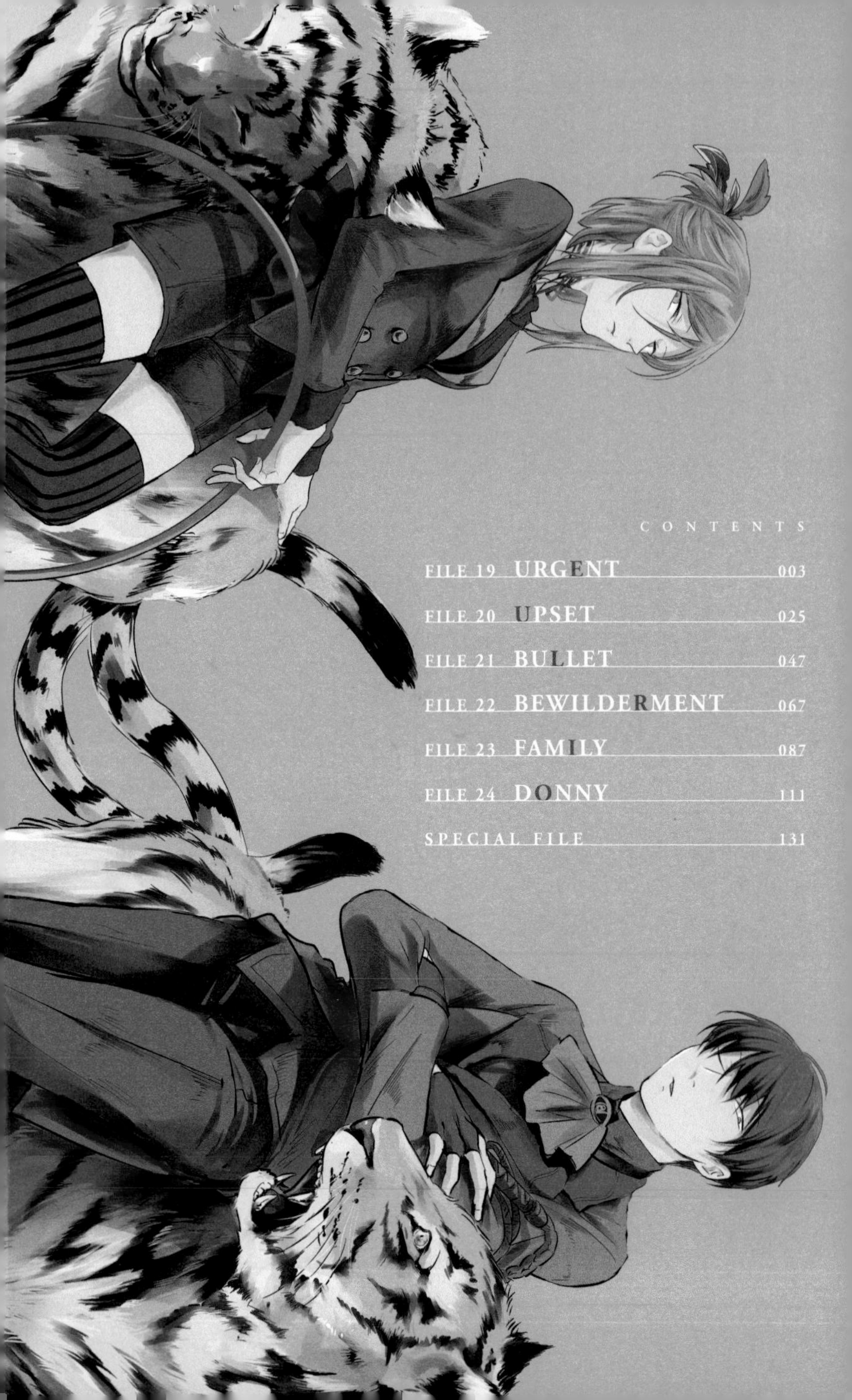

CONTENTS

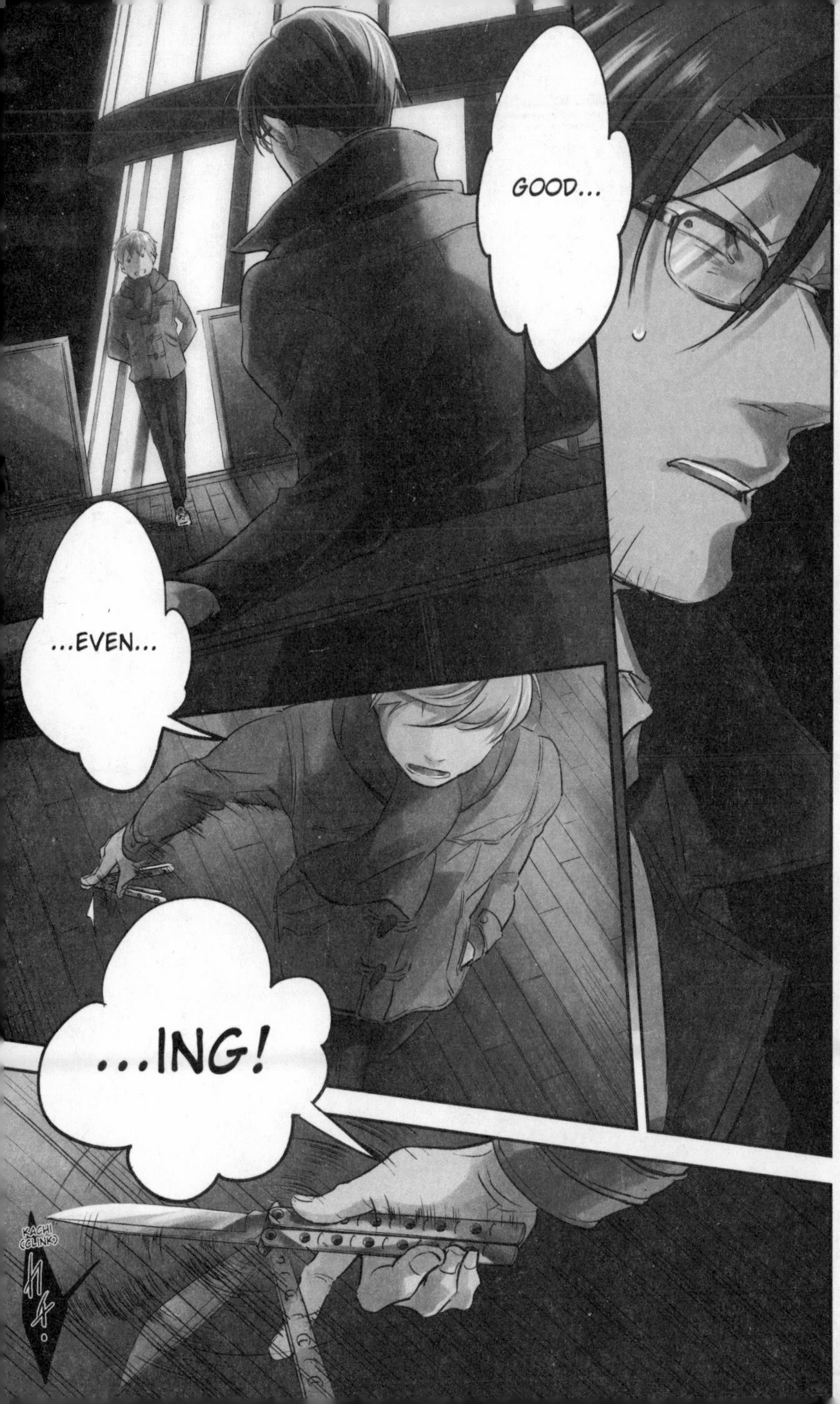
GOOD...
...EVEN...
...ING!
KACHI (CLINK)

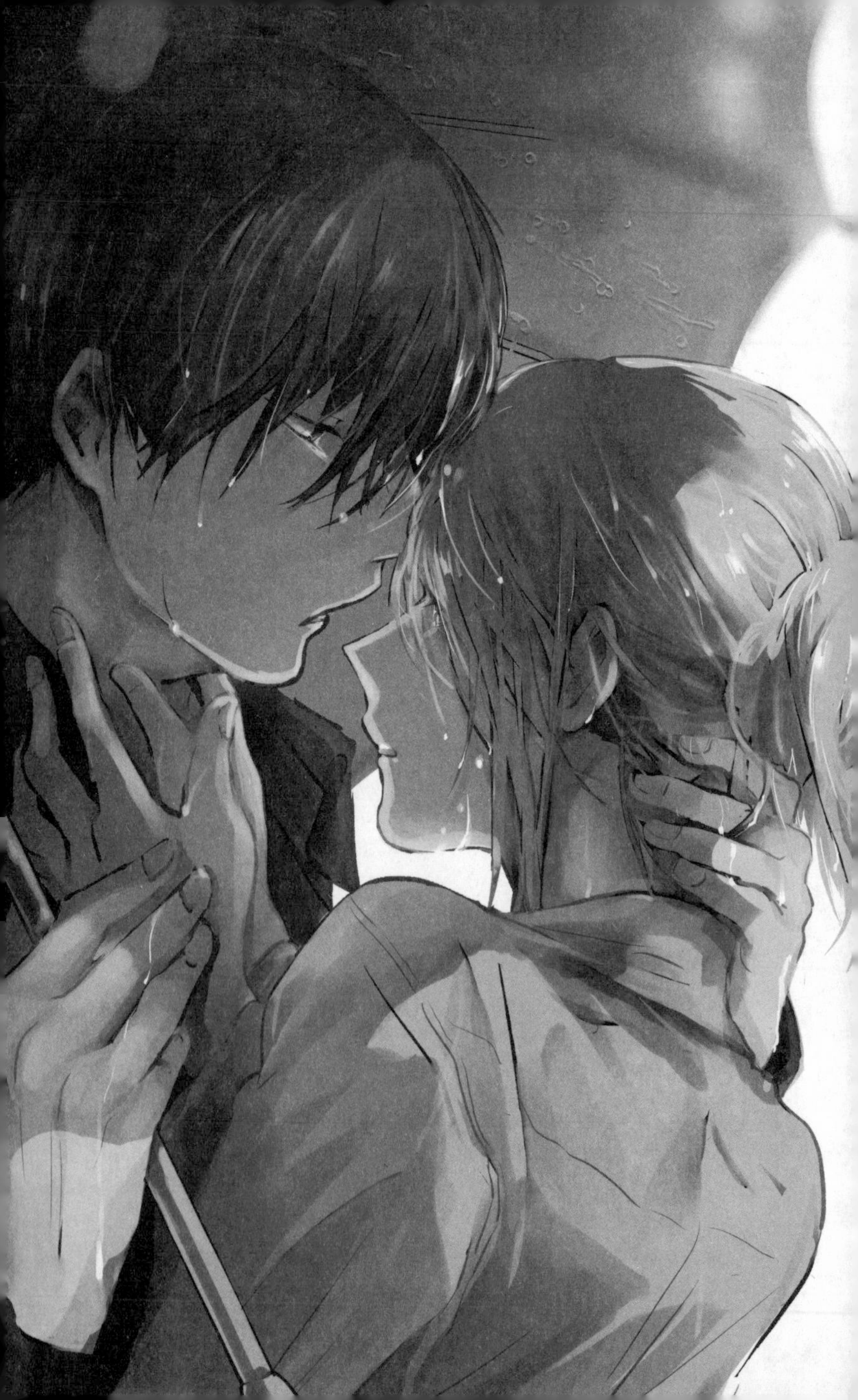

FILE 19 URGENT

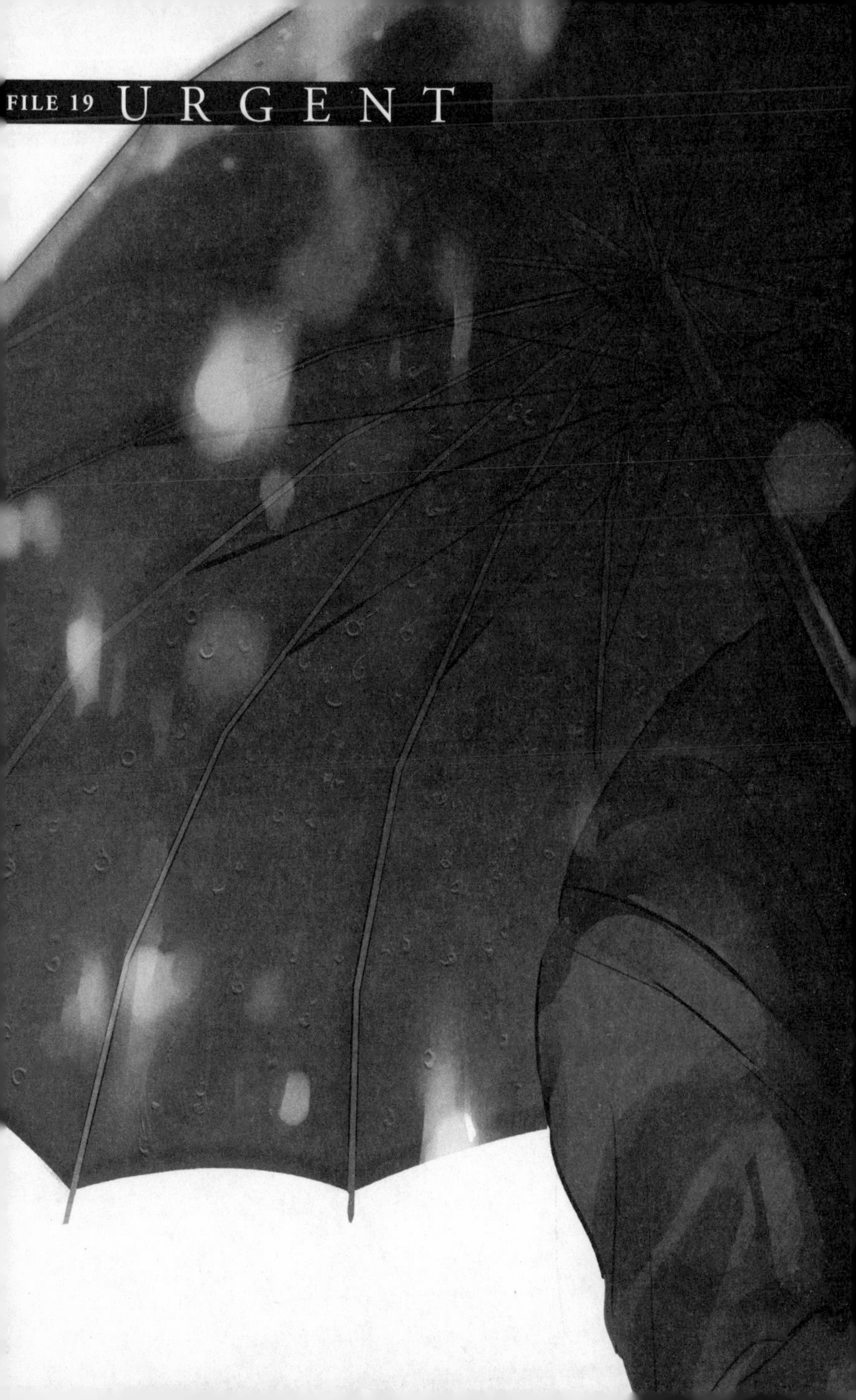

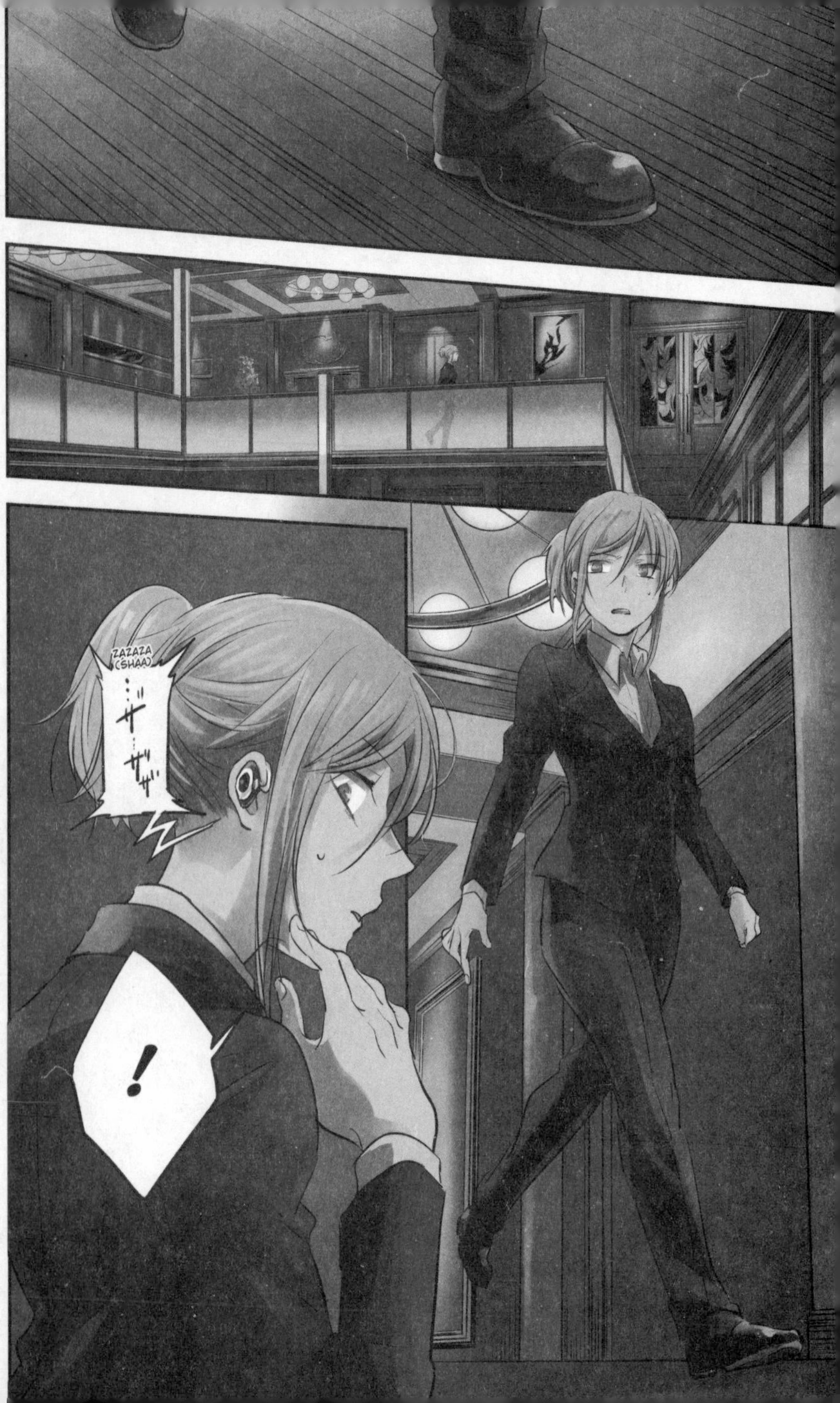
ZAZAZA (SHAA)
…ザ…ザザ
!

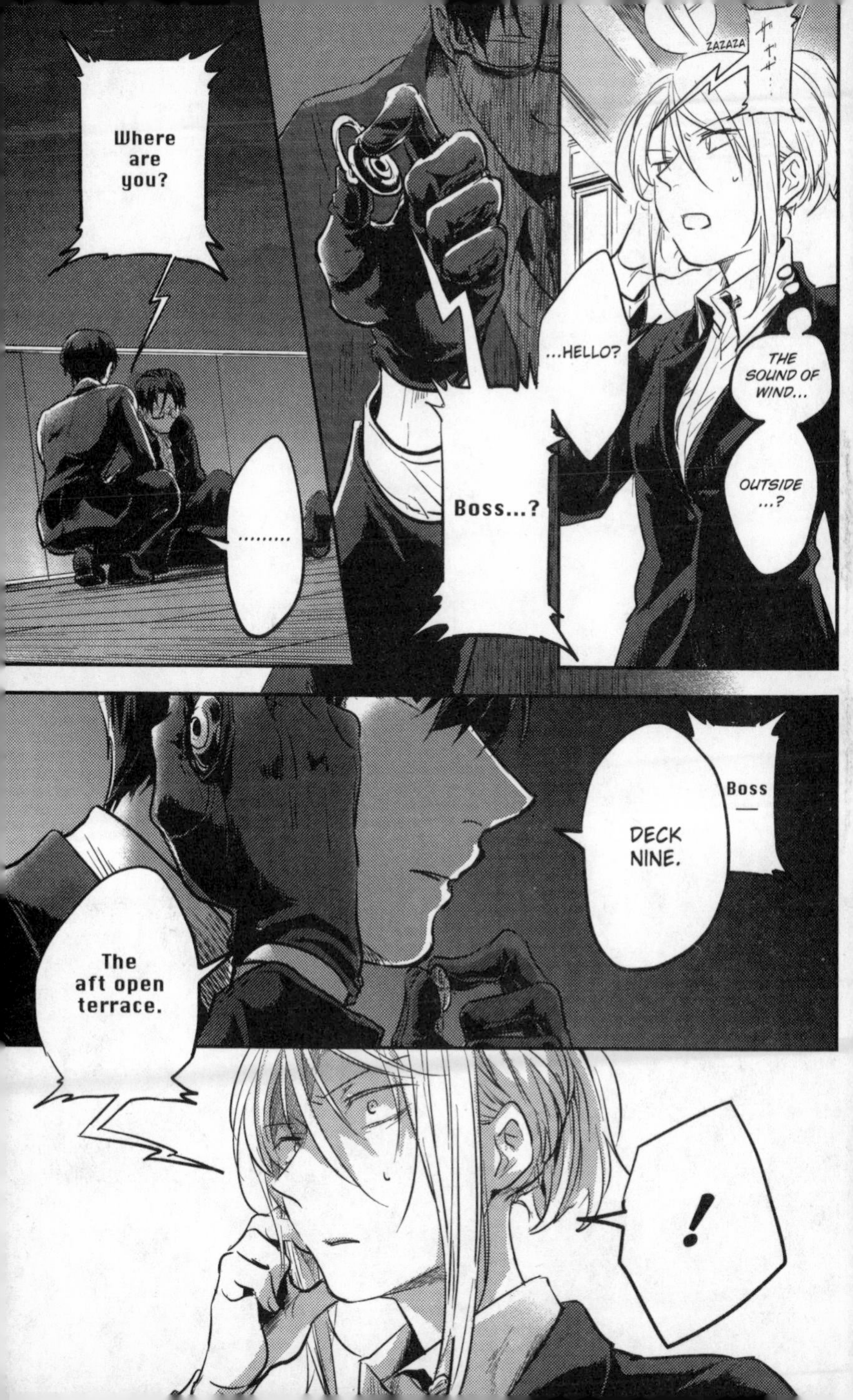
ZAZAZA
ザザザ…
...HELLO?
THE SOUND OF WIND...
OUTSIDE ...?
Boss...?
Where are you?
....
Boss —
DECK NINE.
The aft open terrace.
!

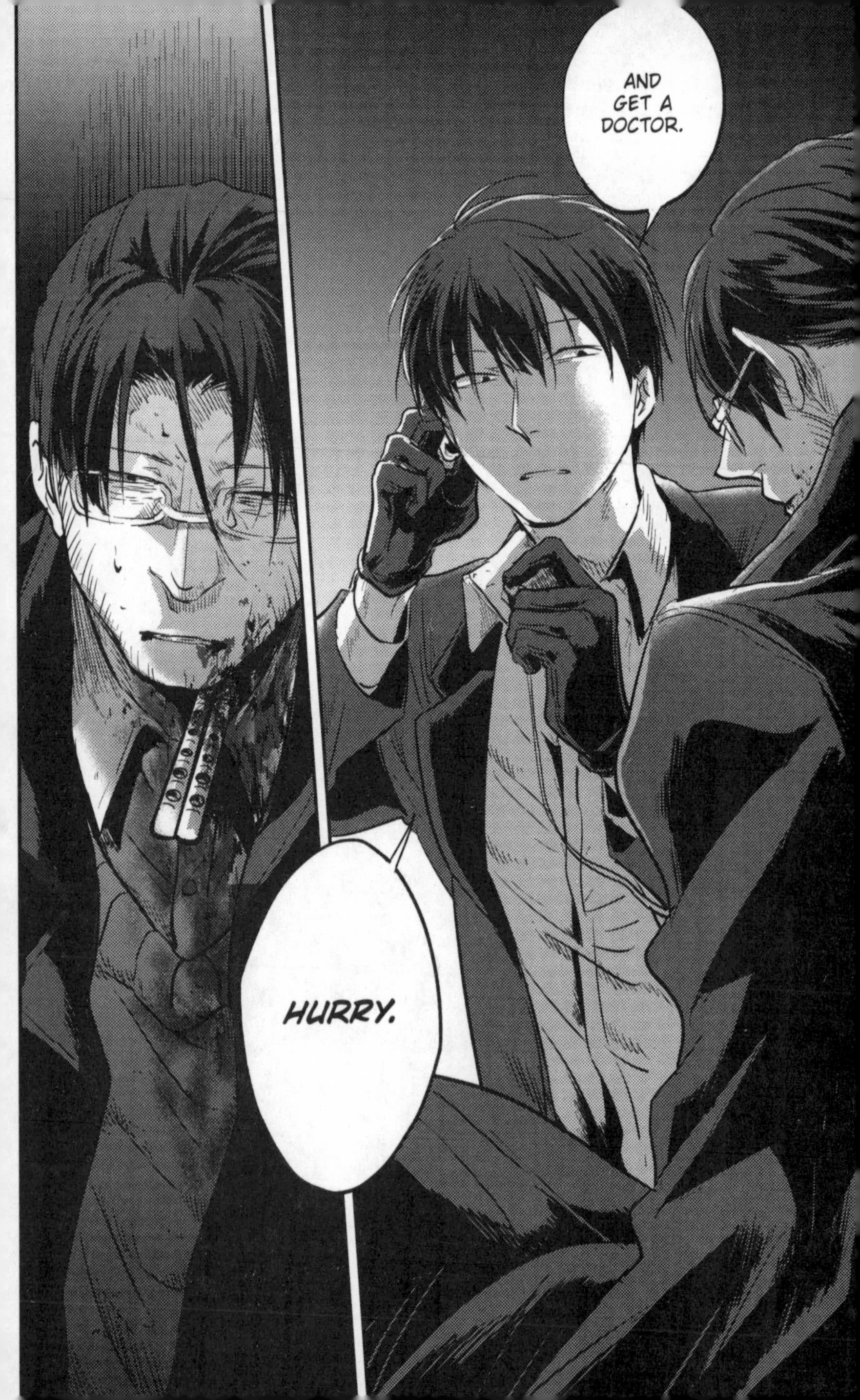
AND GET A DOCTOR.
HURRY.

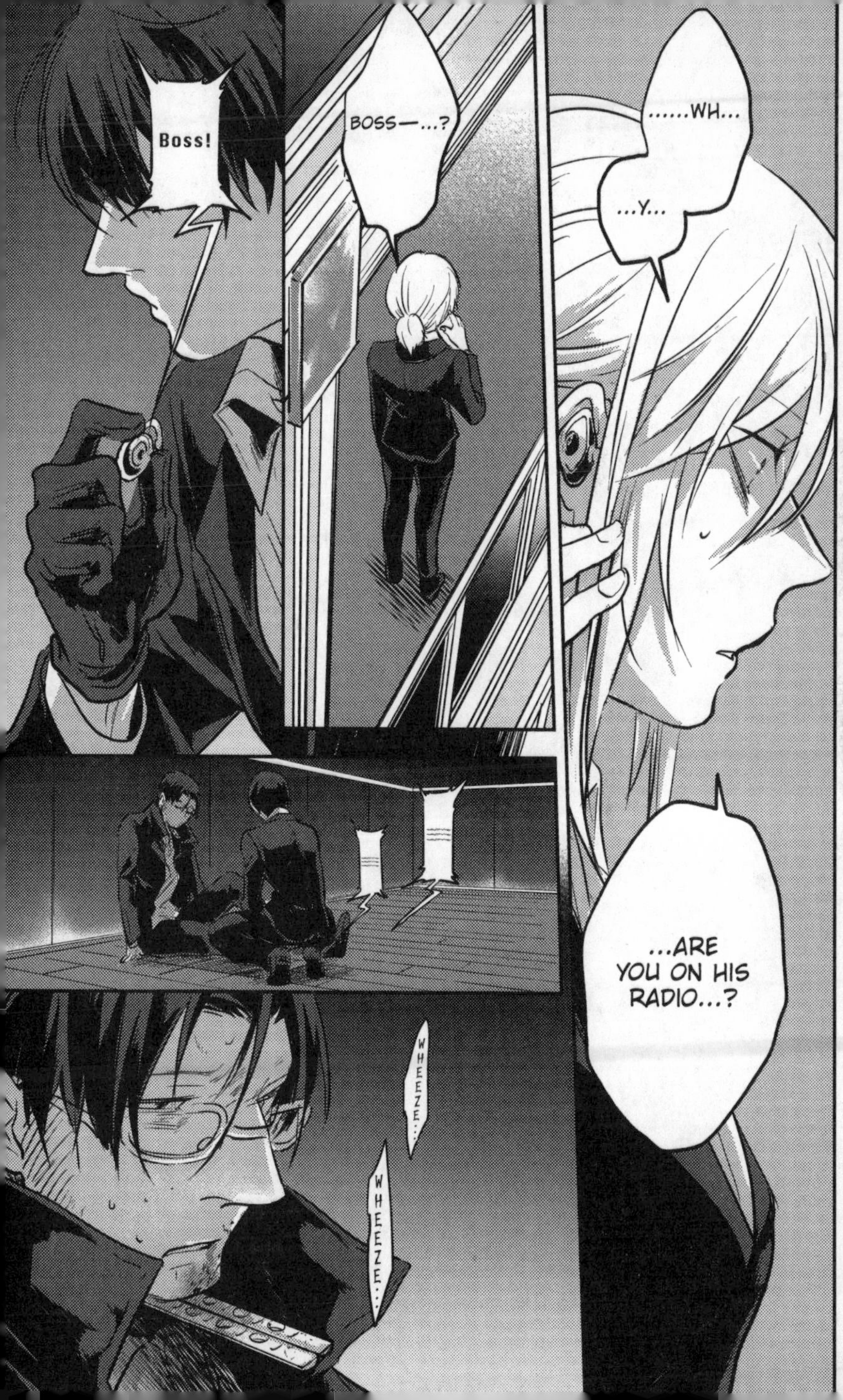

......WH...
...Y...
...ARE YOU ON HIS RADIO...?
BOSS—...?
Boss!
WHEEZE...
WHEEZE...

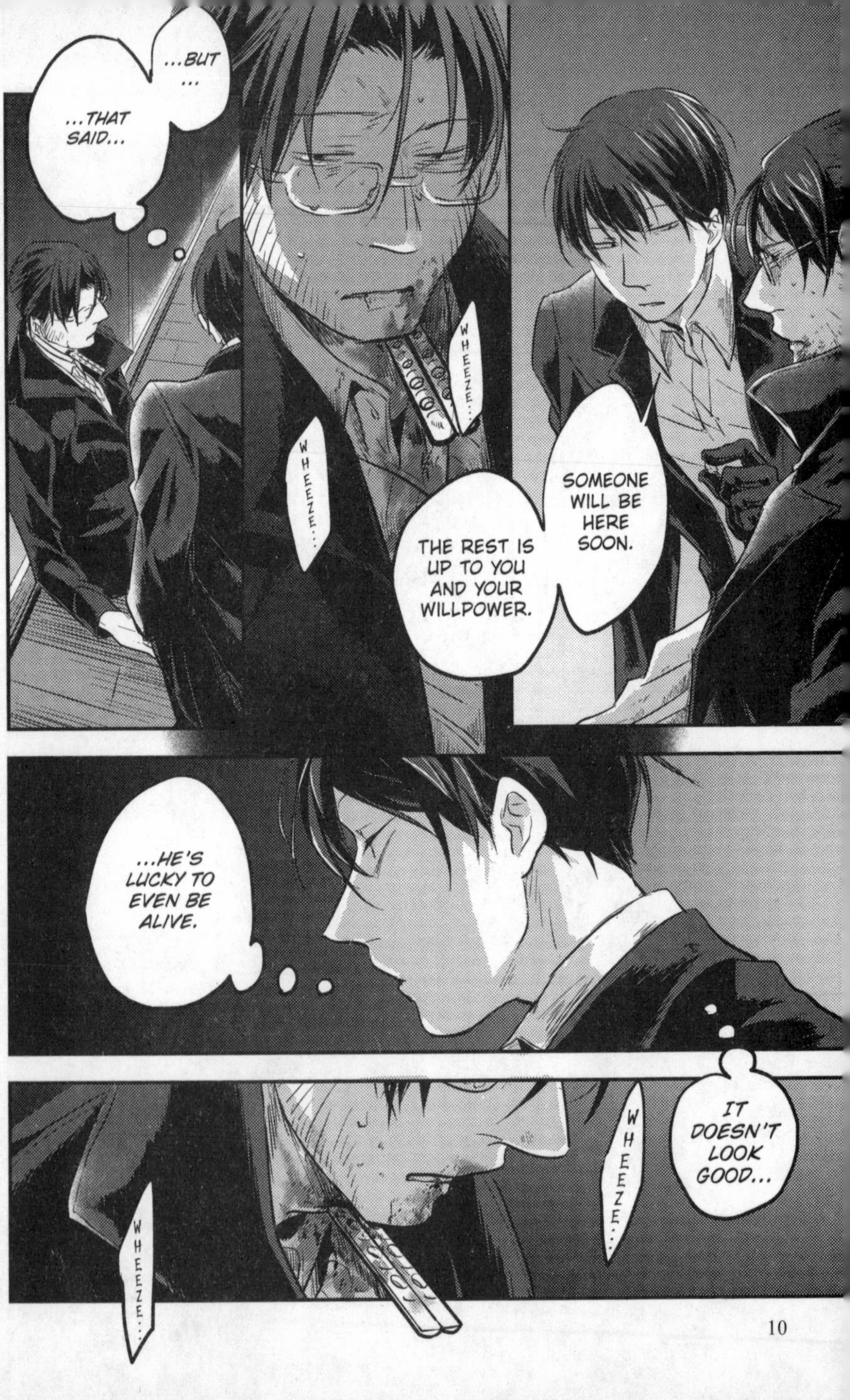
SOMEONE WILL BE HERE SOON.
THE REST IS UP TO YOU AND YOUR WILLPOWER.
WHEEZE...
WHEEZE...
...BUT...
...THAT SAID...
...HE'S LUCKY TO EVEN BE ALIVE.
IT DOESN'T LOOK GOOD...
WHEEZE...
WHEEZE...

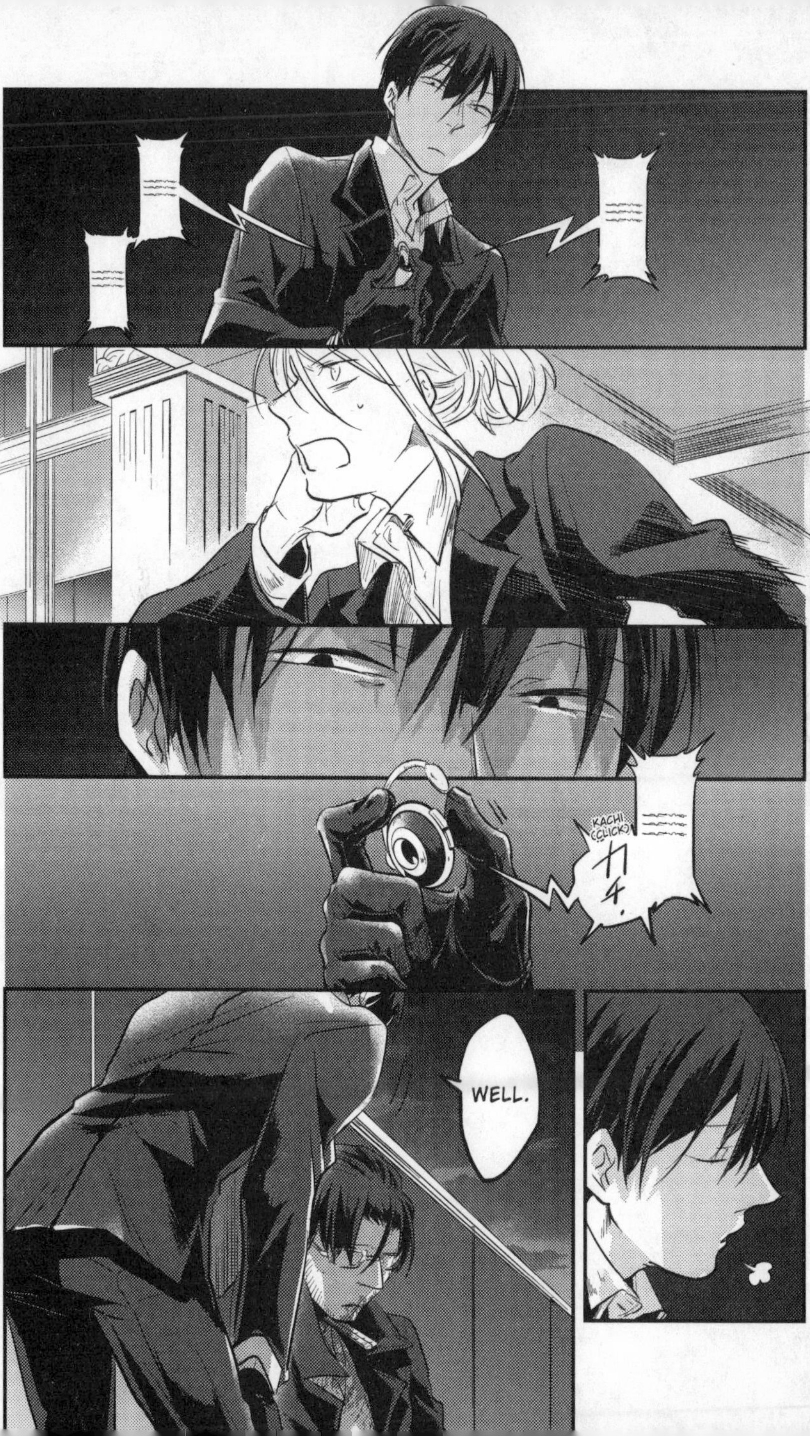
カチ.
KACHI (CLICK)
WELL.

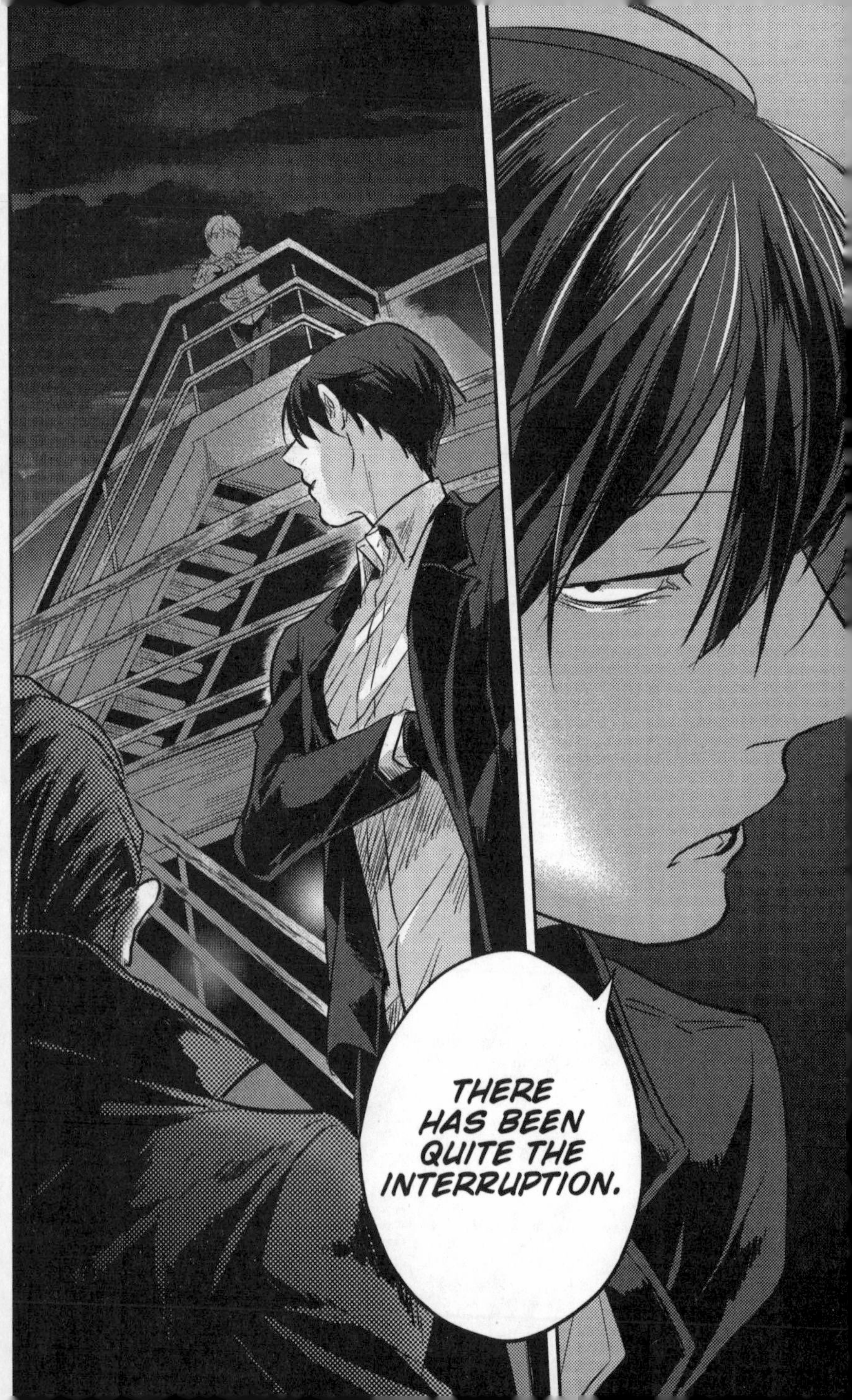
THERE HAS BEEN QUITE THE INTERRUPTION.

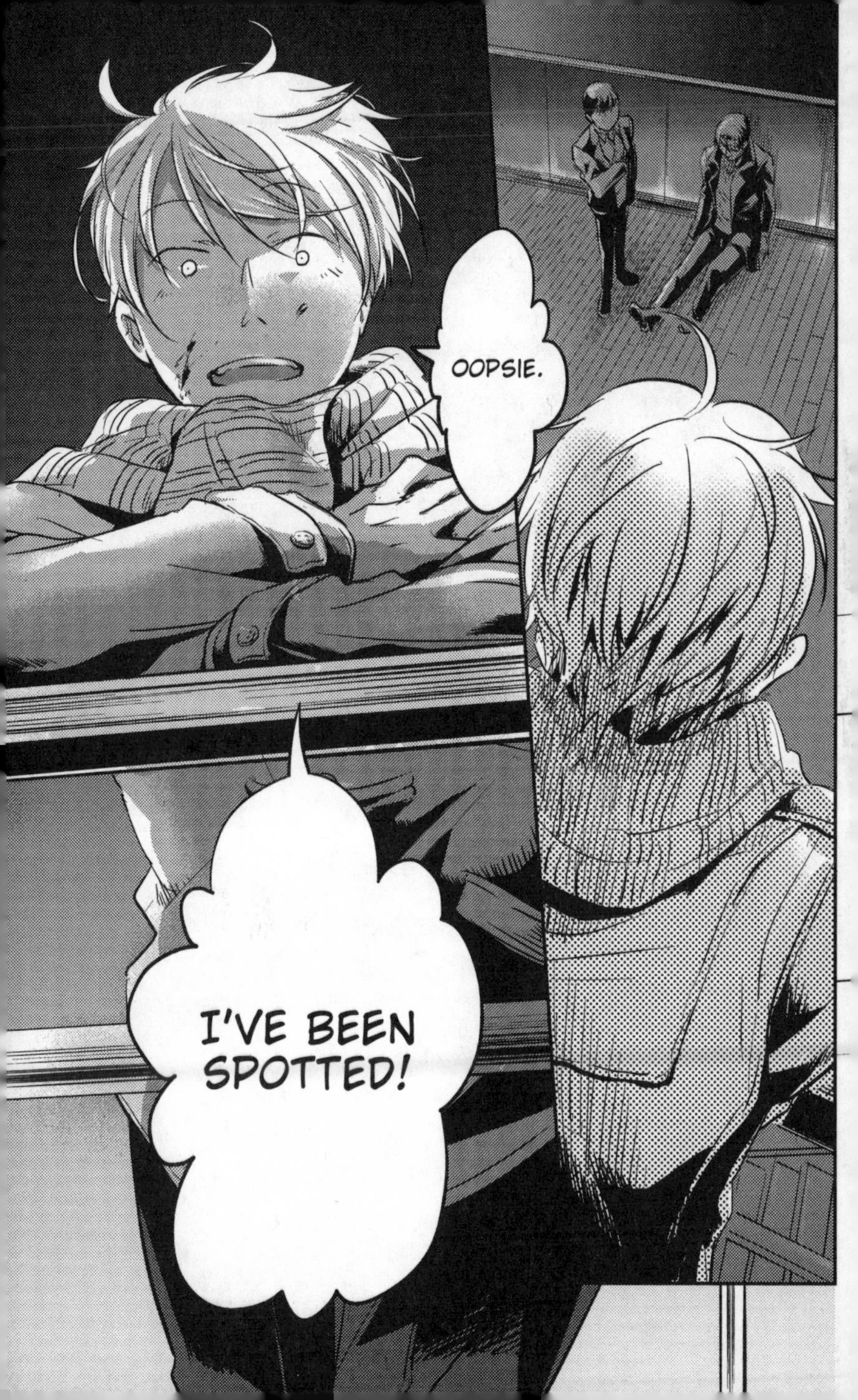
OOPSIE.
I'VE BEEN SPOTTED!

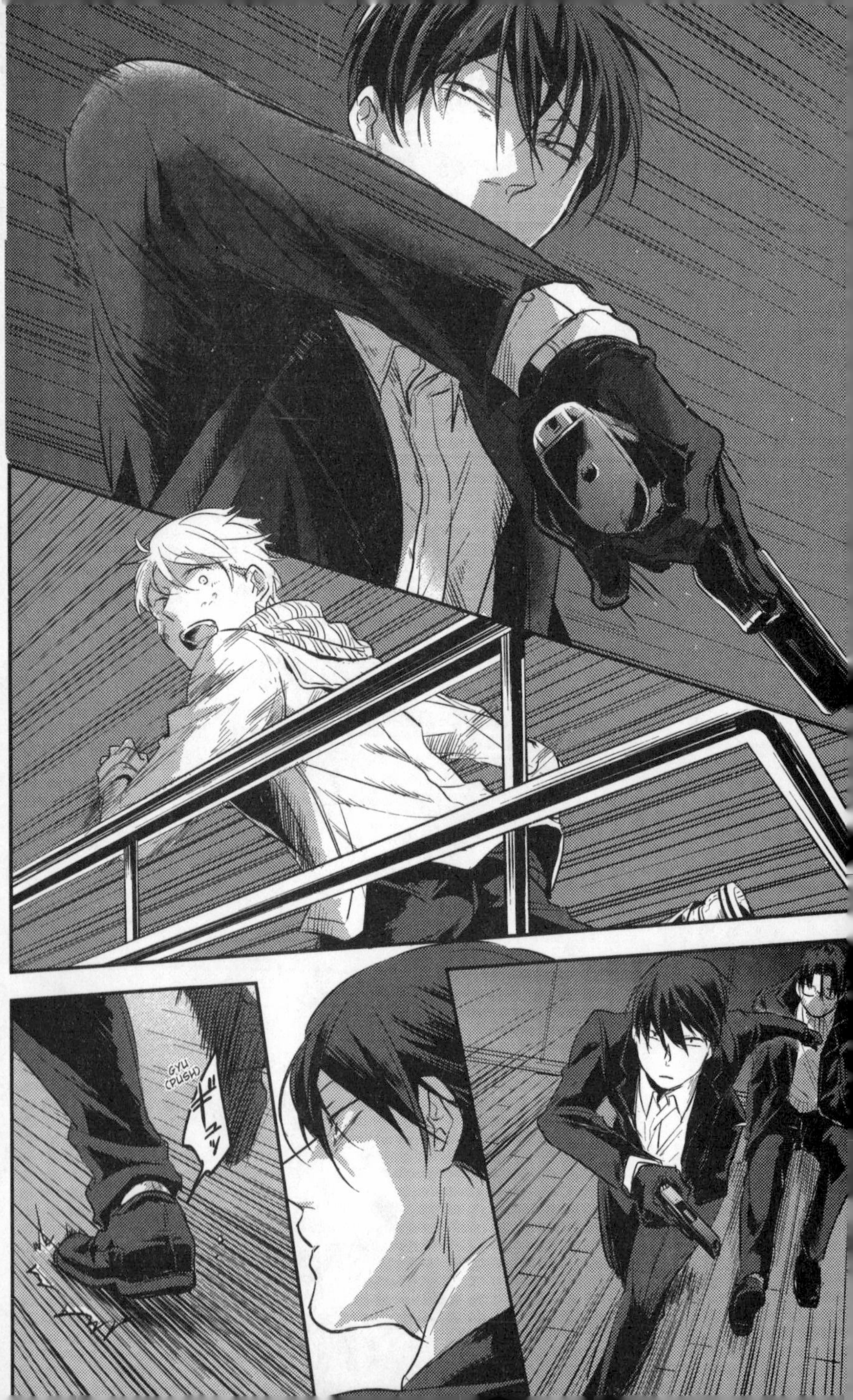
ギュッ
GYU (PUSH)

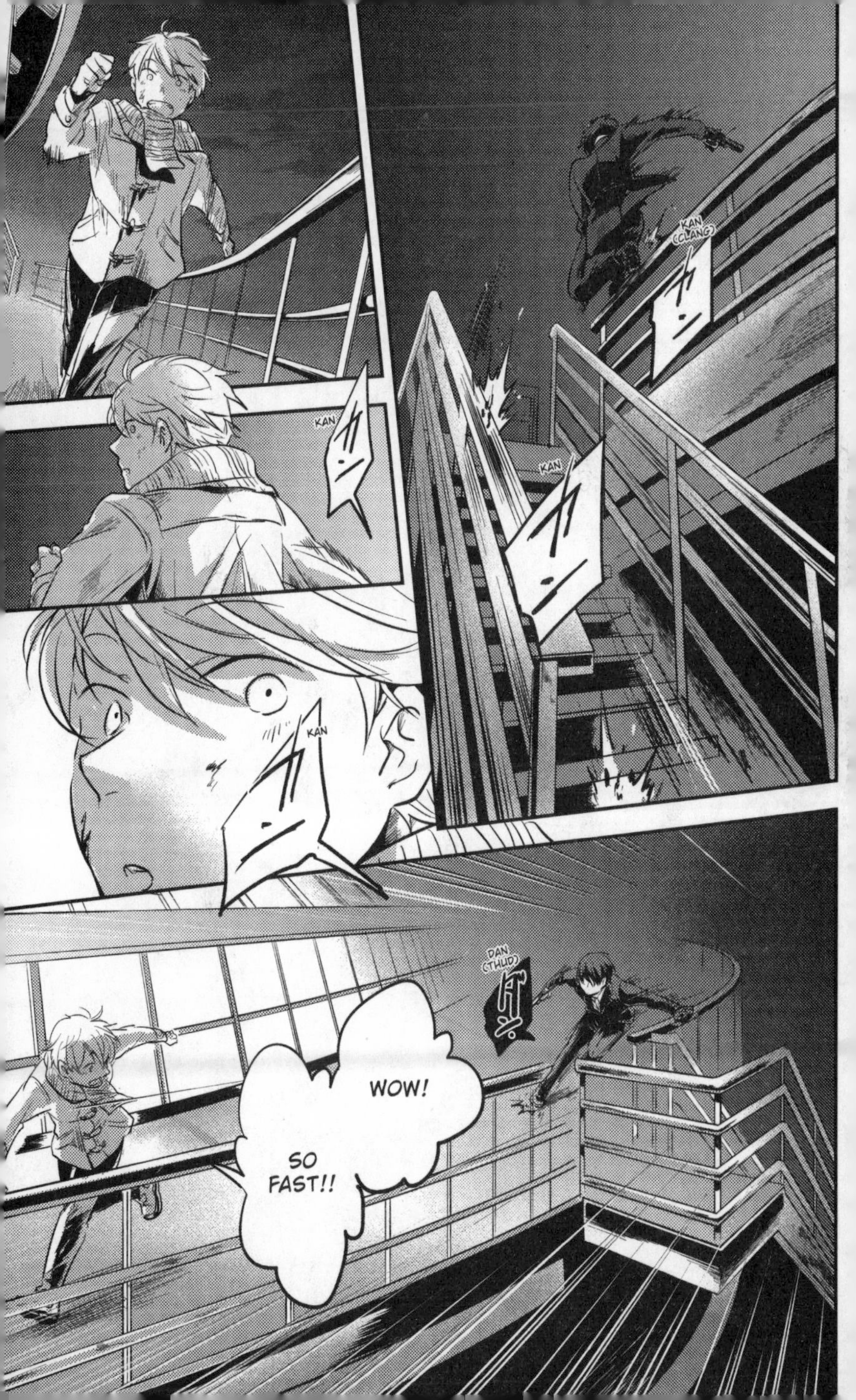
KAN (CLANG)
KAN
KAN
KAN
DAN (THUD)
WOW!
SO FAST!!

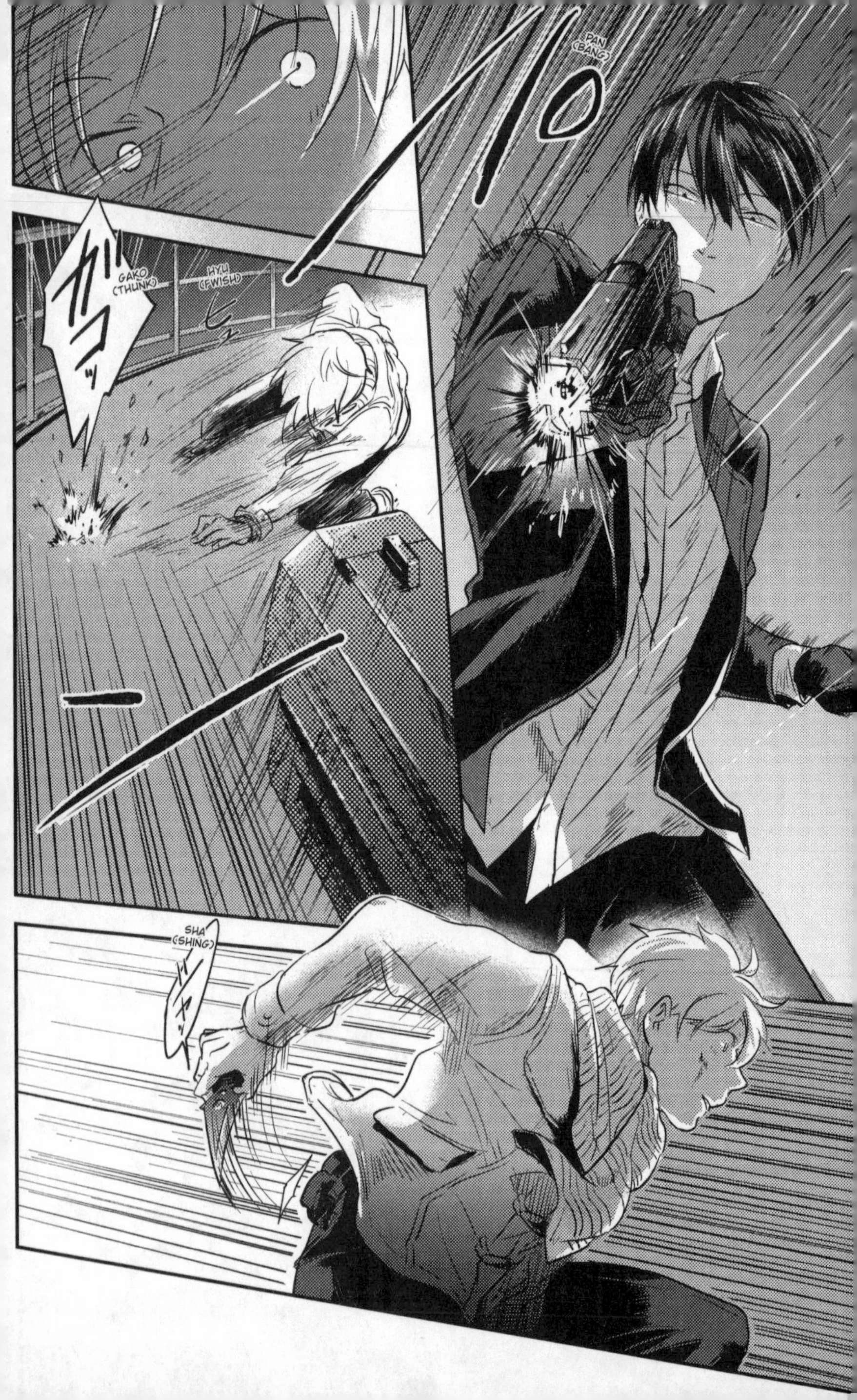
PAN (BANG)
HYU (FWISH)
GAKO (THUNK)
SHA (SHING)

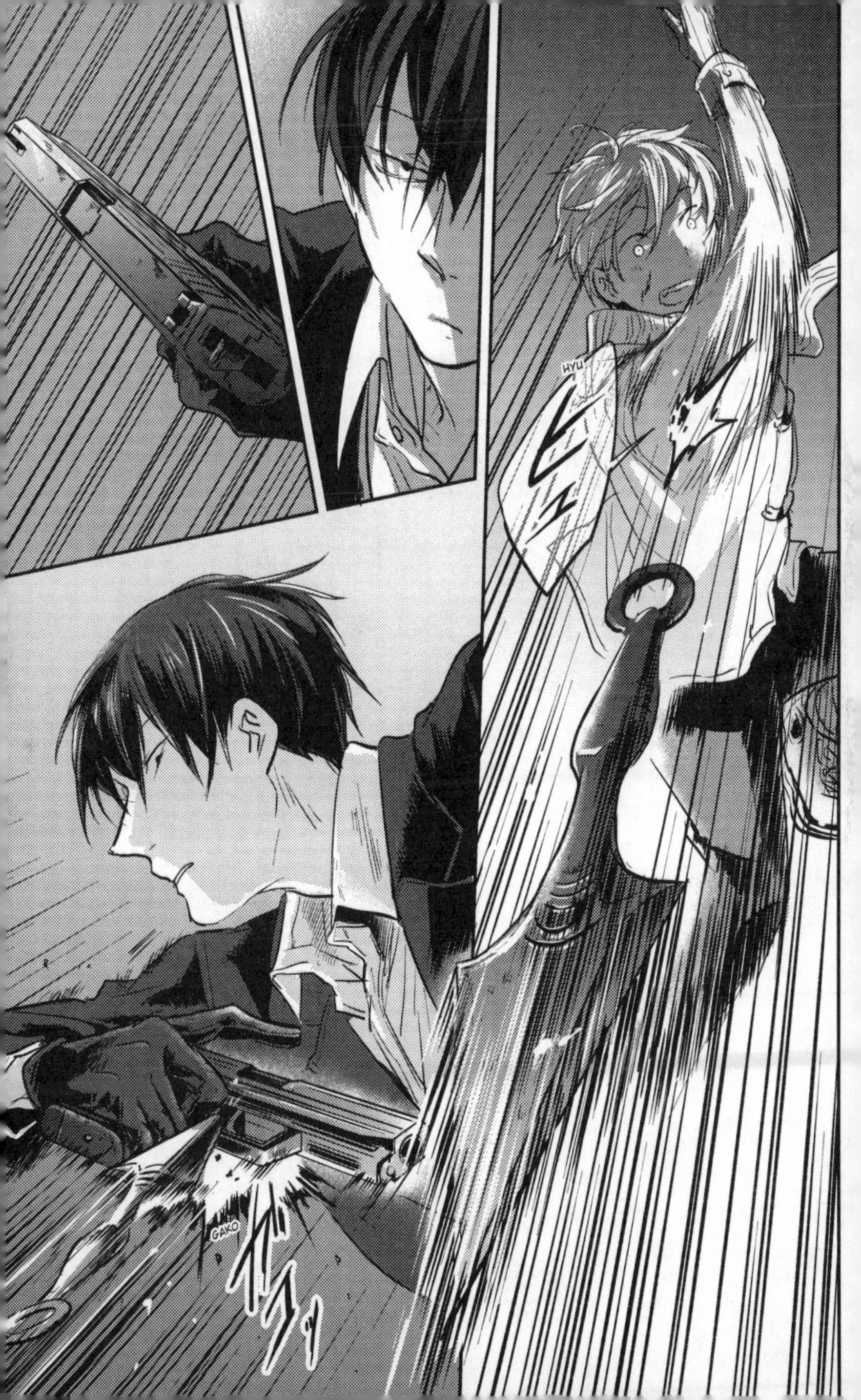
HYU
GAKO

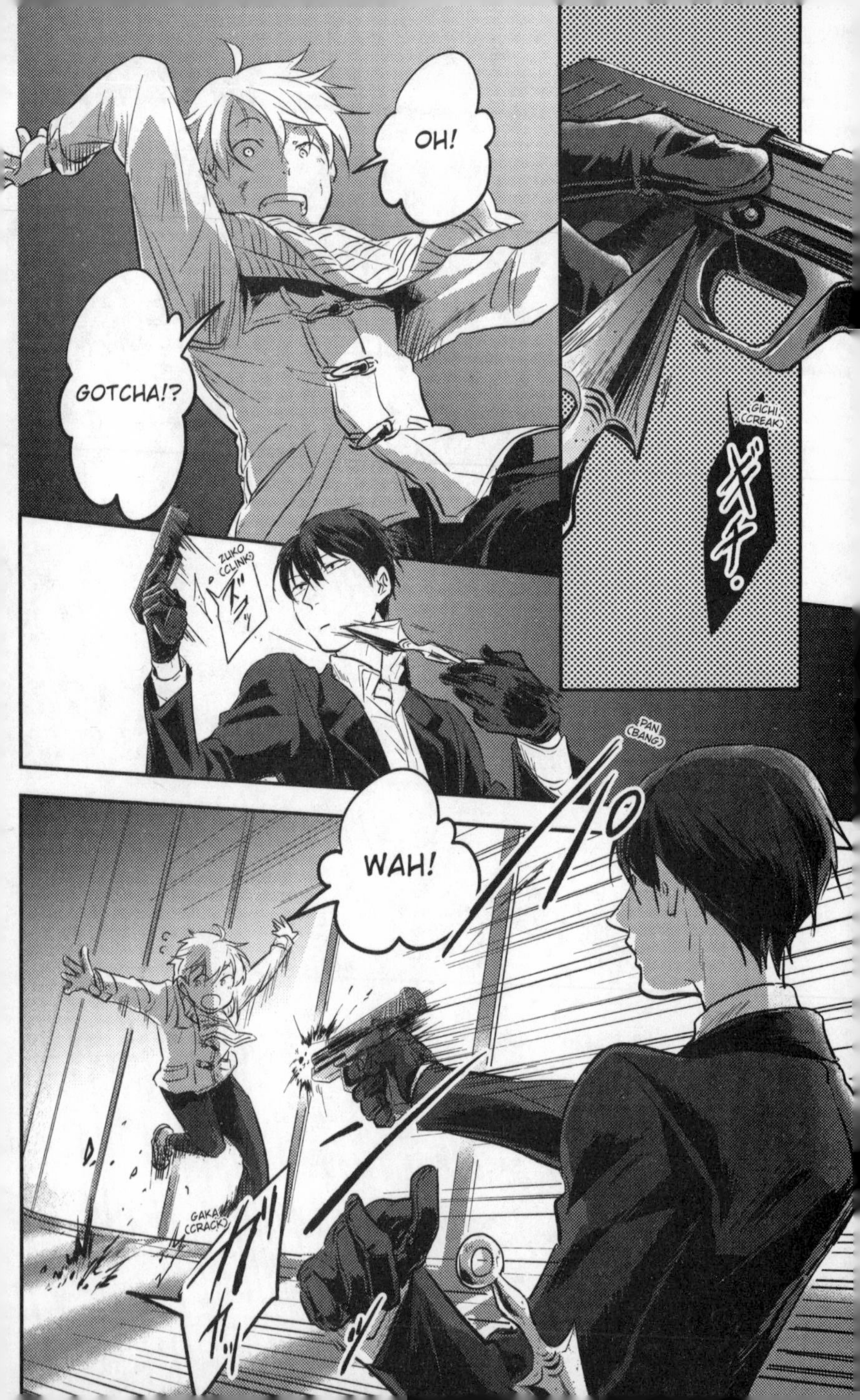
GICHI (CREAK)
OH!
GOTCHA!?
ZUKO (CLINK)
PAN (BANG)
WAH!
GAKA (CRACK)

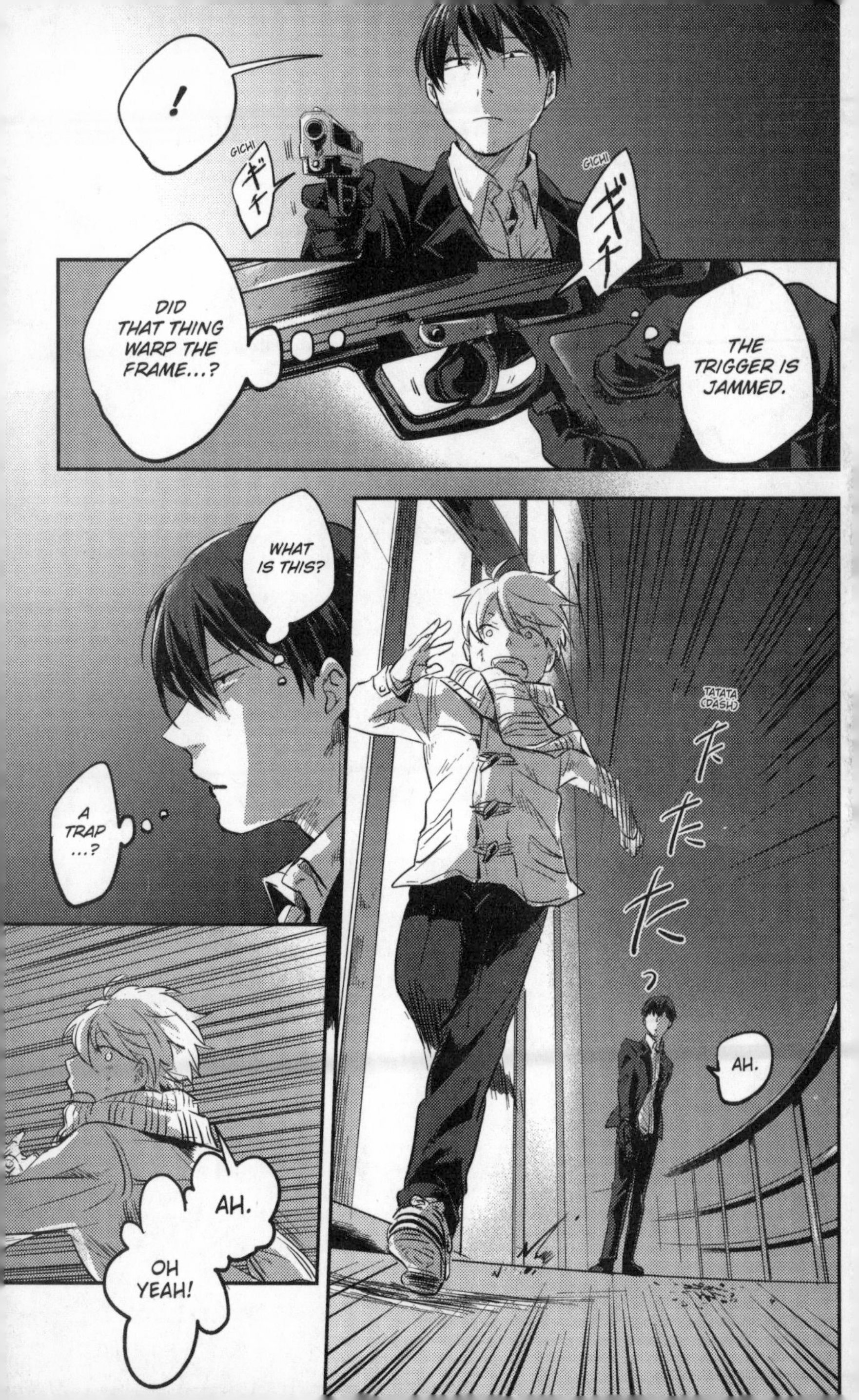

!
GICHI
ギチ
GICHI
ギチ
THE TRIGGER IS JAMMED.
DID THAT THING WARP THE FRAME...?
TATATA (DASH)
たたたっ
AH.
WHAT IS THIS?
A TRAP ...?
AH.
OH YEAH!

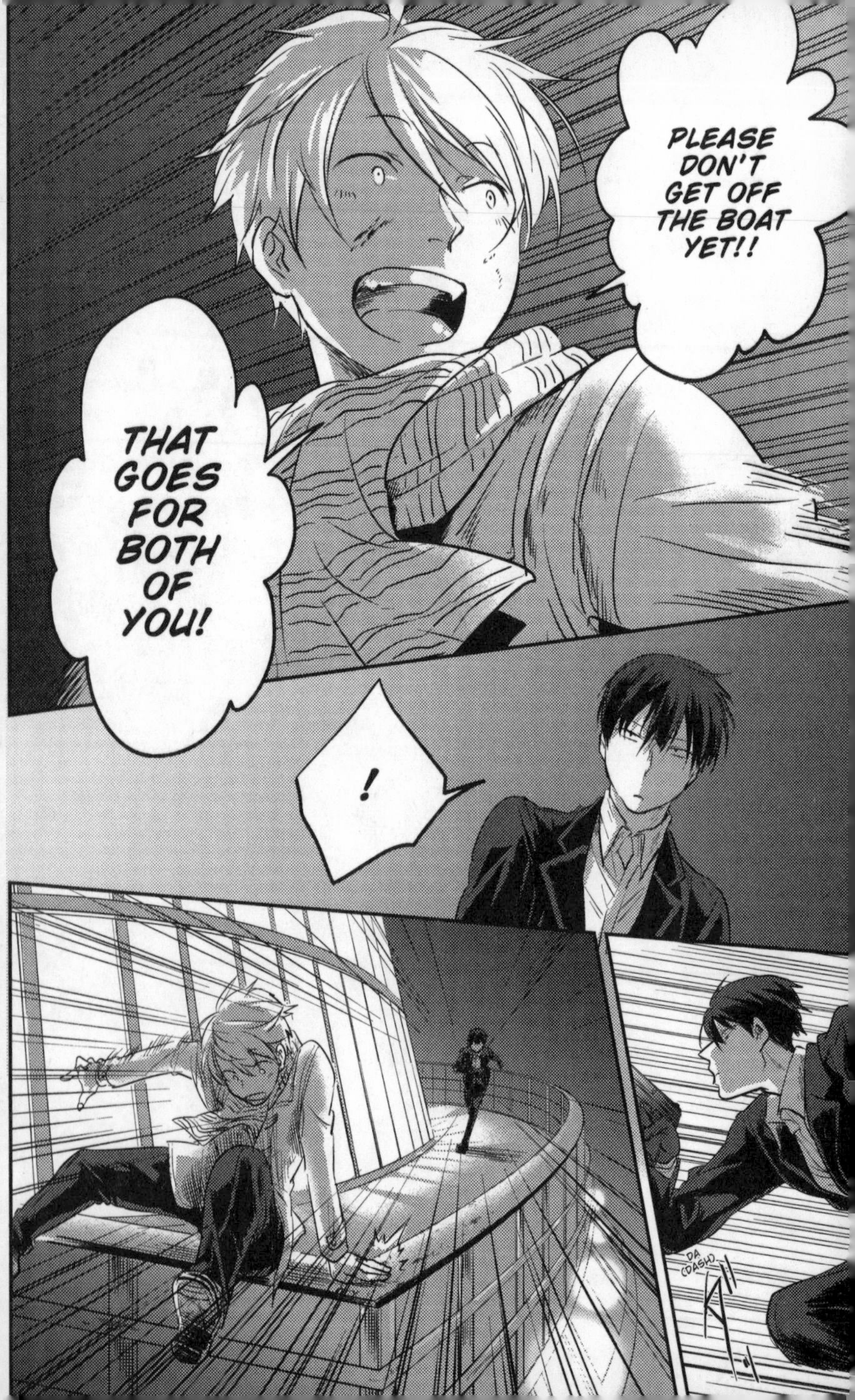
PLEASE DON'T GET OFF THE BOAT YET!!
THAT GOES FOR BOTH OF YOU!
!
DA (DASH)

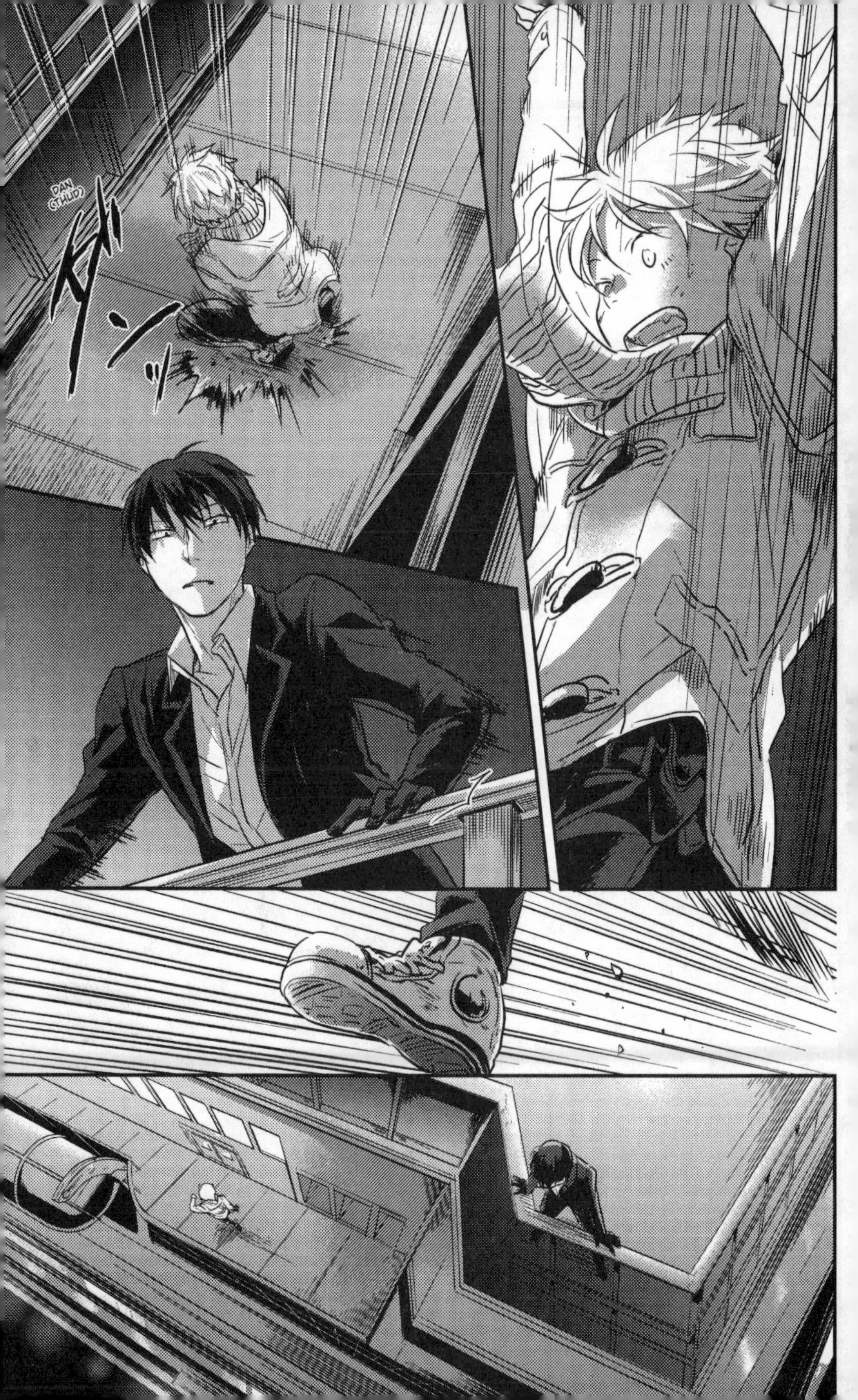
DAN (THUD)
ダンッ

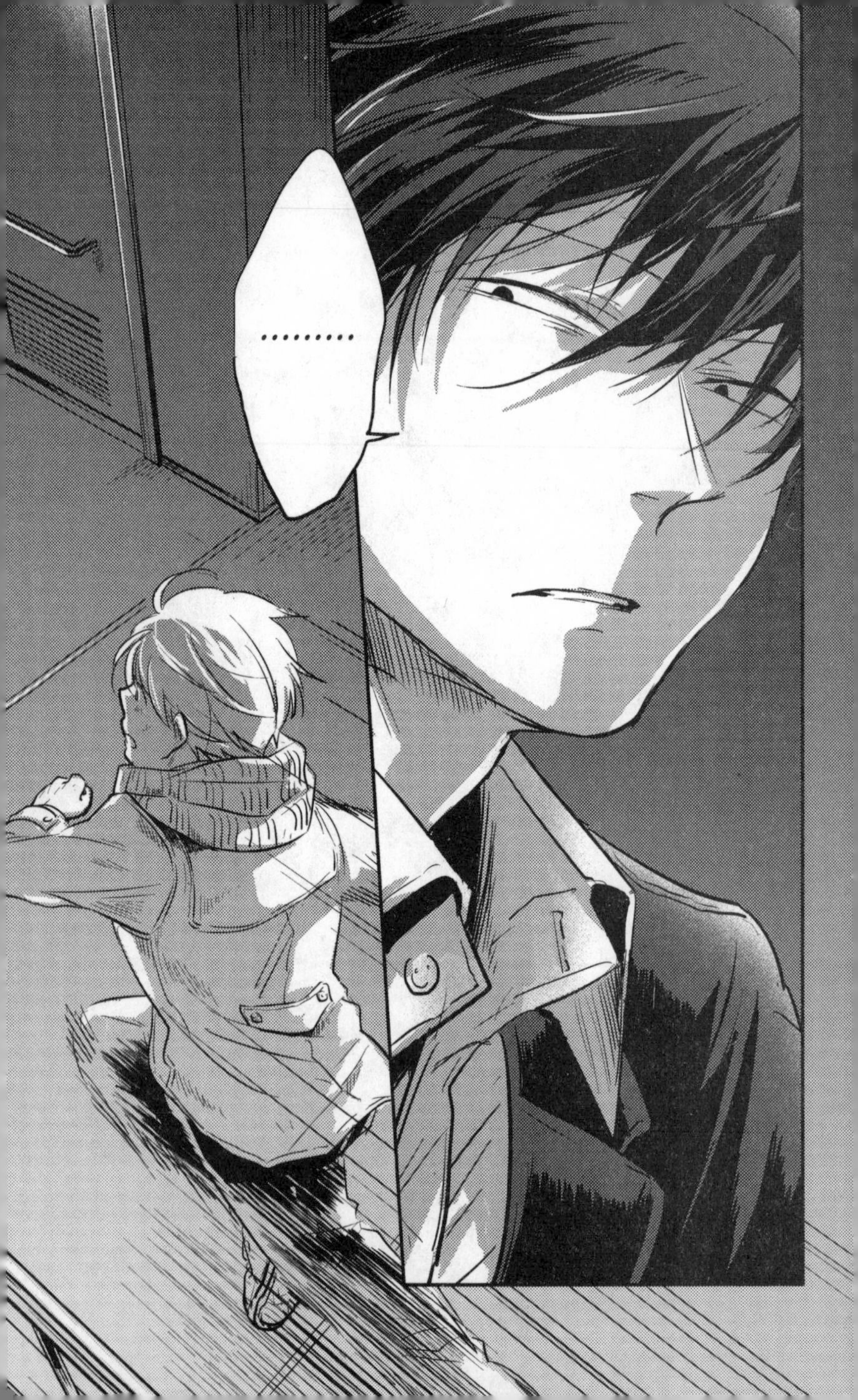
....

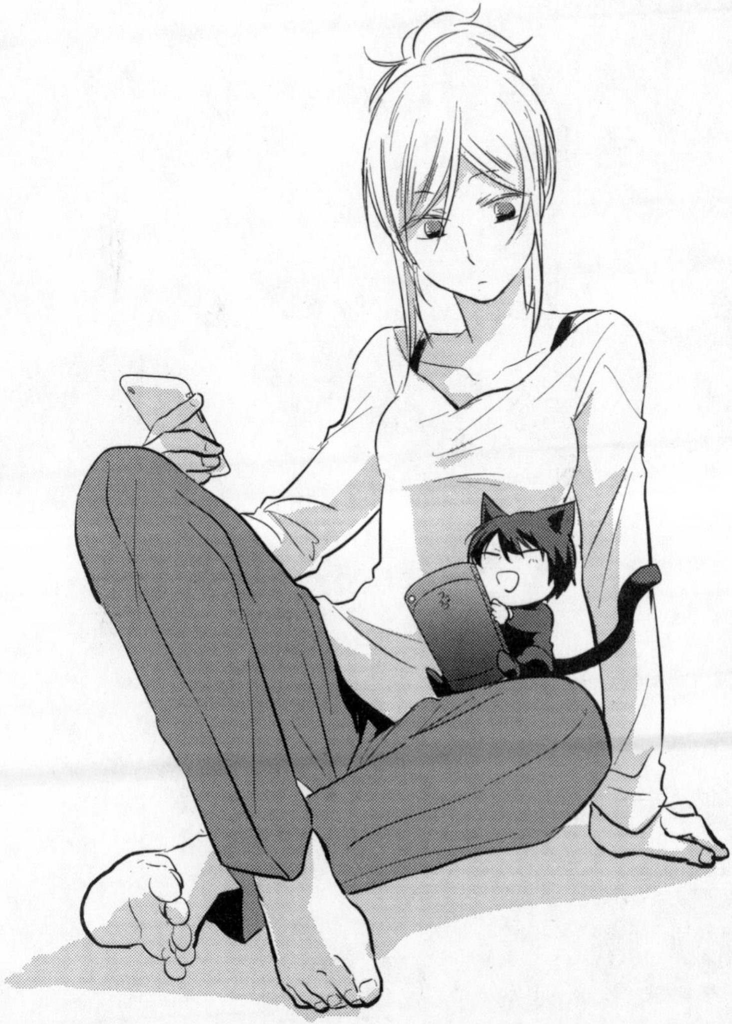

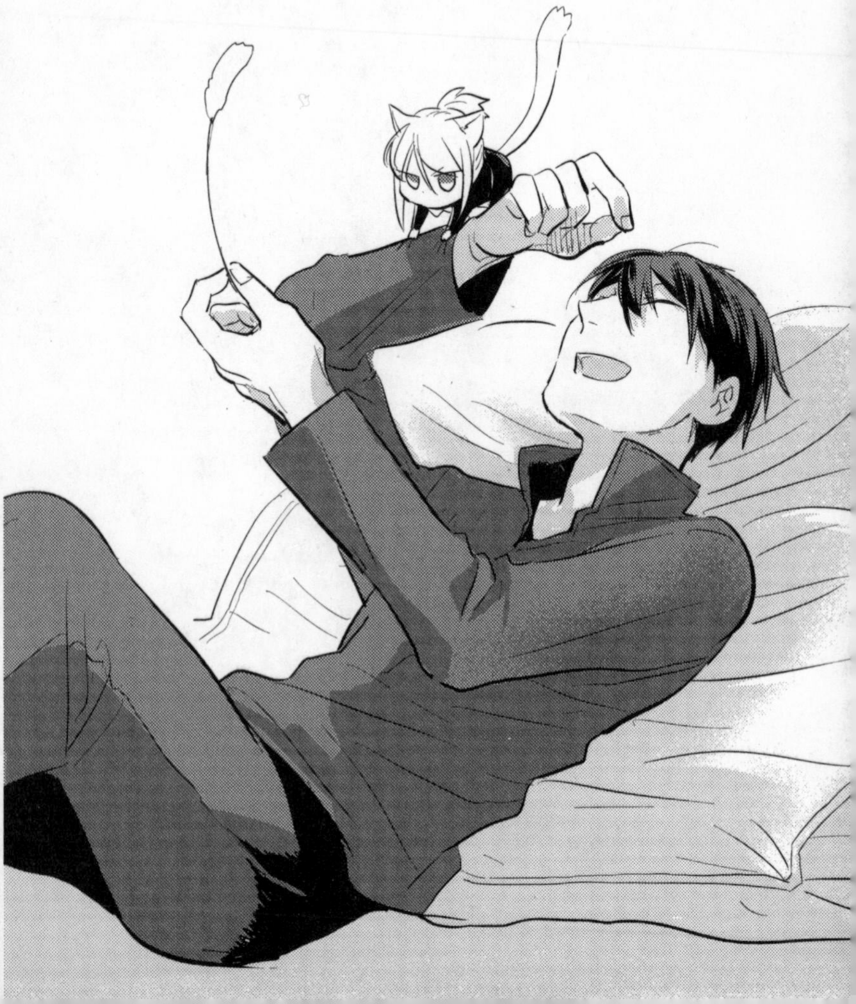

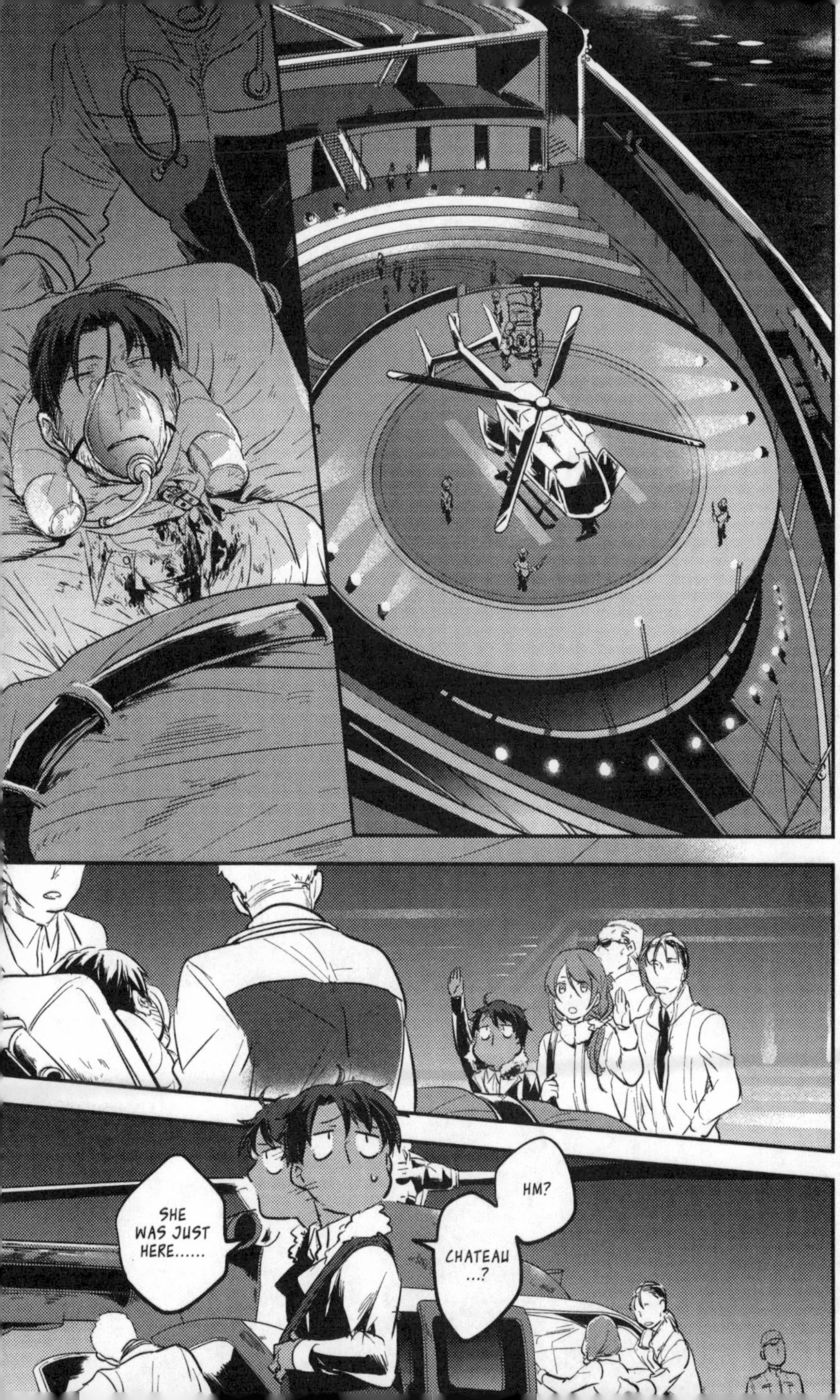
HM?
CHATEAU ...?
SHE WAS JUST HERE......

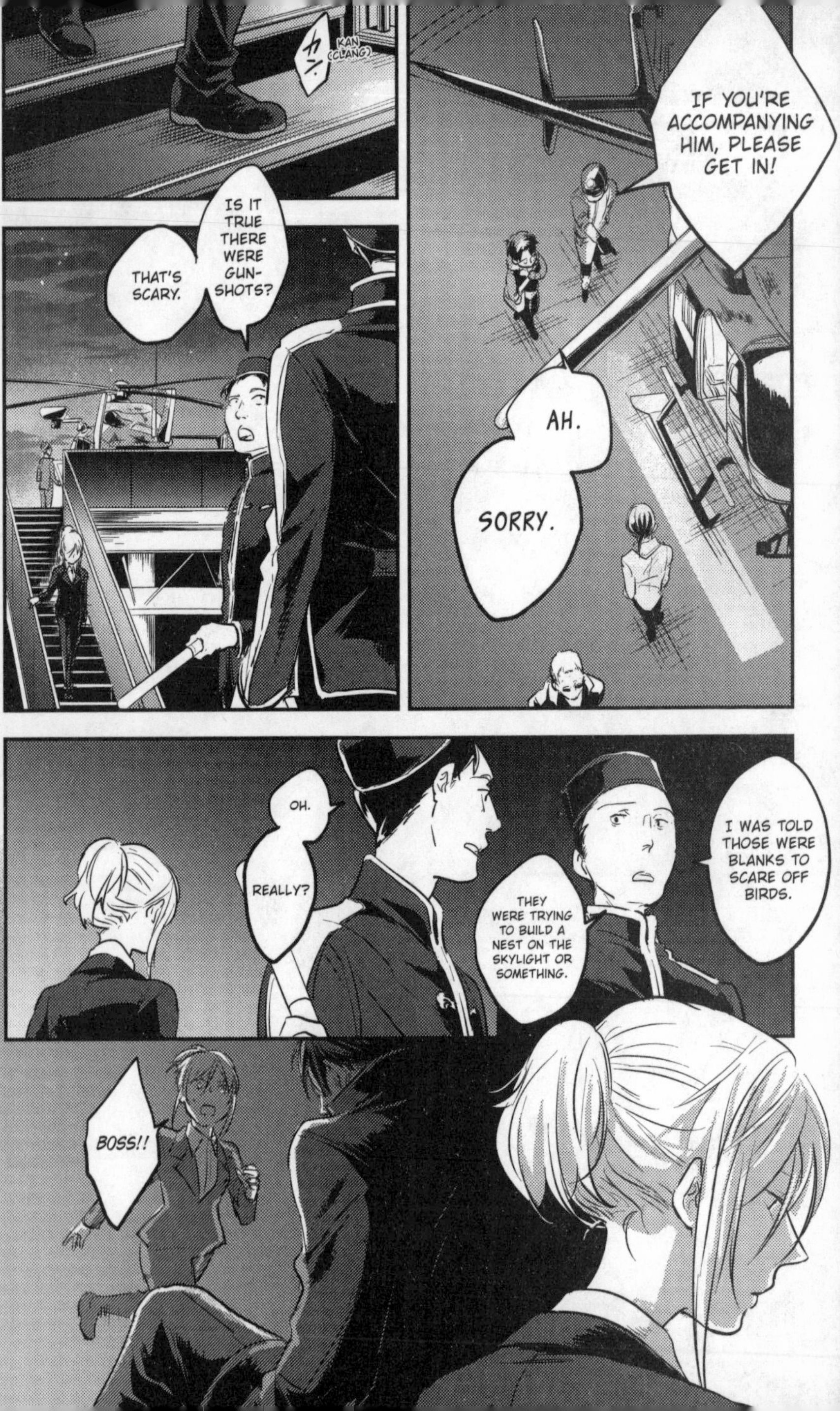
IF YOU'RE ACCOMPANYING HIM, PLEASE GET IN!
AH.
SORRY.
カン
KAN (CLANG)
IS IT TRUE THERE WERE GUN-SHOTS?
THAT'S SCARY.
I WAS TOLD THOSE WERE BLANKS TO SCARE OFF BIRDS.
THEY WERE TRYING TO BUILD A NEST ON THE SKYLIGHT OR SOMETHING.
OH.
REALLY?
BOSS!!

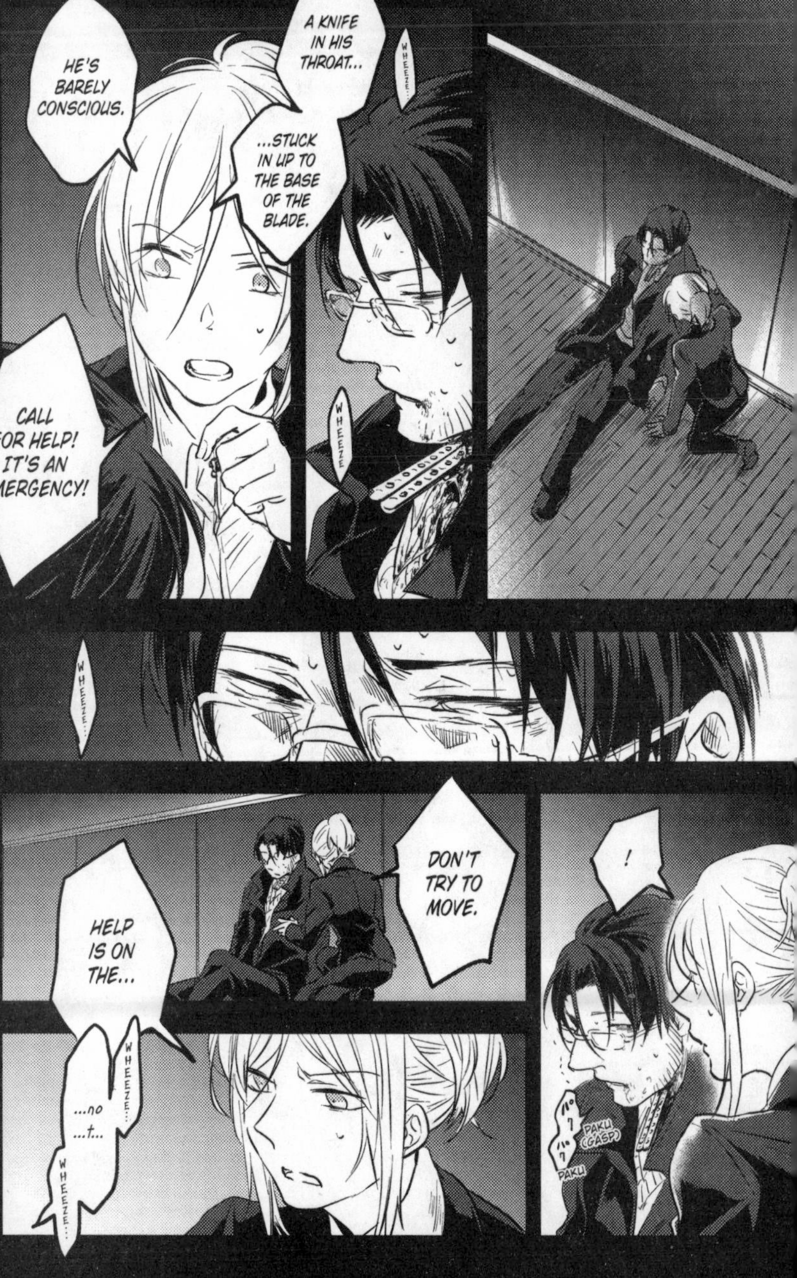
WHEEZE...
A KNIFE IN HIS THROAT...
...STUCK IN UP TO THE BASE OF THE BLADE.
WHEEZE
HE'S BARELY CONSCIOUS.
CALL FOR HELP! IT'S AN EMERGENCY!
WHEEZE...
!
パク
パク
PAKU (GASP)
PAKU
DON'T TRY TO MOVE.
HELP IS ON THE...
WHEEZE...
...no
...t...
WHEEZE...

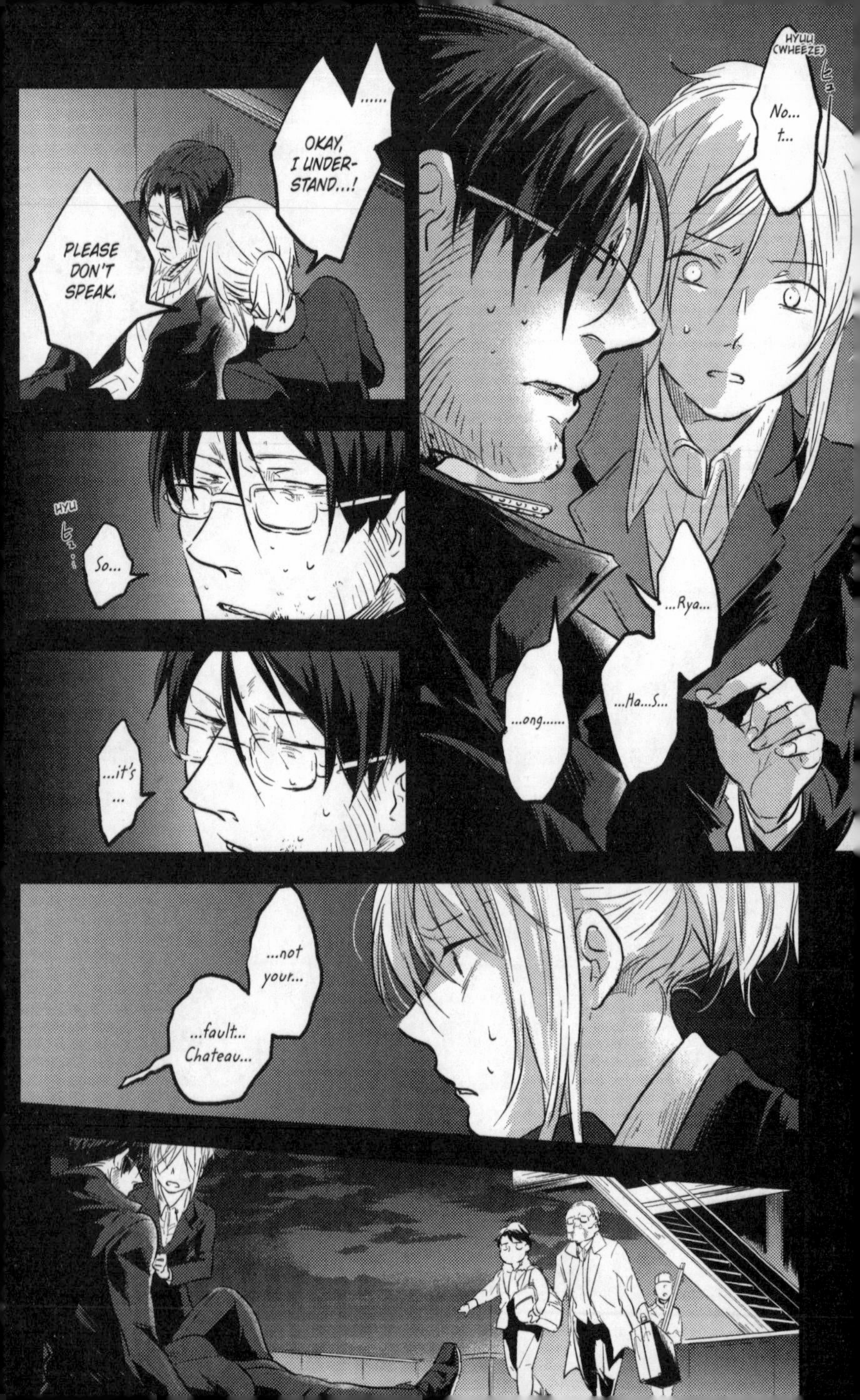
HYUU (WHEEZE)
No... t...
...Rya...
...Ha...S...
...ong......
......
OKAY, I UNDER-STAND...!
PLEASE DON'T SPEAK.
HYU
So...
...it's ...
...not your...
...fault... Chateau...

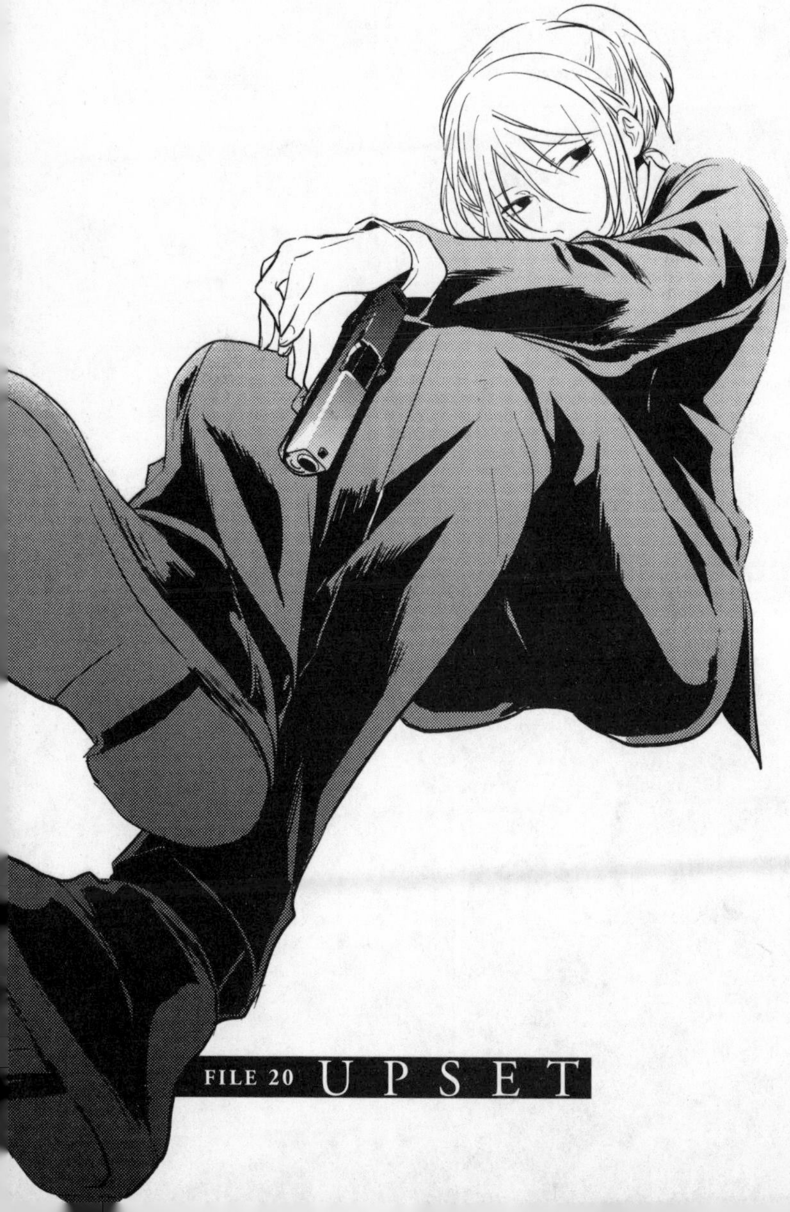

FILE 20 UPSET

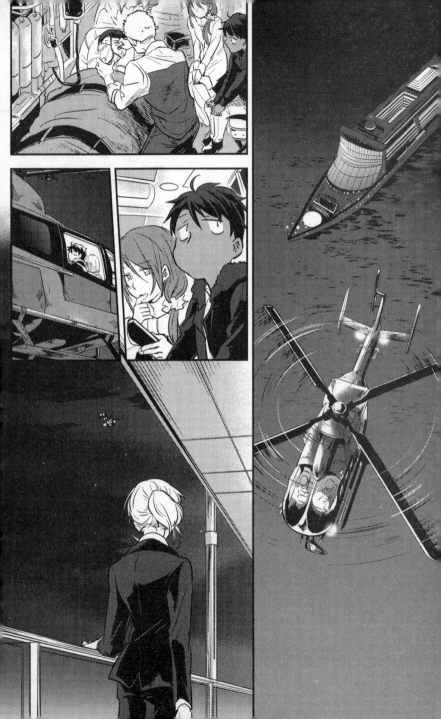

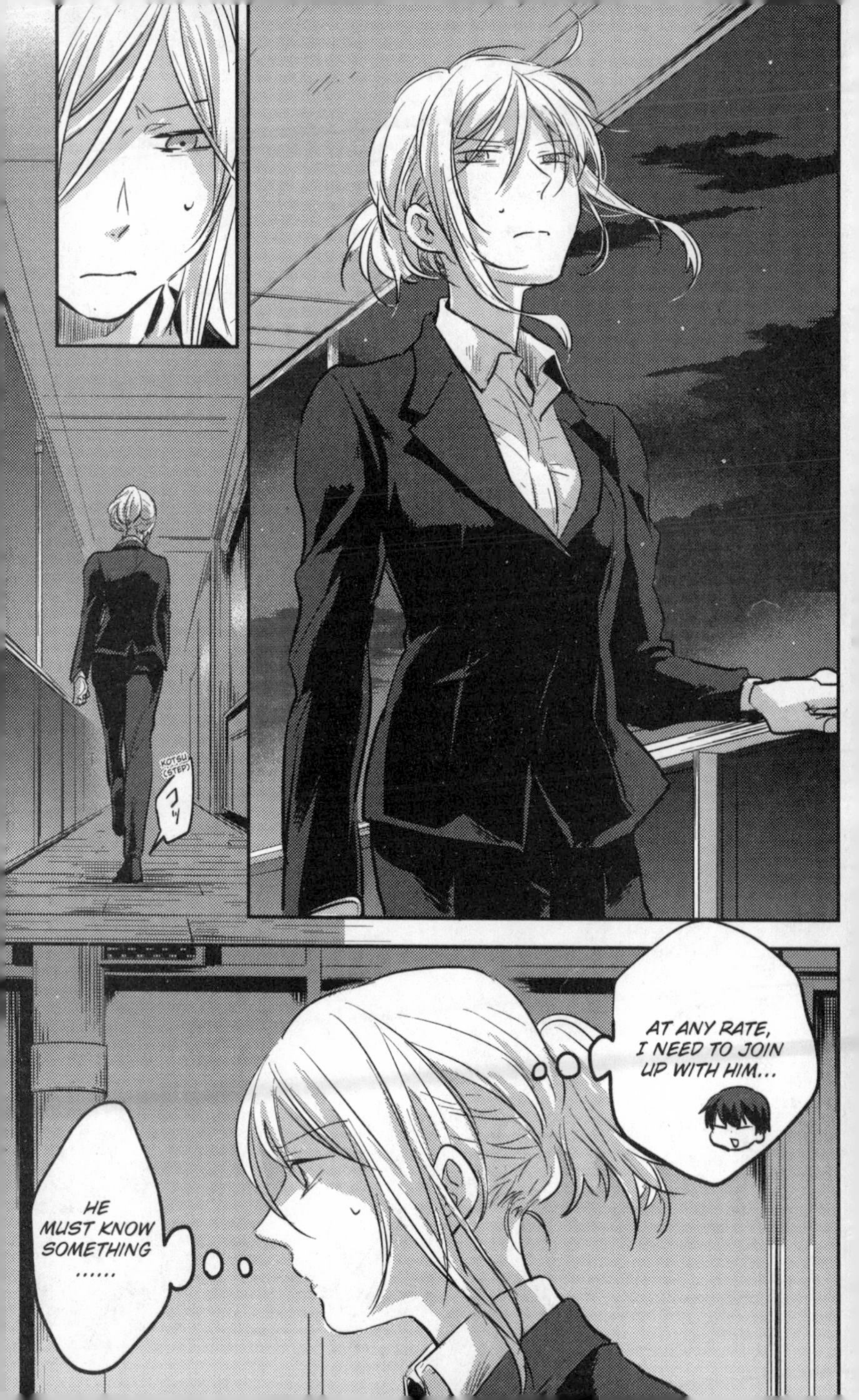
KOTSU (STEP)
コツ
AT ANY RATE, I NEED TO JOIN UP WITH HIM...
HE MUST KNOW SOMETHING ......

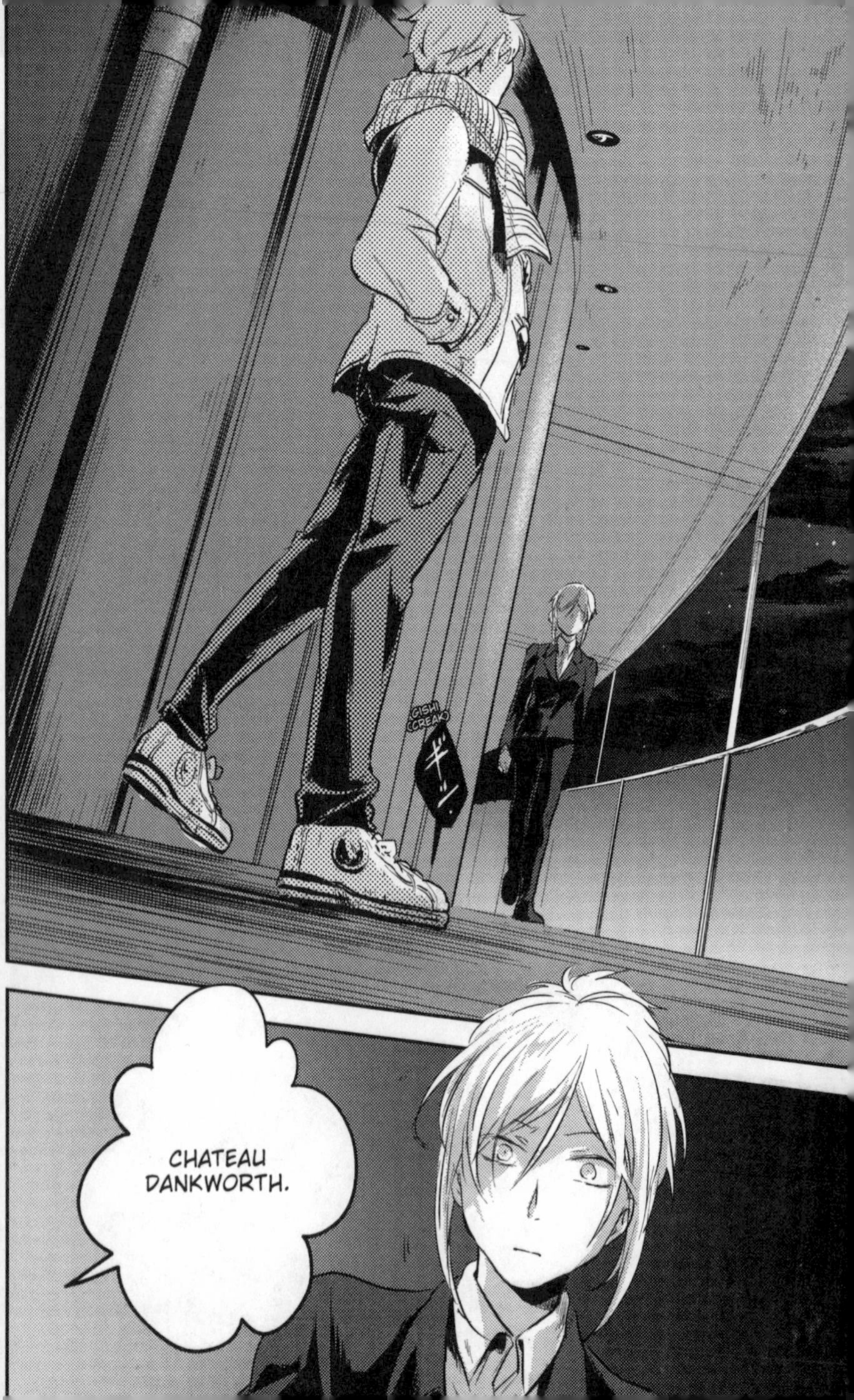
GISHI (CREAK)
ギシッ
CHATEAU DANKWORTH.

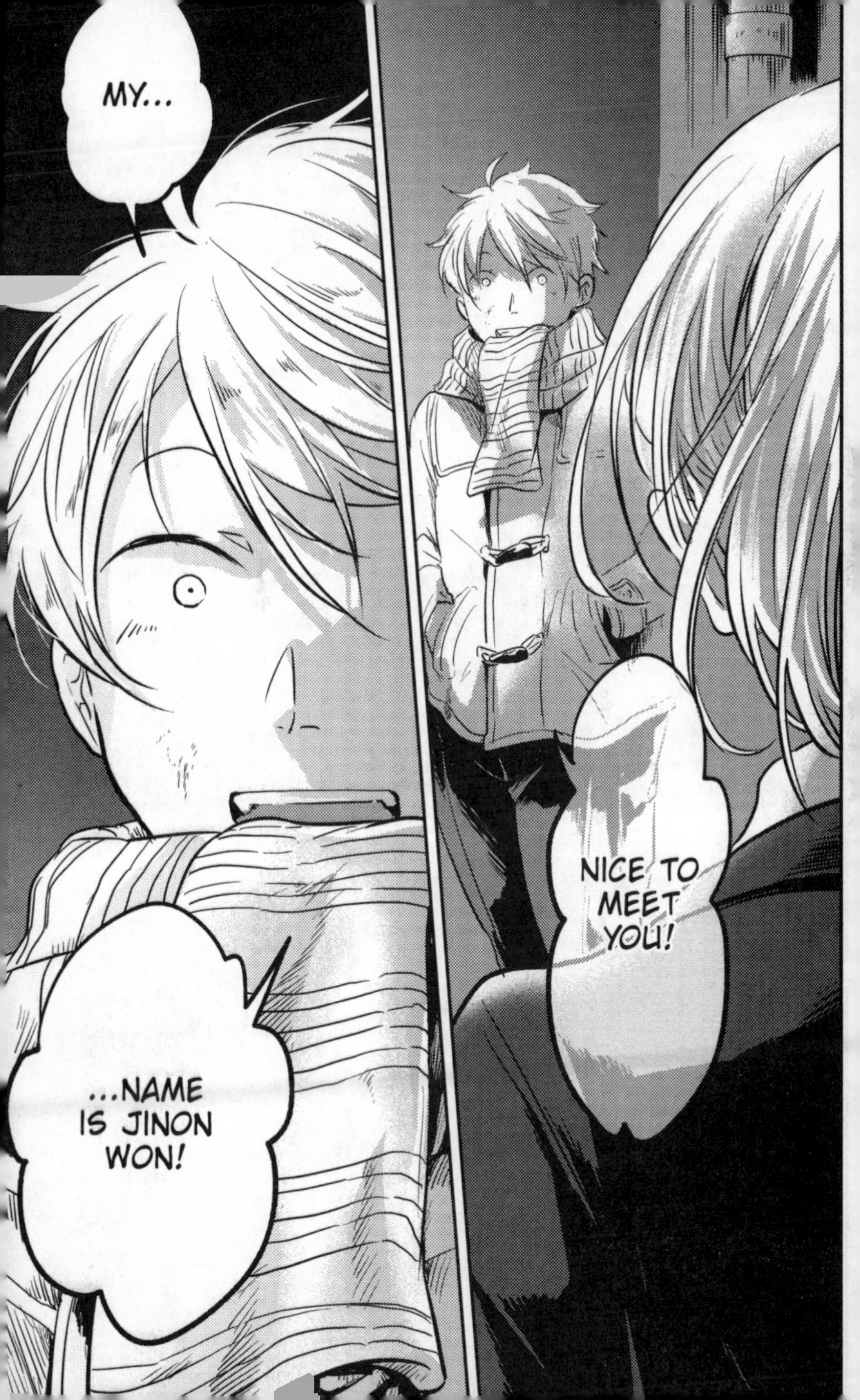
NICE TO MEET YOU!
MY...
...NAME IS JINON WON!

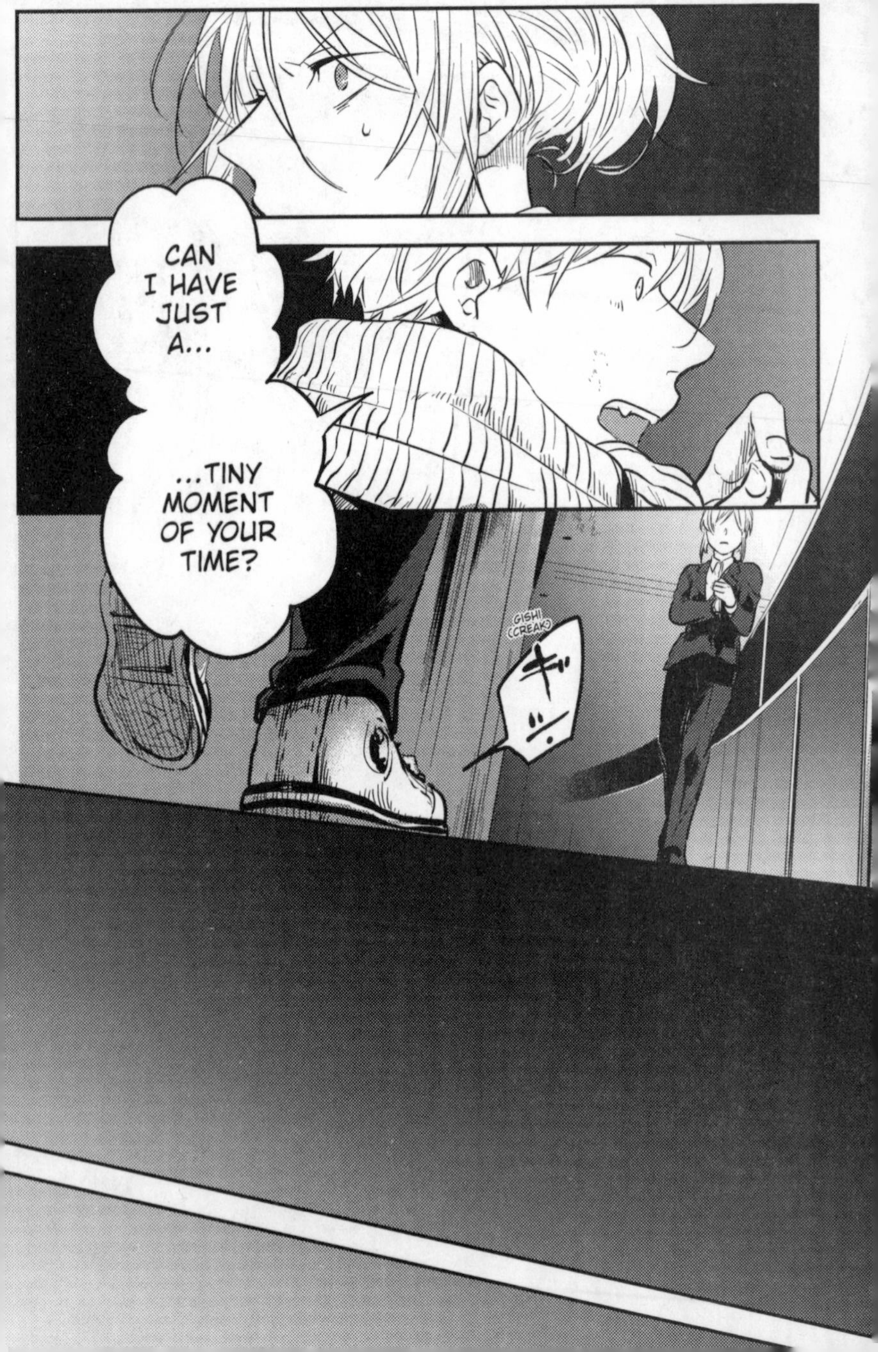
CAN I HAVE JUST A...
...TINY MOMENT OF YOUR TIME?
GISHI (CREAK)
ギッ

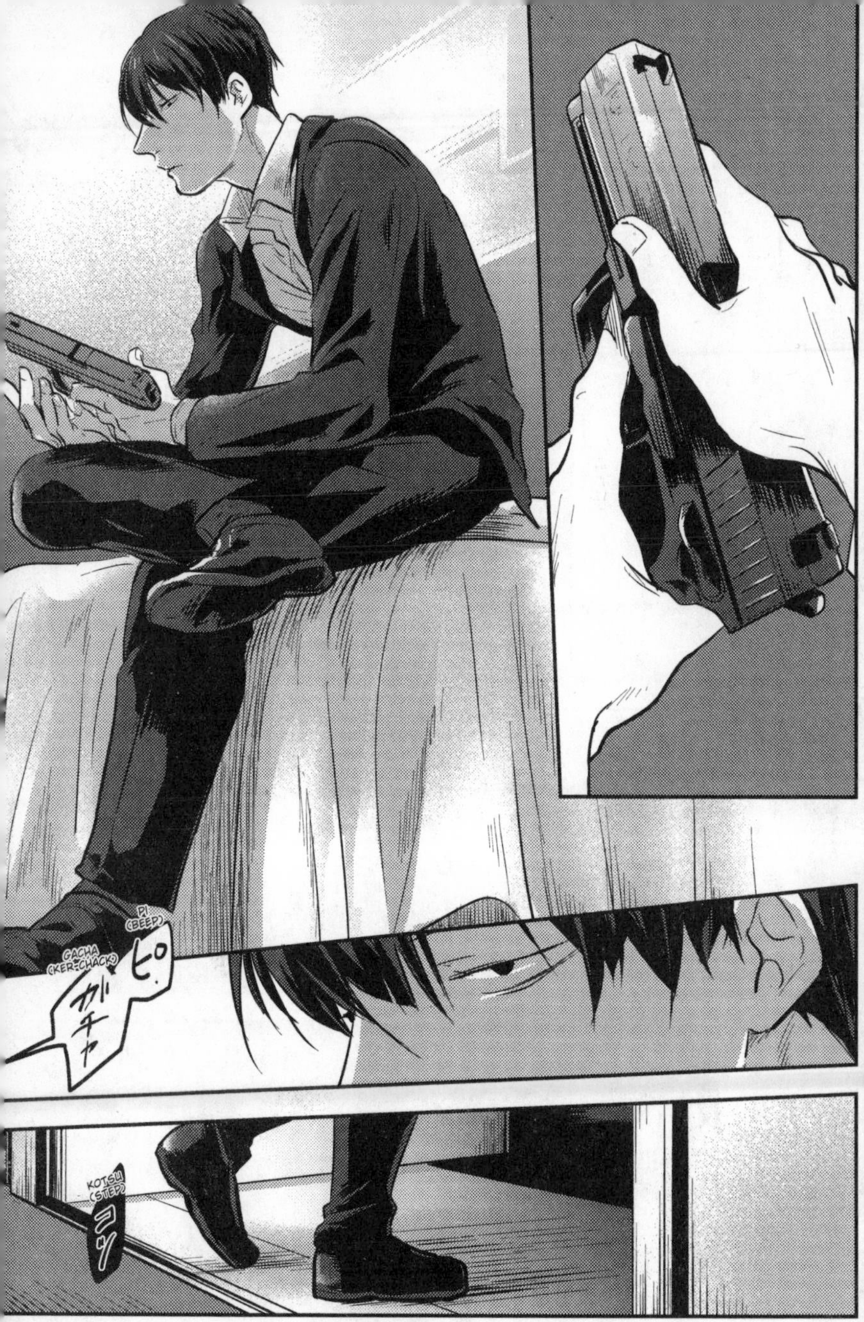
PI (BEEP)
ピ。
GACHA (KER-CHACK)
ガチャ
KOTSU (STEP)
コツ

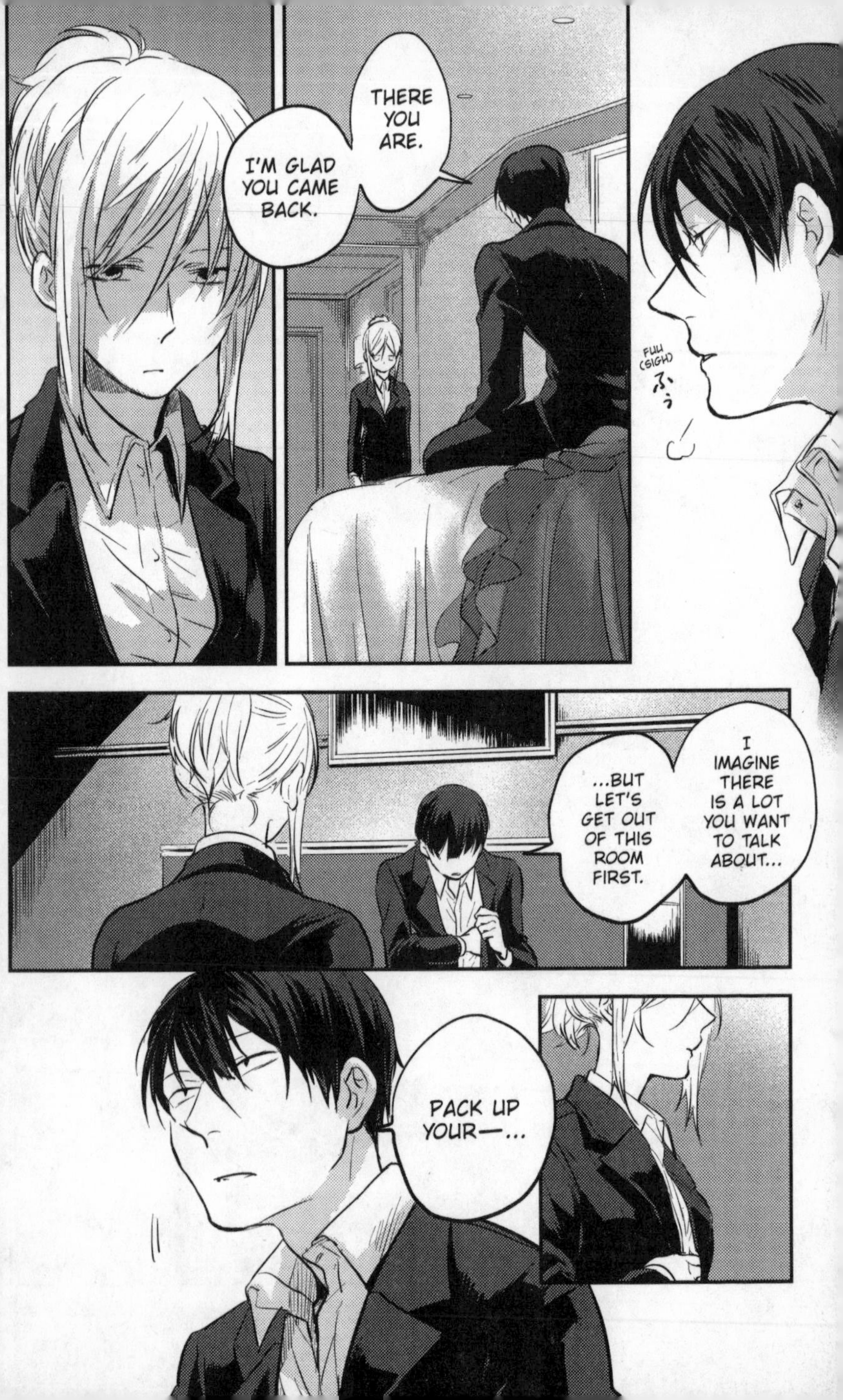
FUU (SIGH)
ふぅ
THERE YOU ARE.
I'M GLAD YOU CAME BACK.
I IMAGINE THERE IS A LOT YOU WANT TO TALK ABOUT...
...BUT LET'S GET OUT OF THIS ROOM FIRST.
PACK UP YOUR—...

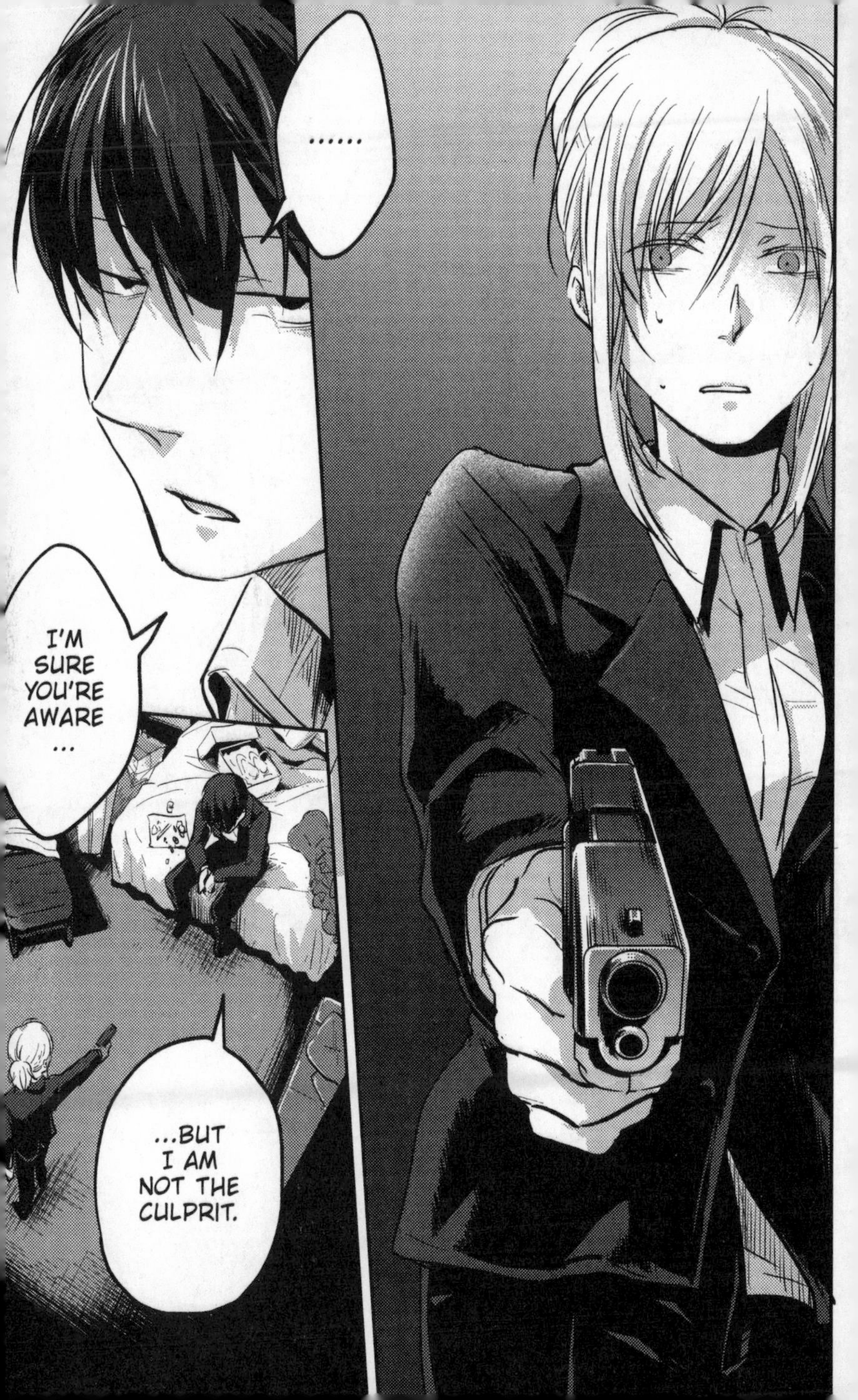
......
I'M SURE YOU'RE AWARE ...
...BUT I AM NOT THE CULPRIT.

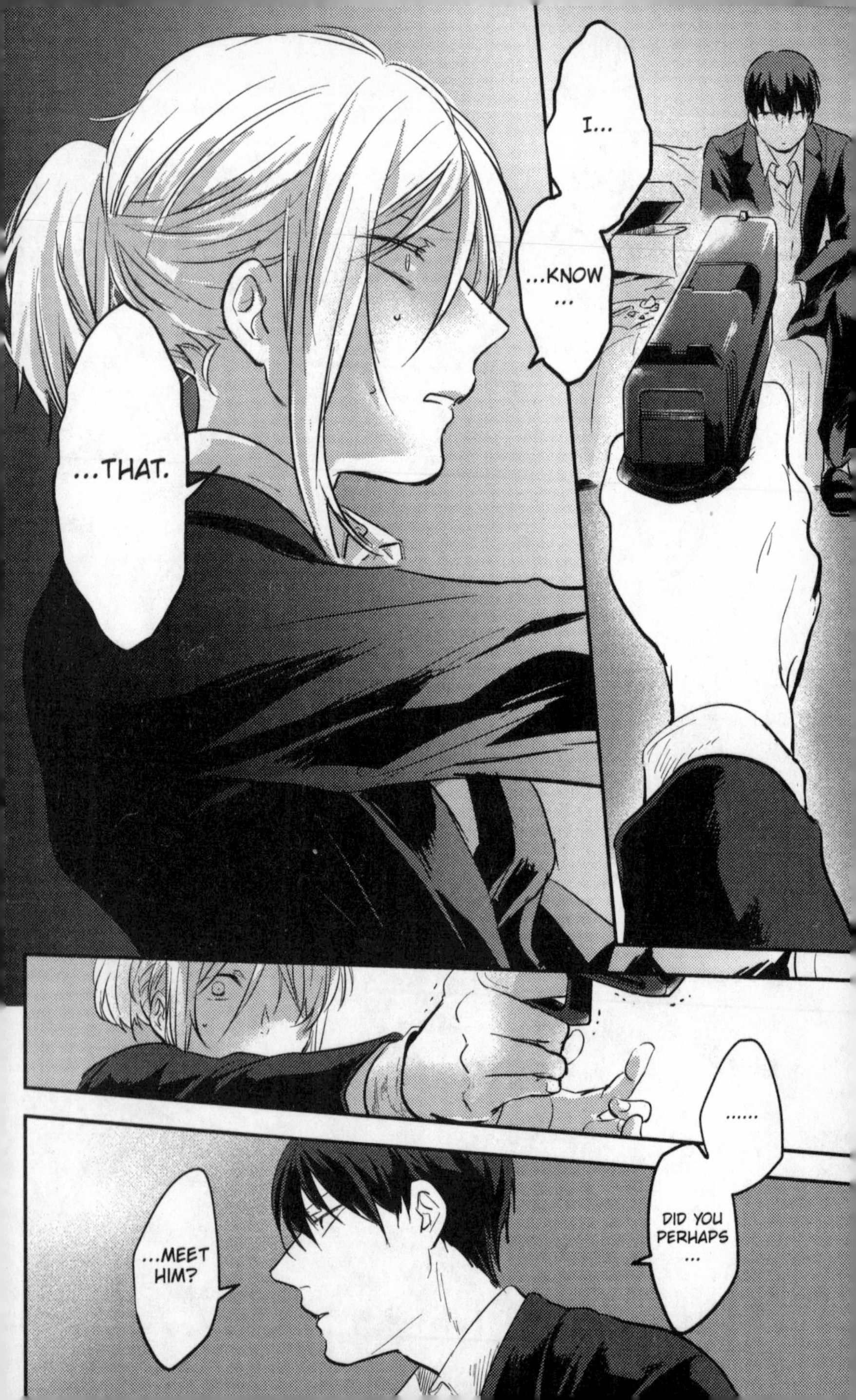
I...
...KNOW ...
...THAT.
......
DID YOU PERHAPS ...
...MEET HIM?

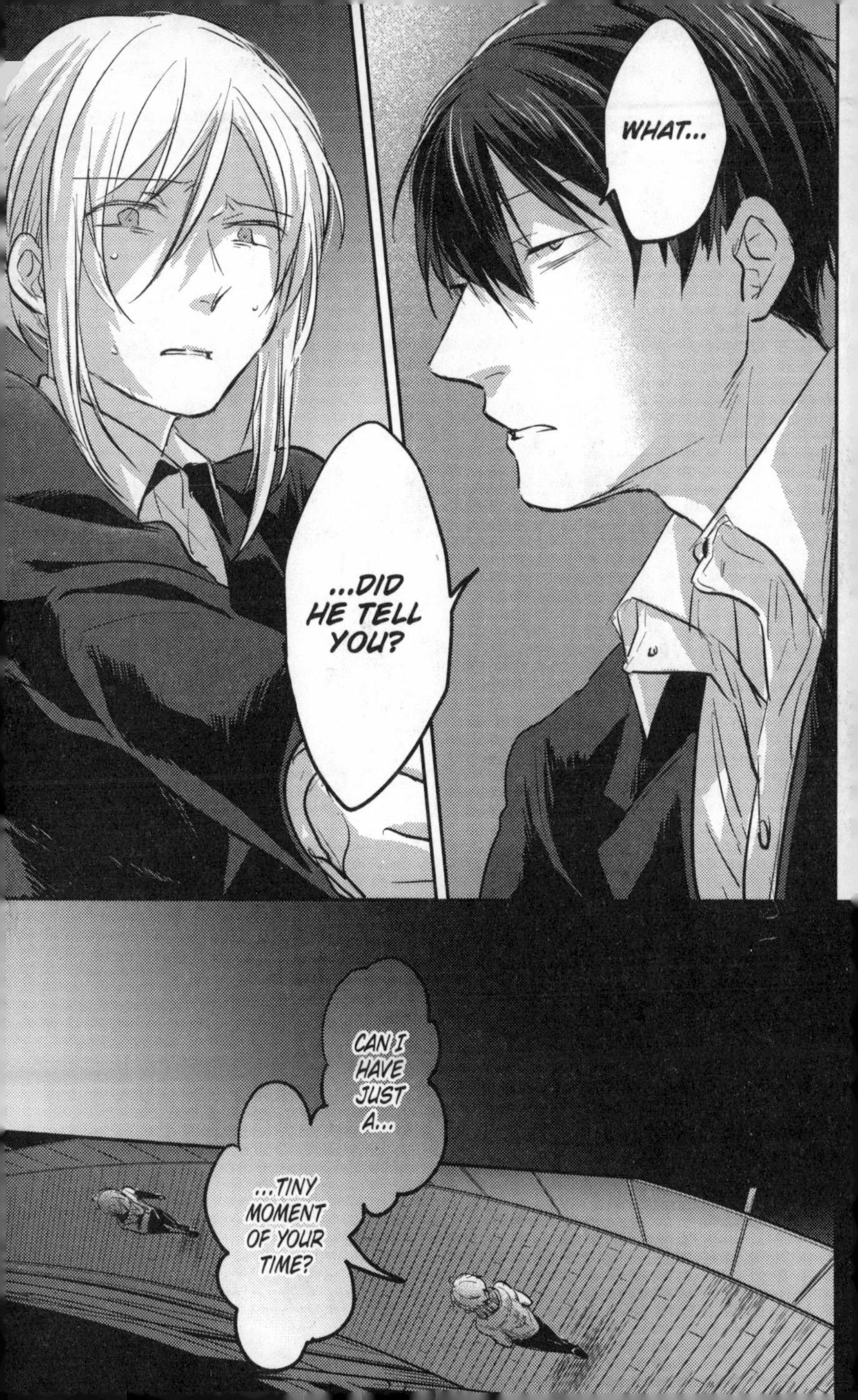
WHAT...
...DID HE TELL YOU?
CAN I HAVE JUST A...
...TINY MOMENT OF YOUR TIME?

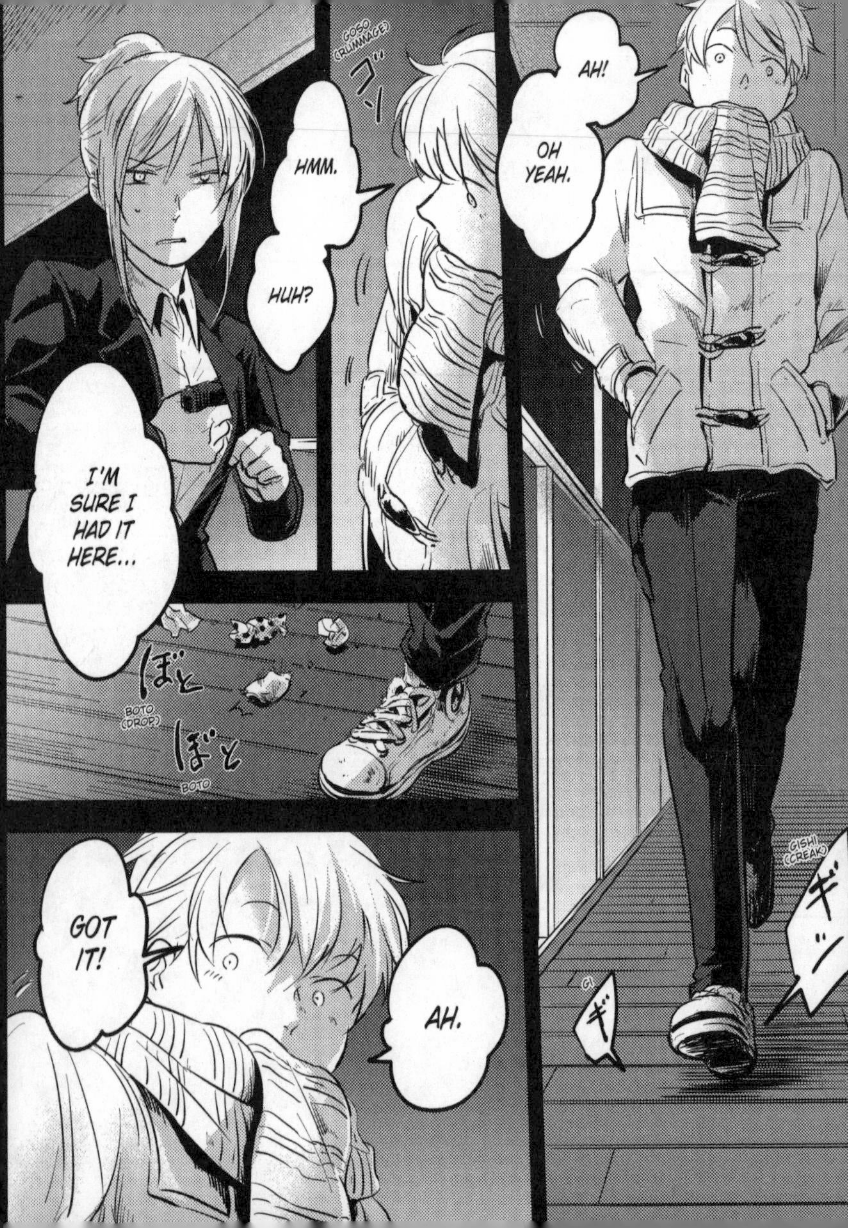
AH!
OH YEAH.
GISHI (CREAK)
GI
GOSO (RUMMAGE)
HMM.
HUH?
I'M SURE I HAD IT HERE...
BOTO (DROP)
BOTO
AH.
GOT IT!

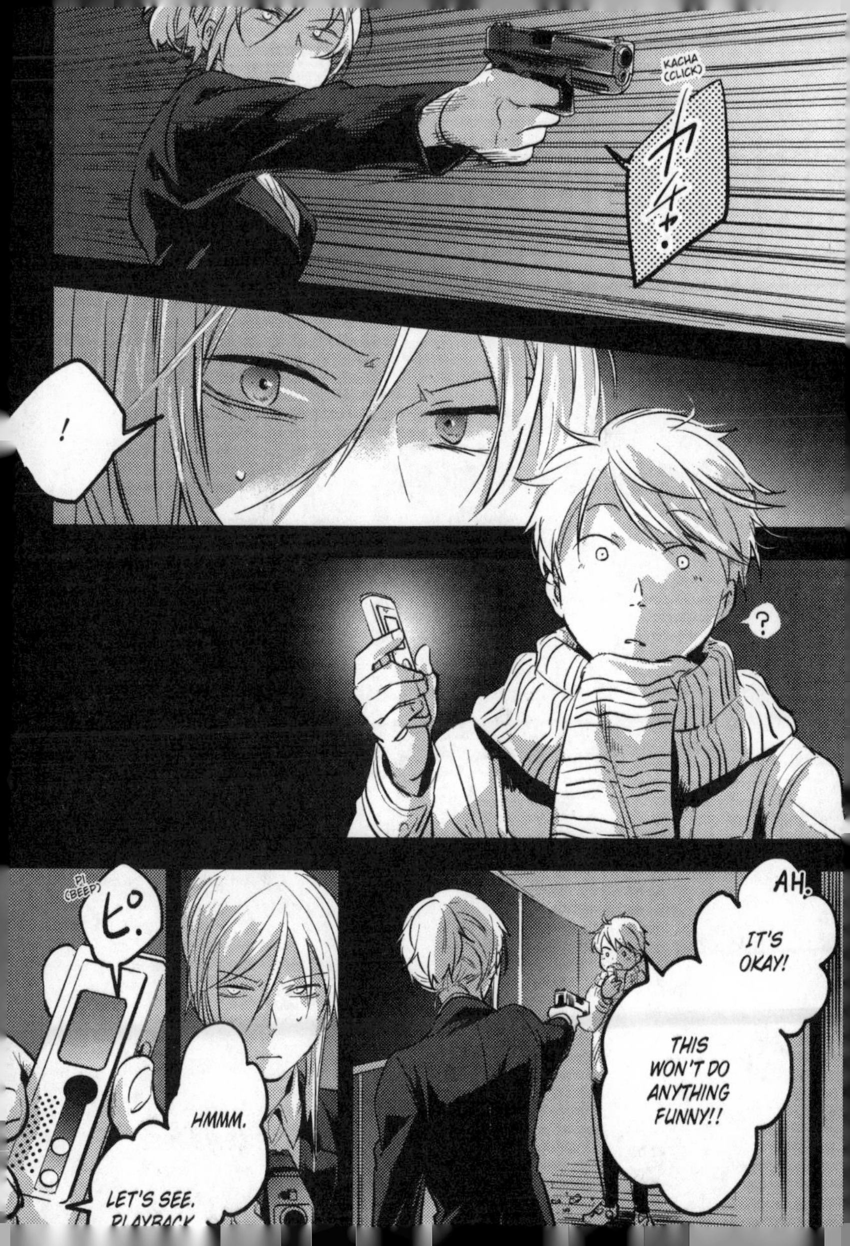
KACHA (CLICK)
カチャ
!
?
AH.
IT'S OKAY!
THIS WON'T DO ANYTHING FUNNY!!
HMMM.
LET'S SEE.
PI (BEEP)
ピ

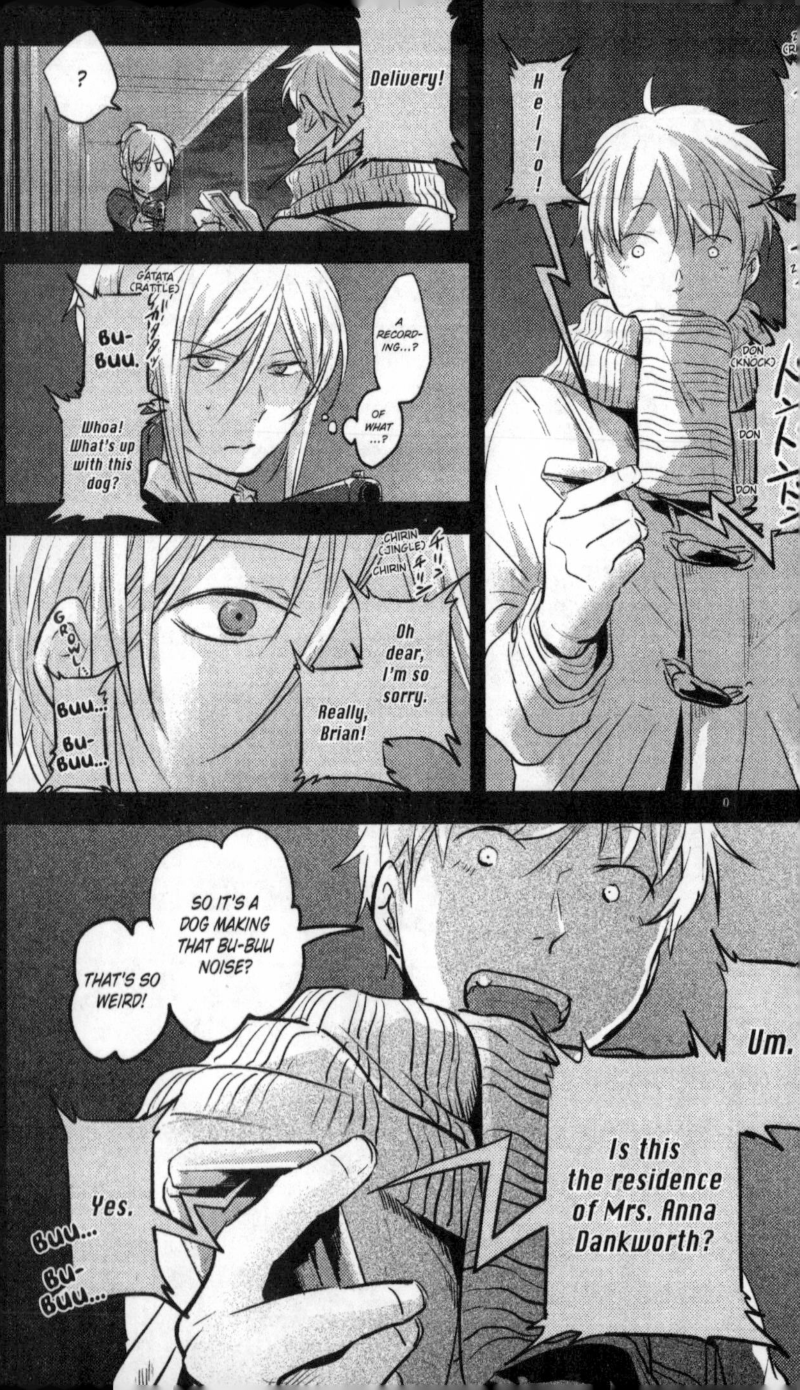
Hello!
DON (KNOCK)
DON
DON
Delivery!
?
A RECORDING...?
OF WHAT...?
GATATA (RATTLE)
BU-BUU.
Whoa! What's up with this dog?
CHIRIN (JINGLE)
CHIRIN
Oh dear, I'm so sorry.
Really, Brian!
GROWL...
BUU...
BU-BUU...
Um.
Is this the residence of Mrs. Anna Dankworth?
SO IT'S A DOG MAKING THAT BU-BUU NOISE?
THAT'S SO WEIRD!
Yes.
BUU...
BU-BUU...

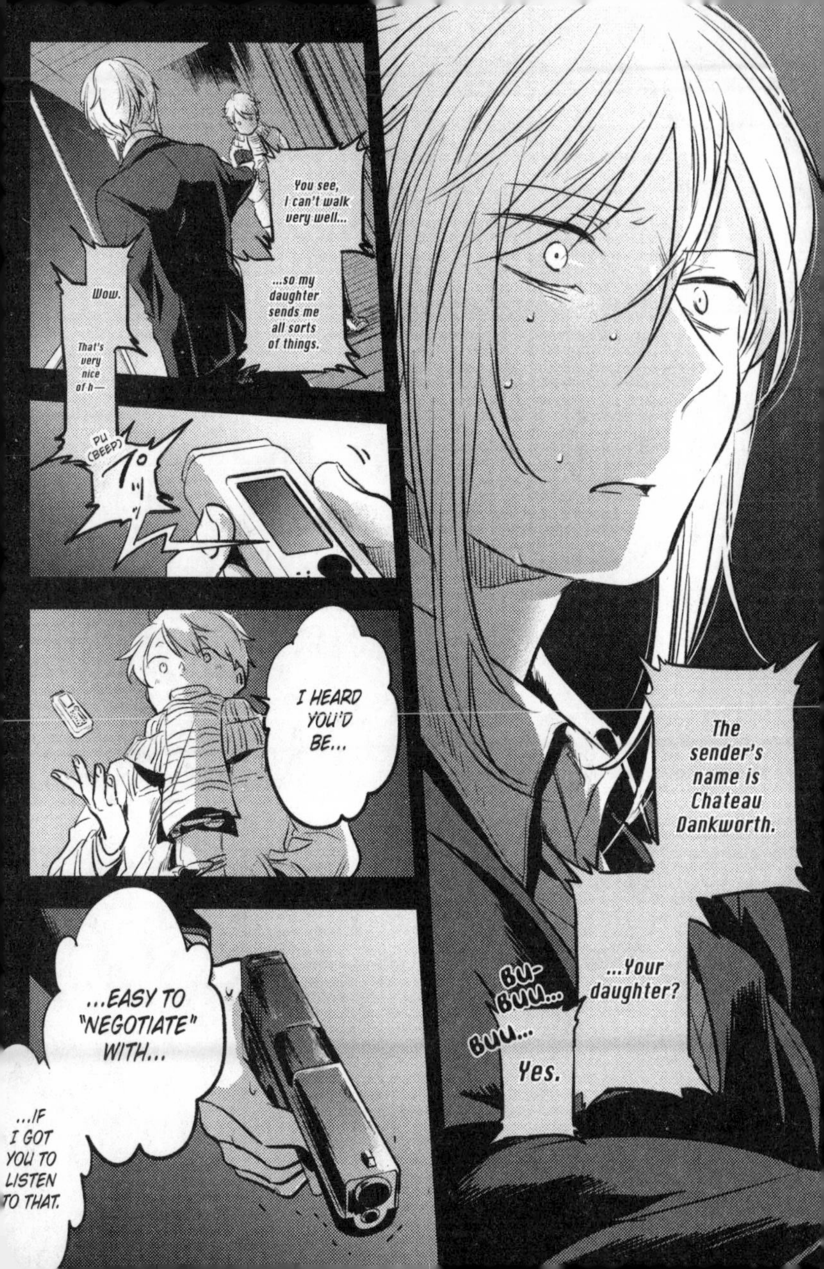
The sender's name is Chateau Dankworth.
...Your daughter?
BU-BUU... BUU...
Yes.
You see, I can't walk very well...
...so my daughter sends me all sorts of things.
Wow.
That's very nice of h—
PU (BEEP)
I HEARD YOU'D BE...
...EASY TO "NEGOTIATE" WITH...
...IF I GOT YOU TO LISTEN TO THAT.

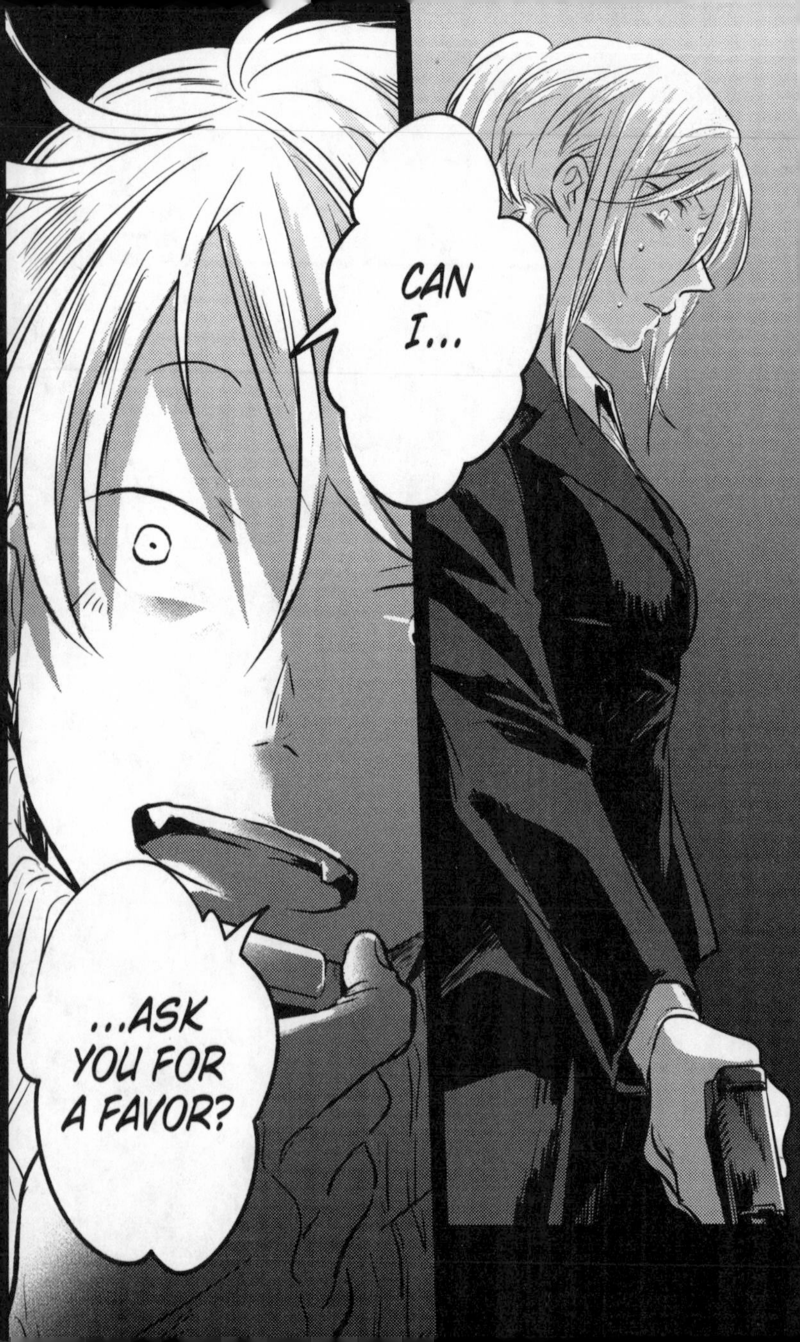
CAN I...
...ASK YOU FOR A FAVOR?

AND NOW, A COMPLETE RIP-OFF OF A
REGULAR SEGMENT FROM *COMIC GENE*!

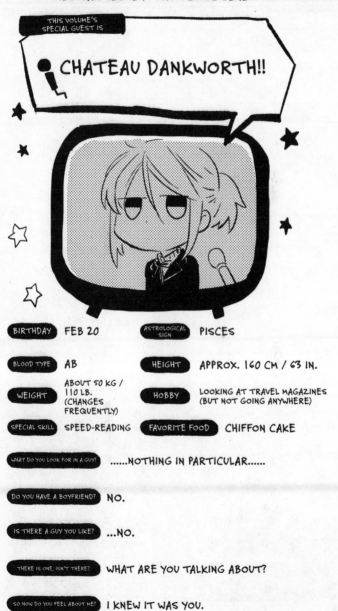

THIS VOLUME'S SPECIAL GUEST IS

CHATEAU DANKWORTH!!

BIRTHDAY	FEB 20	**ASTROLOGICAL SIGN**	PISCES
BLOOD TYPE	AB	**HEIGHT**	APPROX. 160 CM / 63 IN.
WEIGHT	ABOUT 50 KG / 110 LB. (CHANGES FREQUENTLY)	**HOBBY**	LOOKING AT TRAVEL MAGAZINES (BUT NOT GOING ANYWHERE)
SPECIAL SKILL	SPEED-READING	**FAVORITE FOOD**	CHIFFON CAKE

WHAT DO YOU LOOK FOR IN A GUY? ......NOTHING IN PARTICULAR......

DO YOU HAVE A BOYFRIEND? NO.

IS THERE A GUY YOU LIKE? ...NO.

THERE IS ONE, ISN'T THERE? WHAT ARE YOU TALKING ABOUT?

SO HOW DO YOU FEEL ABOUT ME? I KNEW IT WAS YOU.

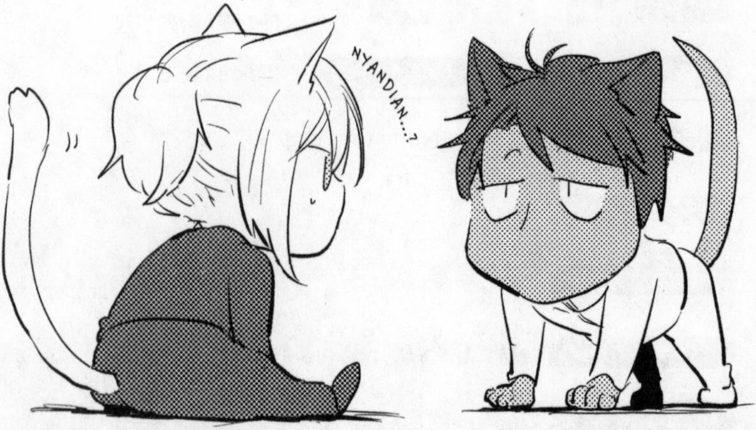
NYANDIAN...?

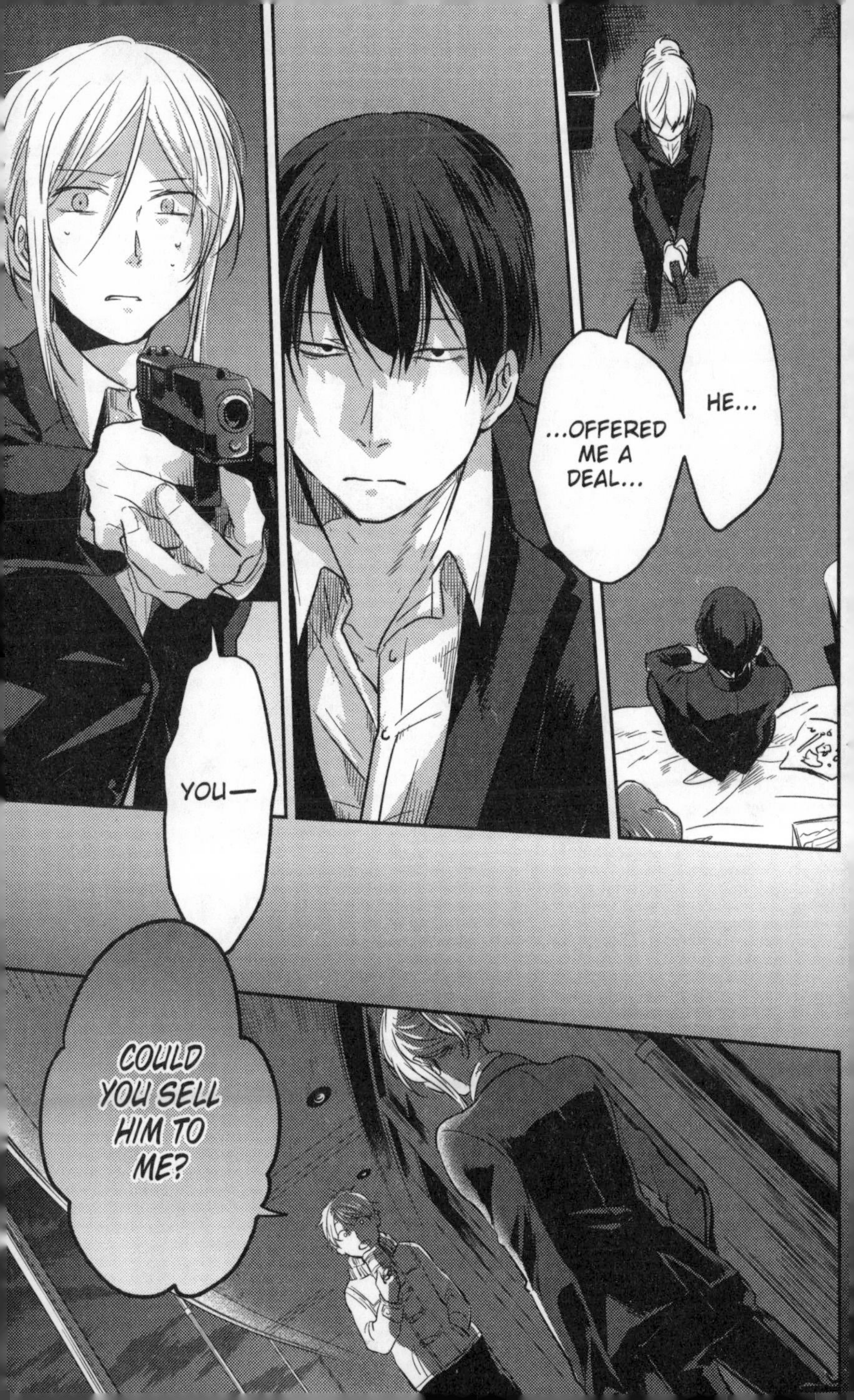
HE...
...OFFERED ME A DEAL...
YOU—
COULD YOU SELL HIM TO ME?

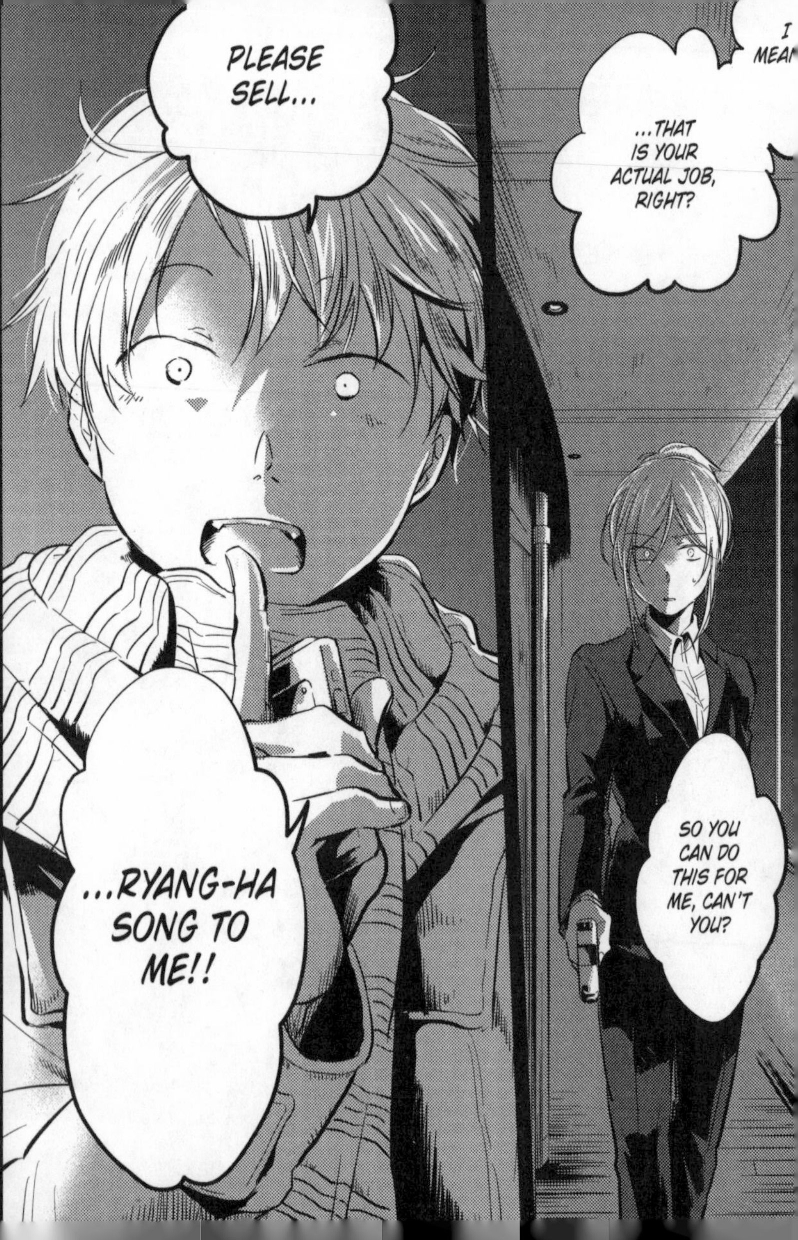
I MEA
...THAT IS YOUR ACTUAL JOB, RIGHT?
SO YOU CAN DO THIS FOR ME, CAN'T YOU?
PLEASE SELL...
...RYANG-HA SONG TO ME!!

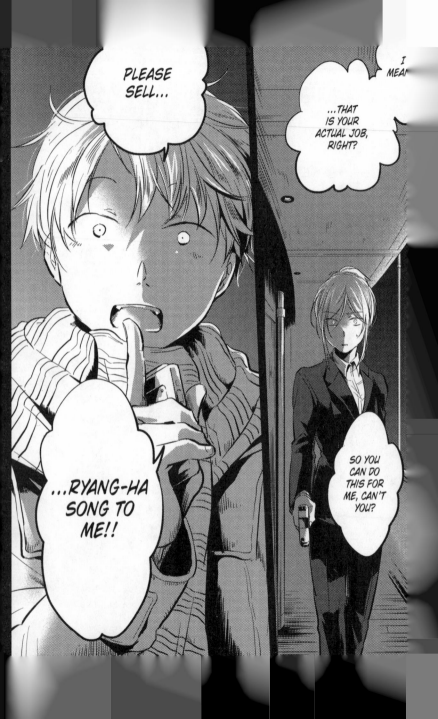

FILE 21 BULLET

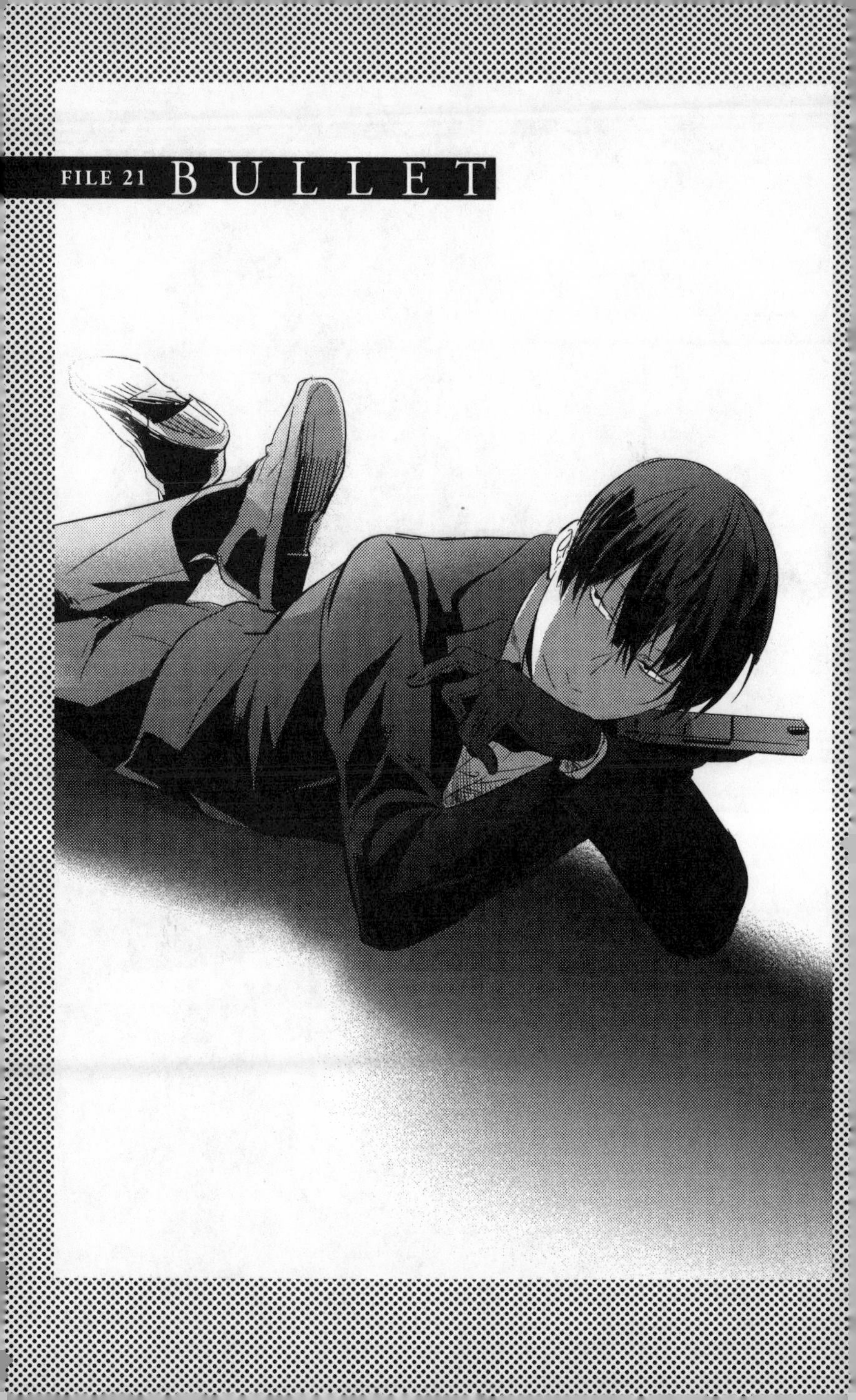

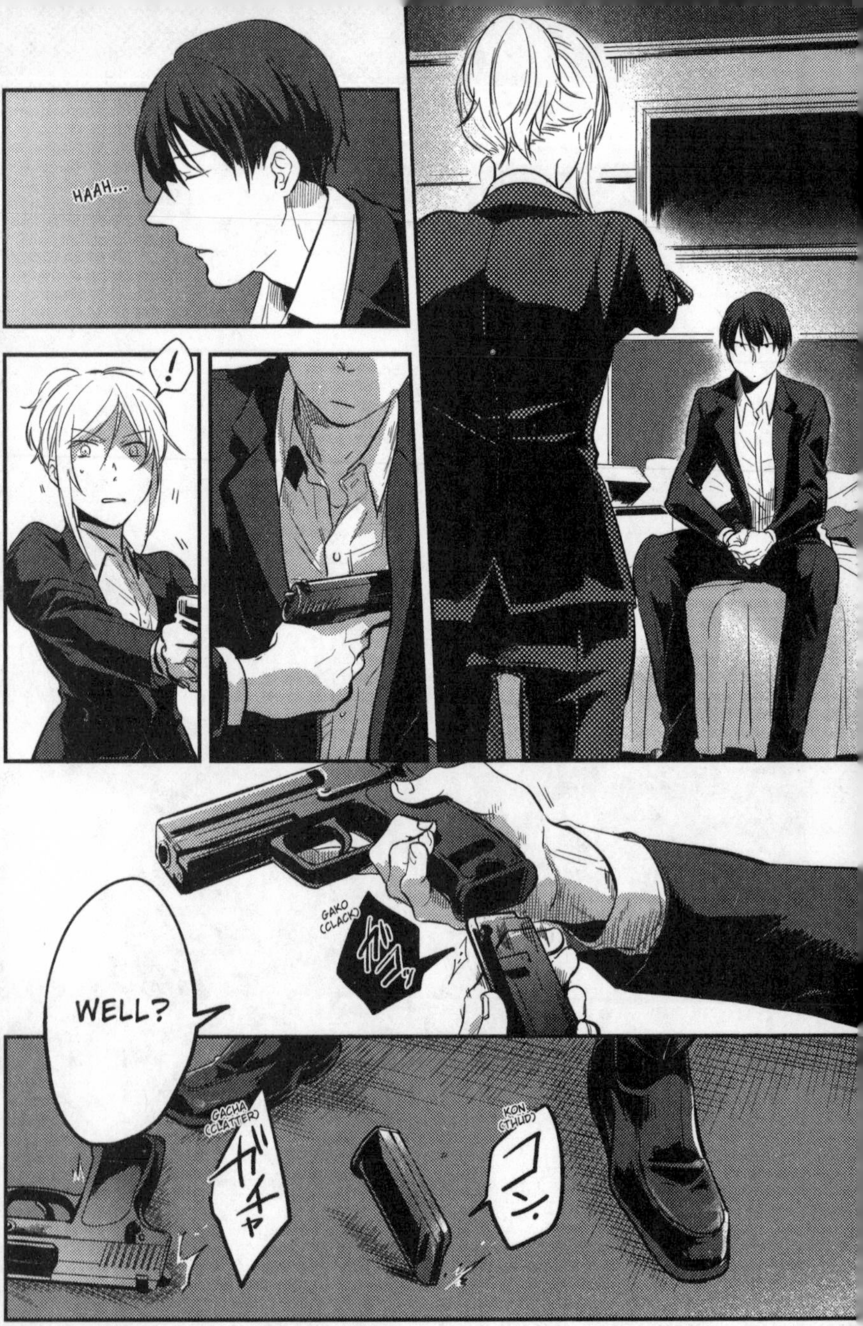
HAAH...
!
GAKO (CLACK)
ガコッ
WELL?
KON (THUD)
コン
GACHA (CLATTER)
ガチャ

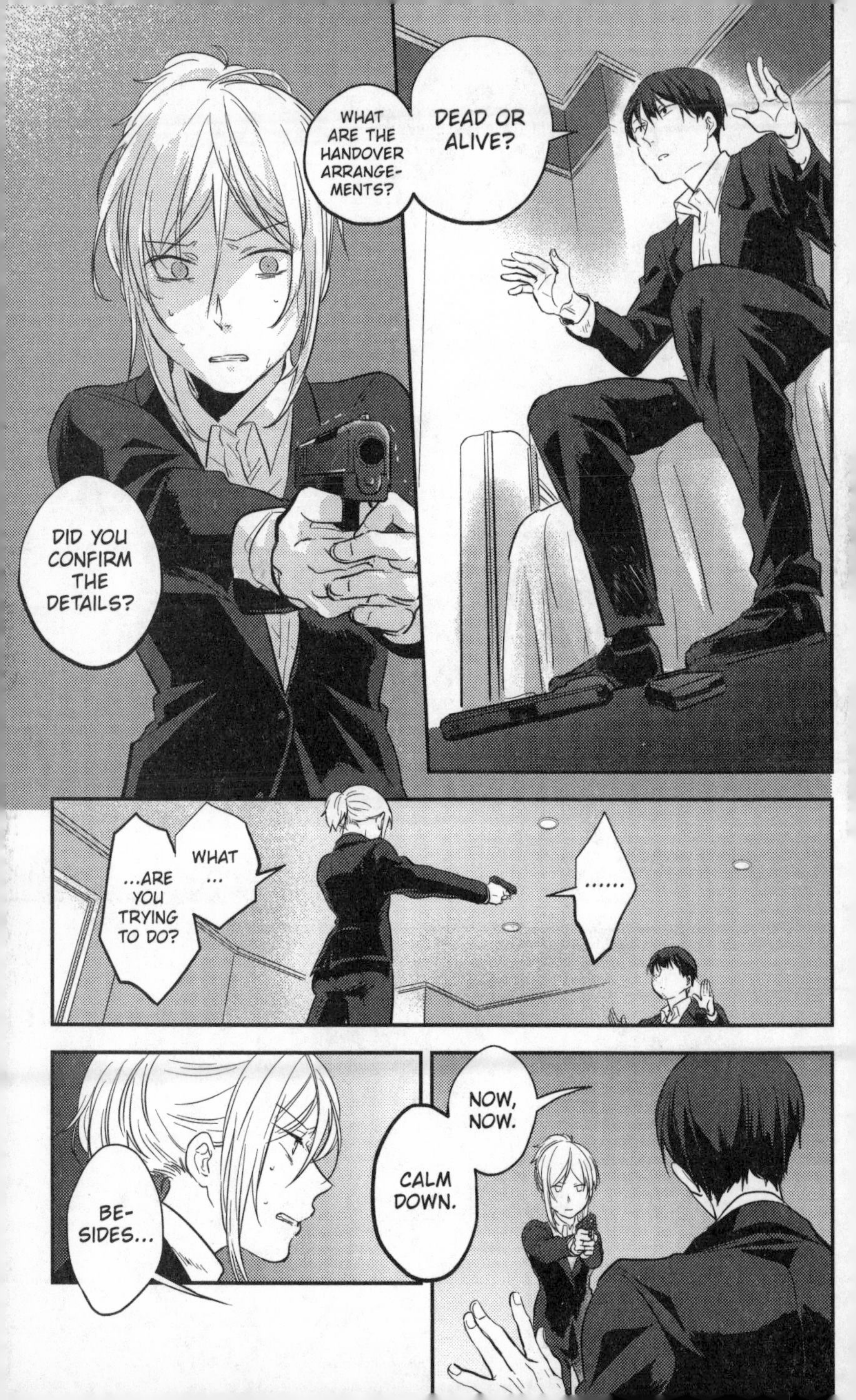
DEAD OR ALIVE?
WHAT ARE THE HANDOVER ARRANGE-MENTS?
DID YOU CONFIRM THE DETAILS?
......
WHAT ...
...ARE YOU TRYING TO DO?
NOW, NOW.
CALM DOWN.
BE-SIDES...

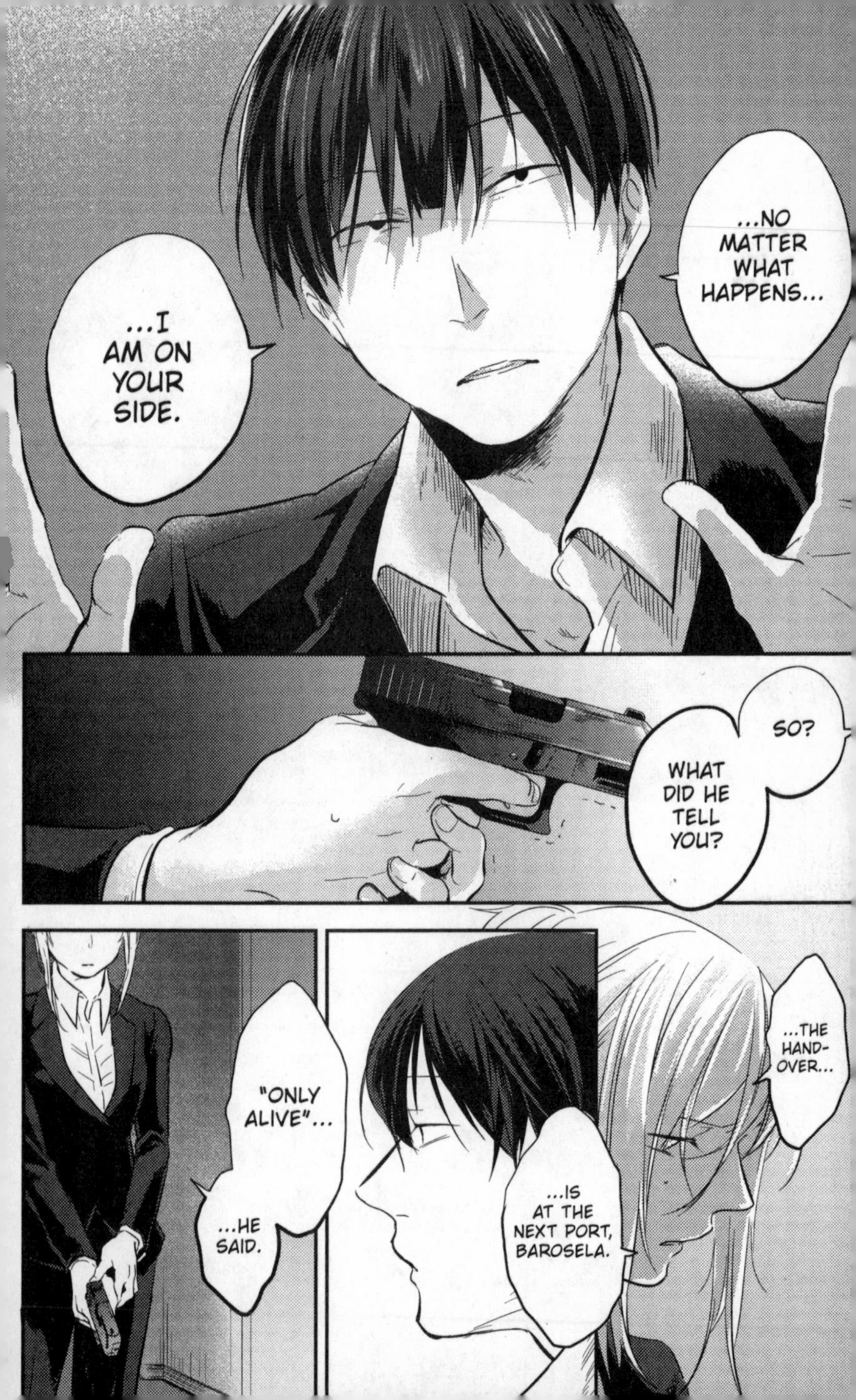
...NO MATTER WHAT HAPPENS...
...I AM ON YOUR SIDE.
SO?
WHAT DID HE TELL YOU?
...THE HAND-OVER...
...IS AT THE NEXT PORT, BAROSELA.
"ONLY ALIVE"...
...HE SAID.

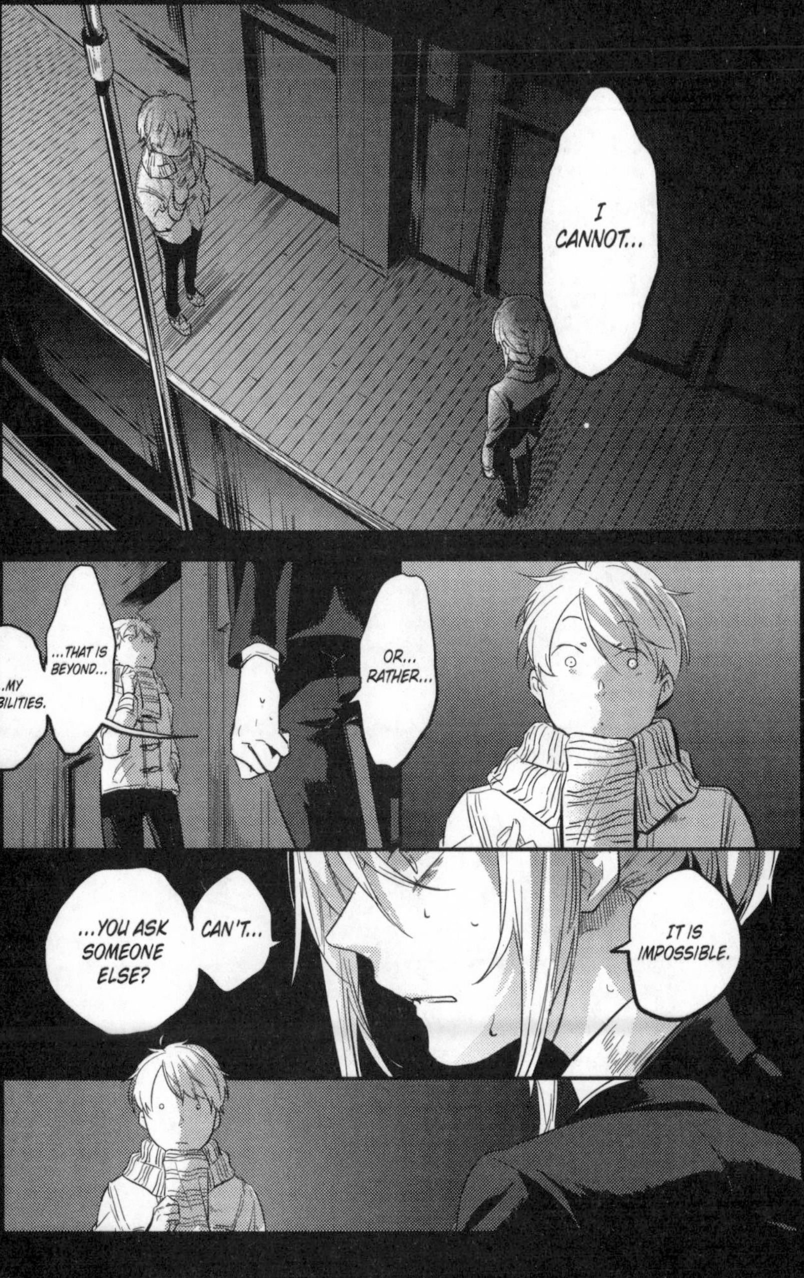
I CANNOT...
OR... RATHER...
...THAT IS BEYOND...
...MY CAPABILITIES.
IT IS IMPOSSIBLE.
CAN'T...
...YOU ASK SOMEONE ELSE?

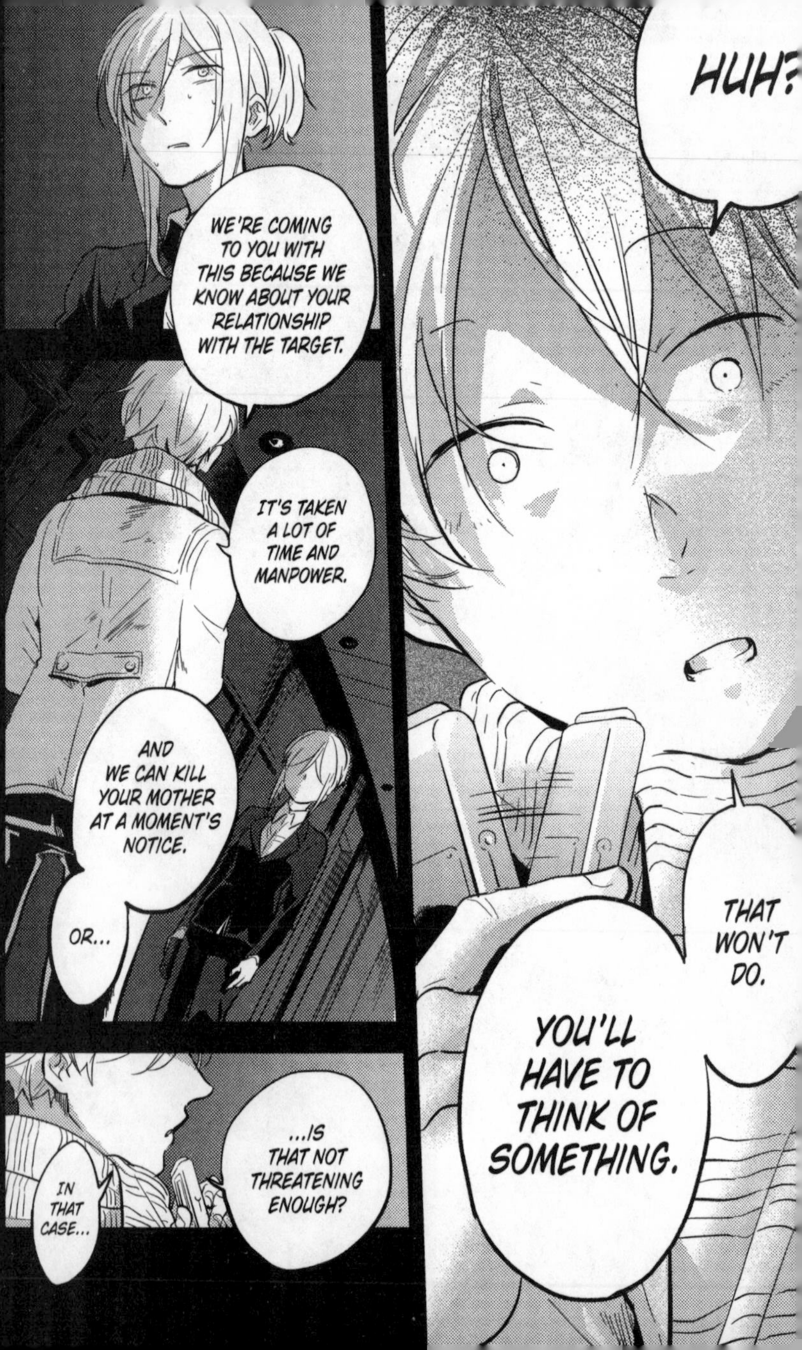
HUH?
THAT WON'T DO.
YOU'LL HAVE TO THINK OF SOMETHING.
WE'RE COMING TO YOU WITH THIS BECAUSE WE KNOW ABOUT YOUR RELATIONSHIP WITH THE TARGET.
IT'S TAKEN A LOT OF TIME AND MANPOWER.
AND WE CAN KILL YOUR MOTHER AT A MOMENT'S NOTICE.
OR...
...IS THAT NOT THREATENING ENOUGH?
IN THAT CASE...

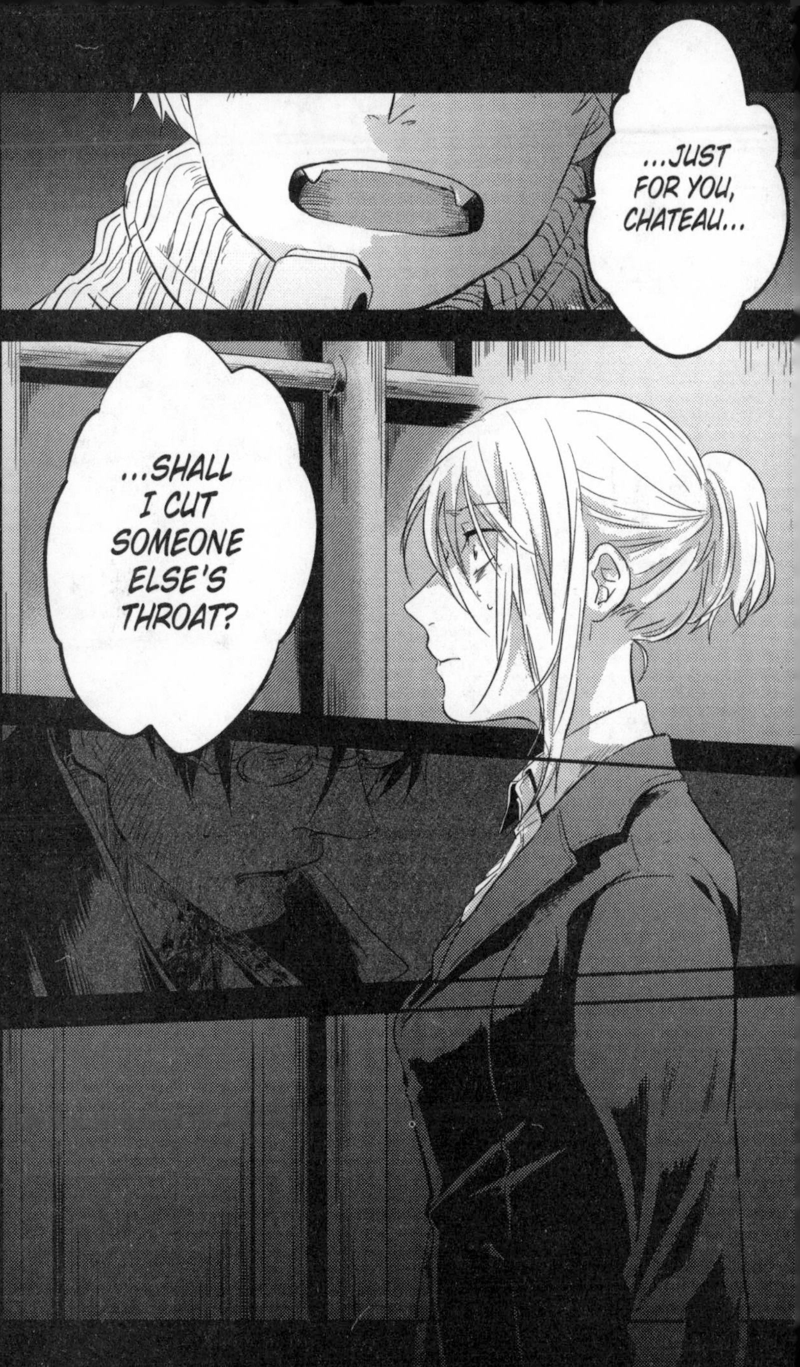
...JUST FOR YOU, CHATEAU...
...SHALL I CUT SOMEONE ELSE'S THROAT?

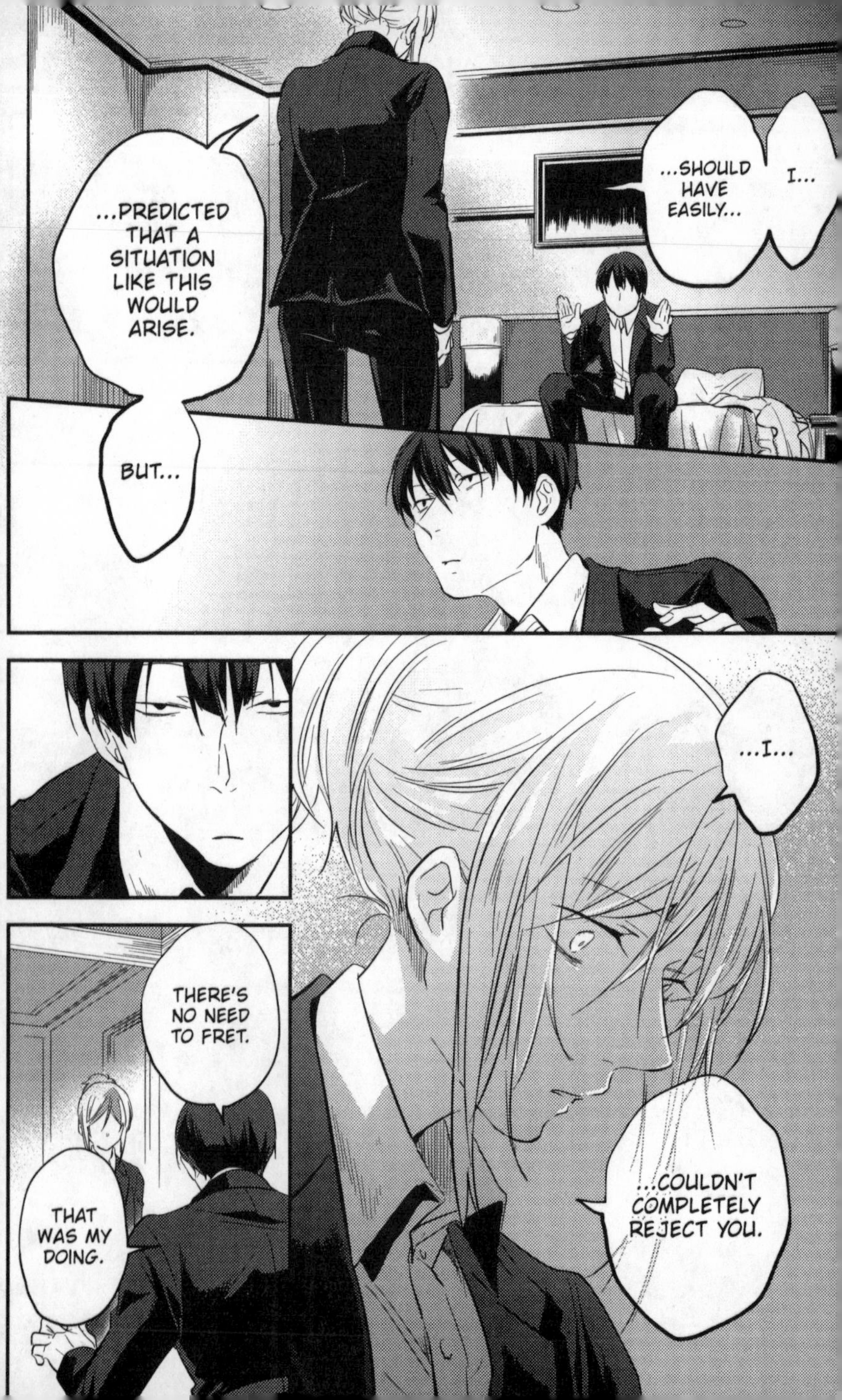
I...
...SHOULD HAVE EASILY...
...PREDICTED THAT A SITUATION LIKE THIS WOULD ARISE.
BUT...
...I...
...COULDN'T COMPLETELY REJECT YOU.
THERE'S NO NEED TO FRET.
THAT WAS MY DOING.

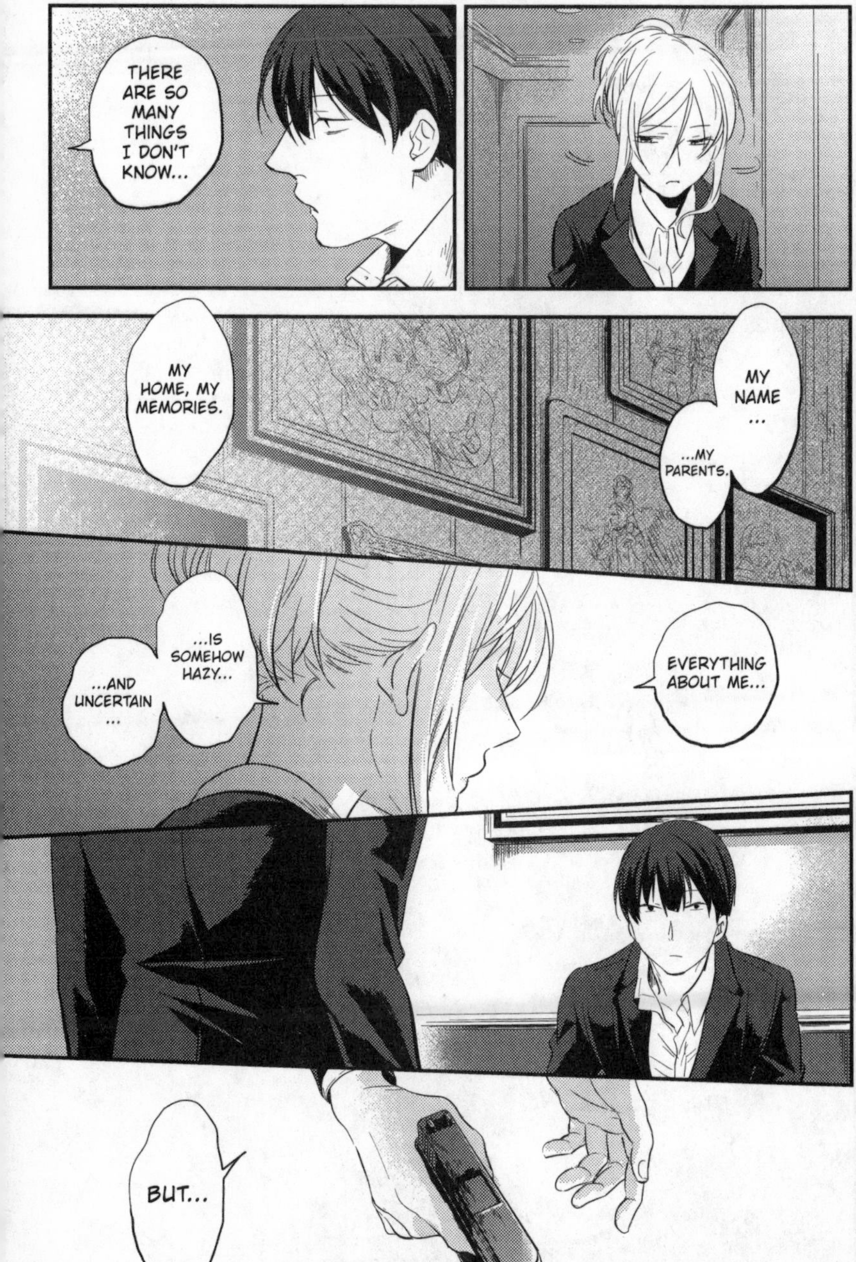
THERE ARE SO MANY THINGS I DON'T KNOW...
MY NAME ...
...MY PARENTS.
MY HOME, MY MEMORIES.
EVERYTHING ABOUT ME...
...IS SOMEHOW HAZY...
...AND UNCERTAIN ...
BUT...

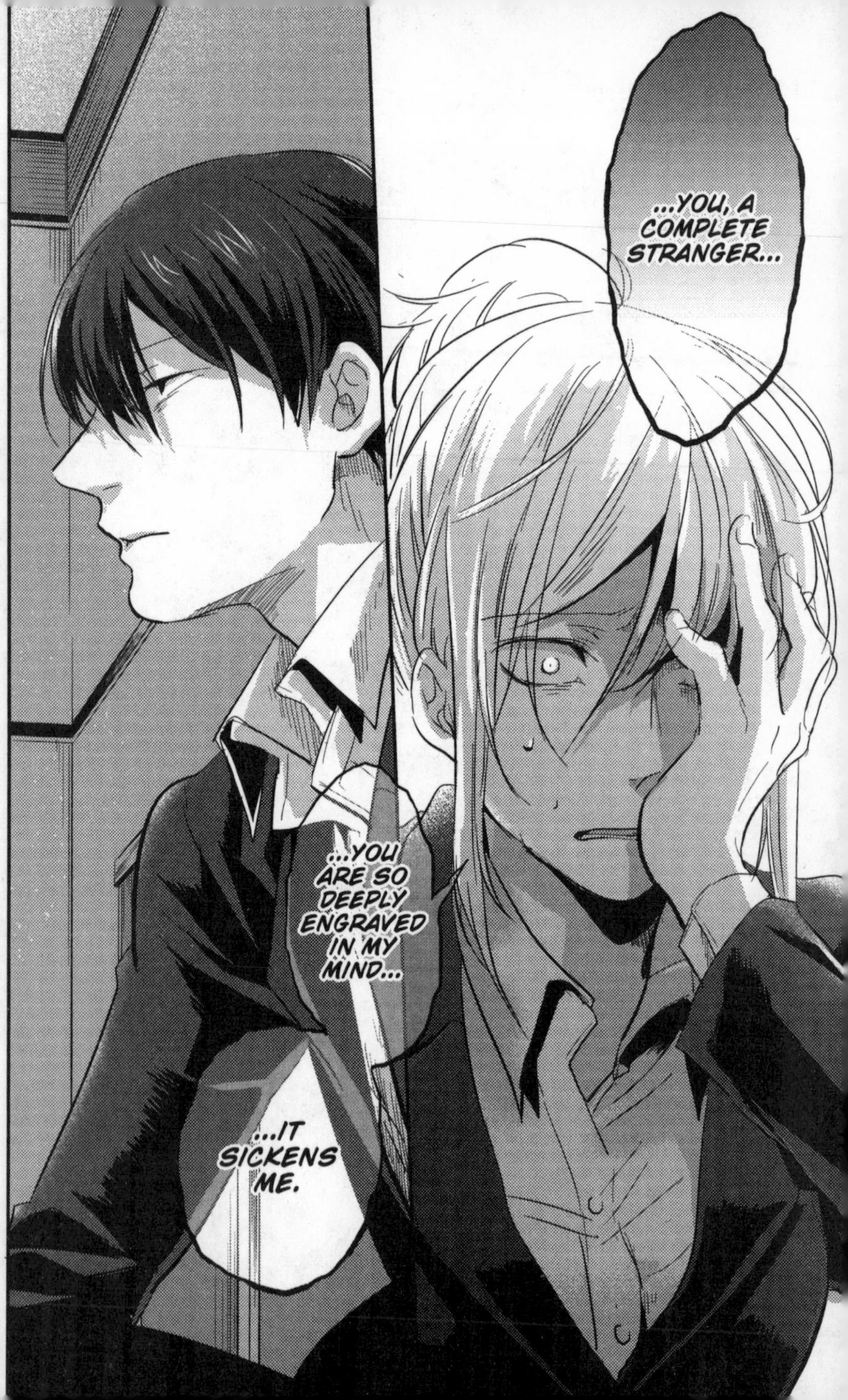
...YOU, A COMPLETE STRANGER...
...YOU ARE SO DEEPLY ENGRAVED IN MY MIND...
...IT SICKENS ME.

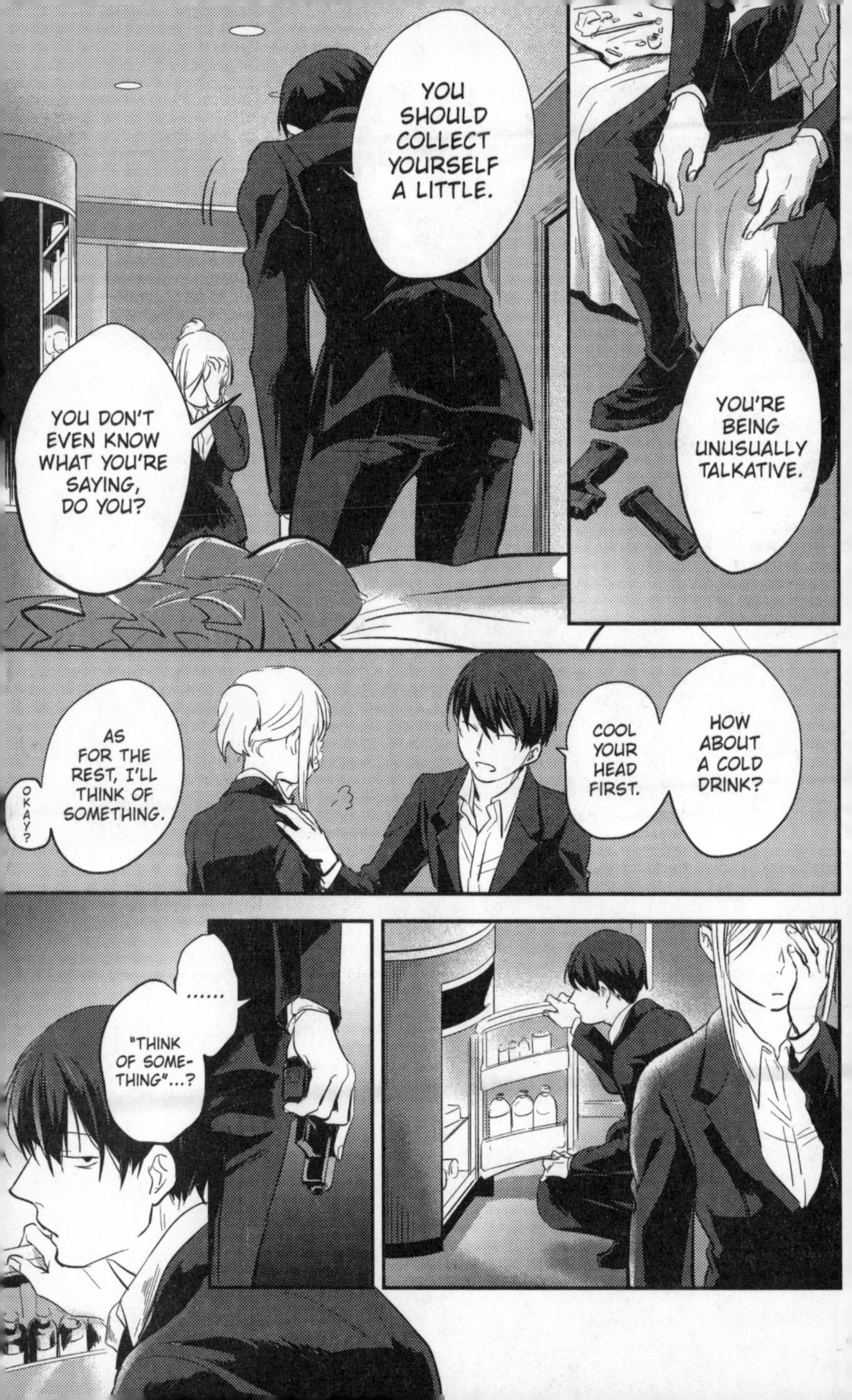
YOU'RE BEING UNUSUALLY TALKATIVE.
YOU SHOULD COLLECT YOURSELF A LITTLE.
YOU DON'T EVEN KNOW WHAT YOU'RE SAYING, DO YOU?
HOW ABOUT A COLD DRINK?
COOL YOUR HEAD FIRST.
AS FOR THE REST, I'LL THINK OF SOMETHING.
OKAY?
......
"THINK OF SOME-THING"...?

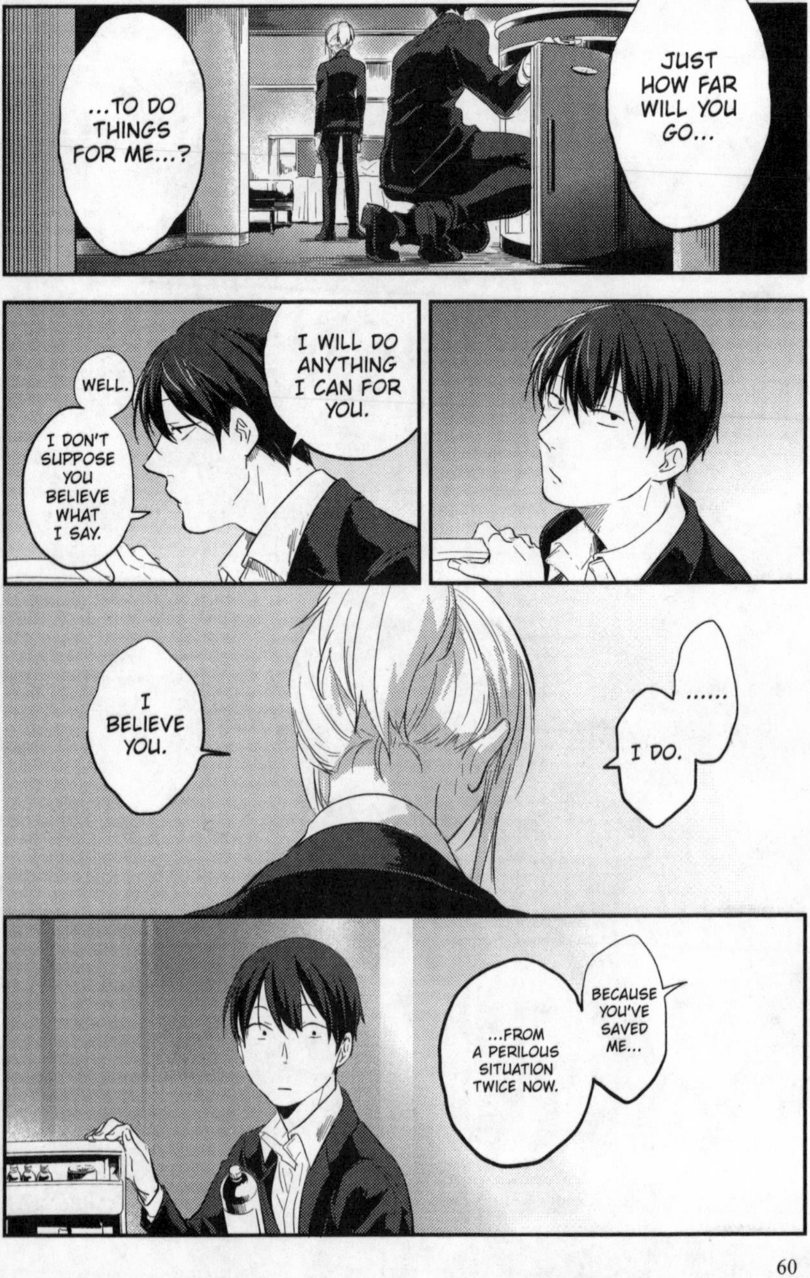
JUST HOW FAR WILL YOU GO...
...TO DO THINGS FOR ME...?
I WILL DO ANYTHING I CAN FOR YOU.
WELL.
I DON'T SUPPOSE YOU BELIEVE WHAT I SAY.
...... I DO.
I BELIEVE YOU.
BECAUSE YOU'VE SAVED ME...
...FROM A PERILOUS SITUATION TWICE NOW.

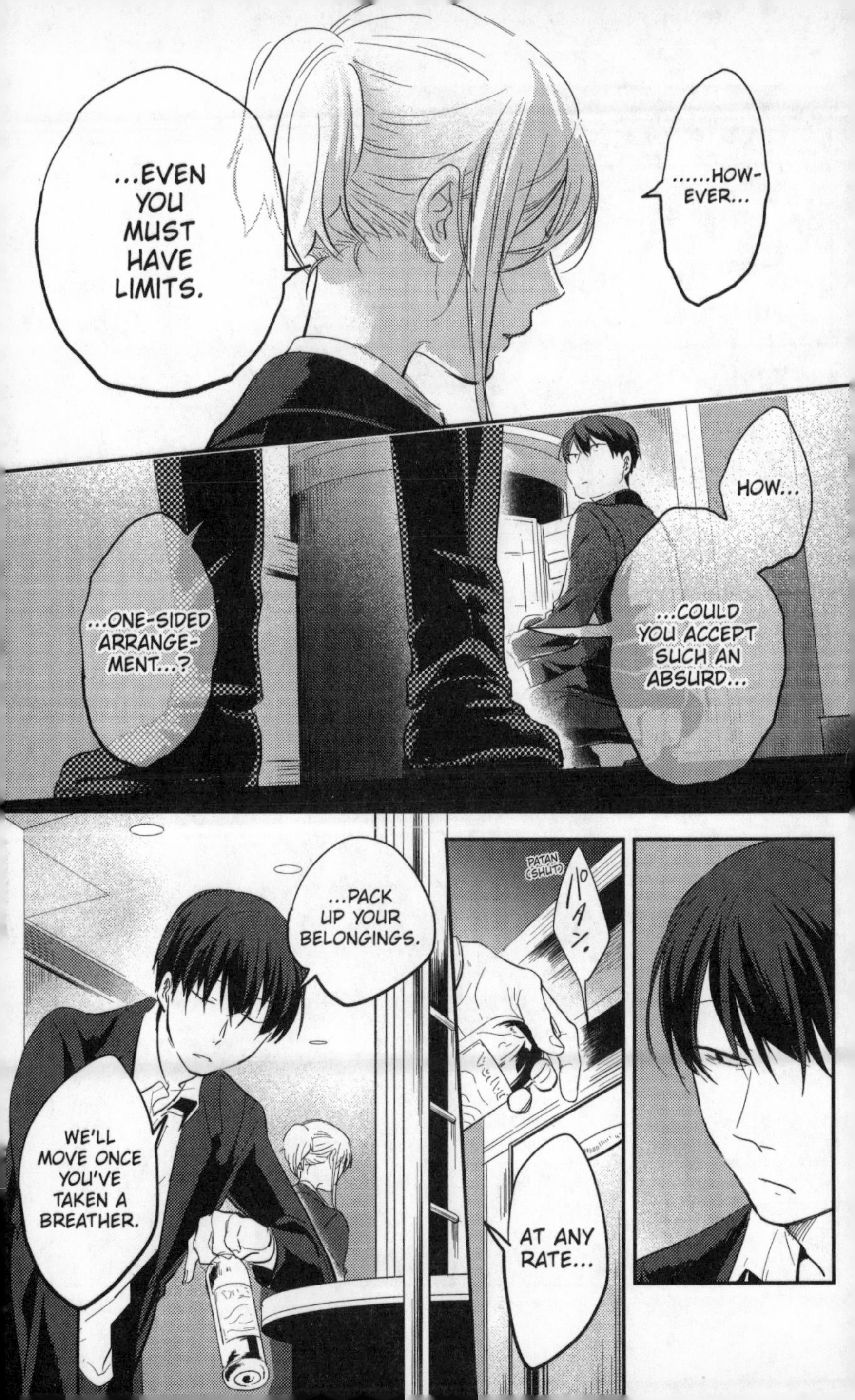
......HOW-EVER...
...EVEN YOU MUST HAVE LIMITS.
HOW...
...COULD YOU ACCEPT SUCH AN ABSURD...
...ONE-SIDED ARRANGE-MENT...?
PATAN (SHUT)
AT ANY RATE...
...PACK UP YOUR BELONGINGS.
WE'LL MOVE ONCE YOU'VE TAKEN A BREATHER.

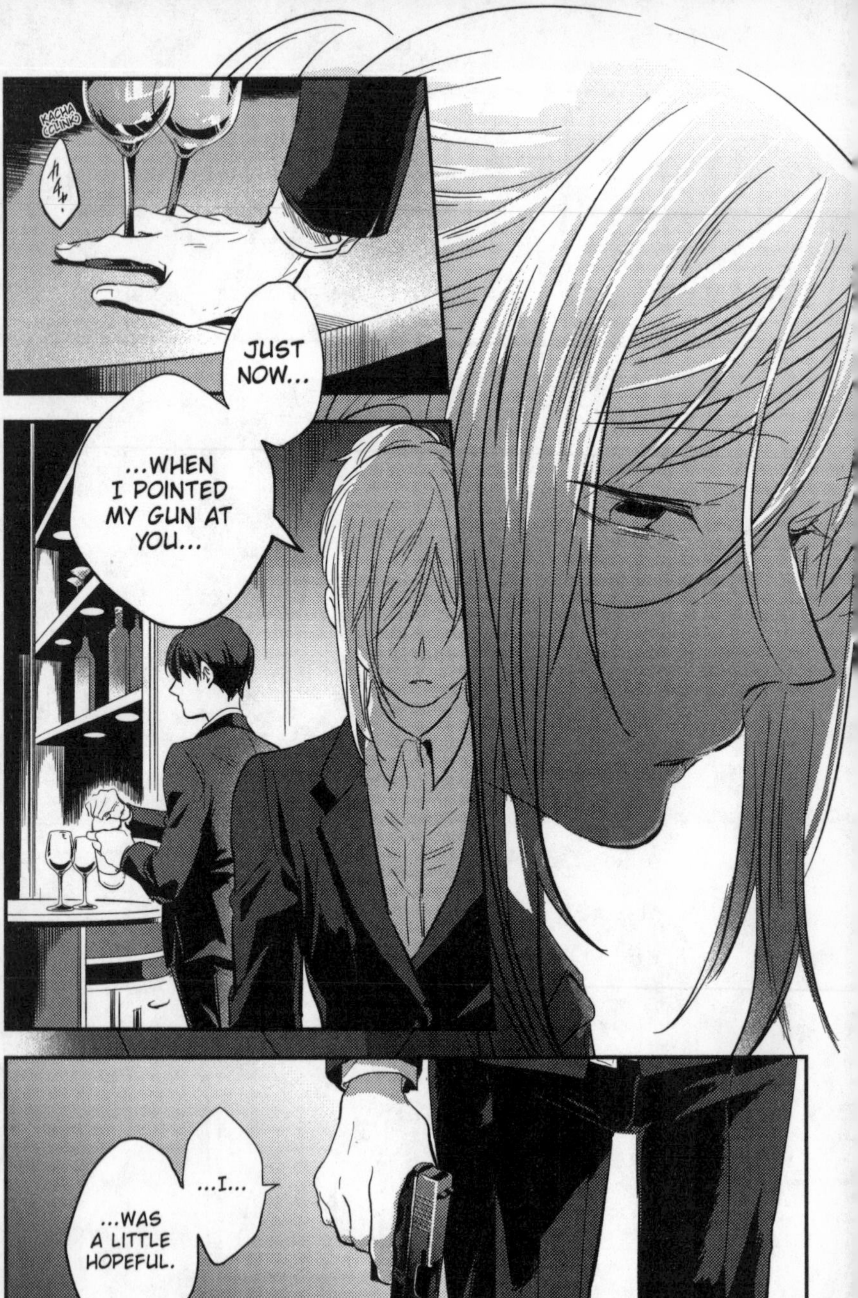
KACHA (CLINK)
JUST NOW...
...WHEN I POINTED MY GUN AT YOU...
...I...
...WAS A LITTLE HOPEFUL.

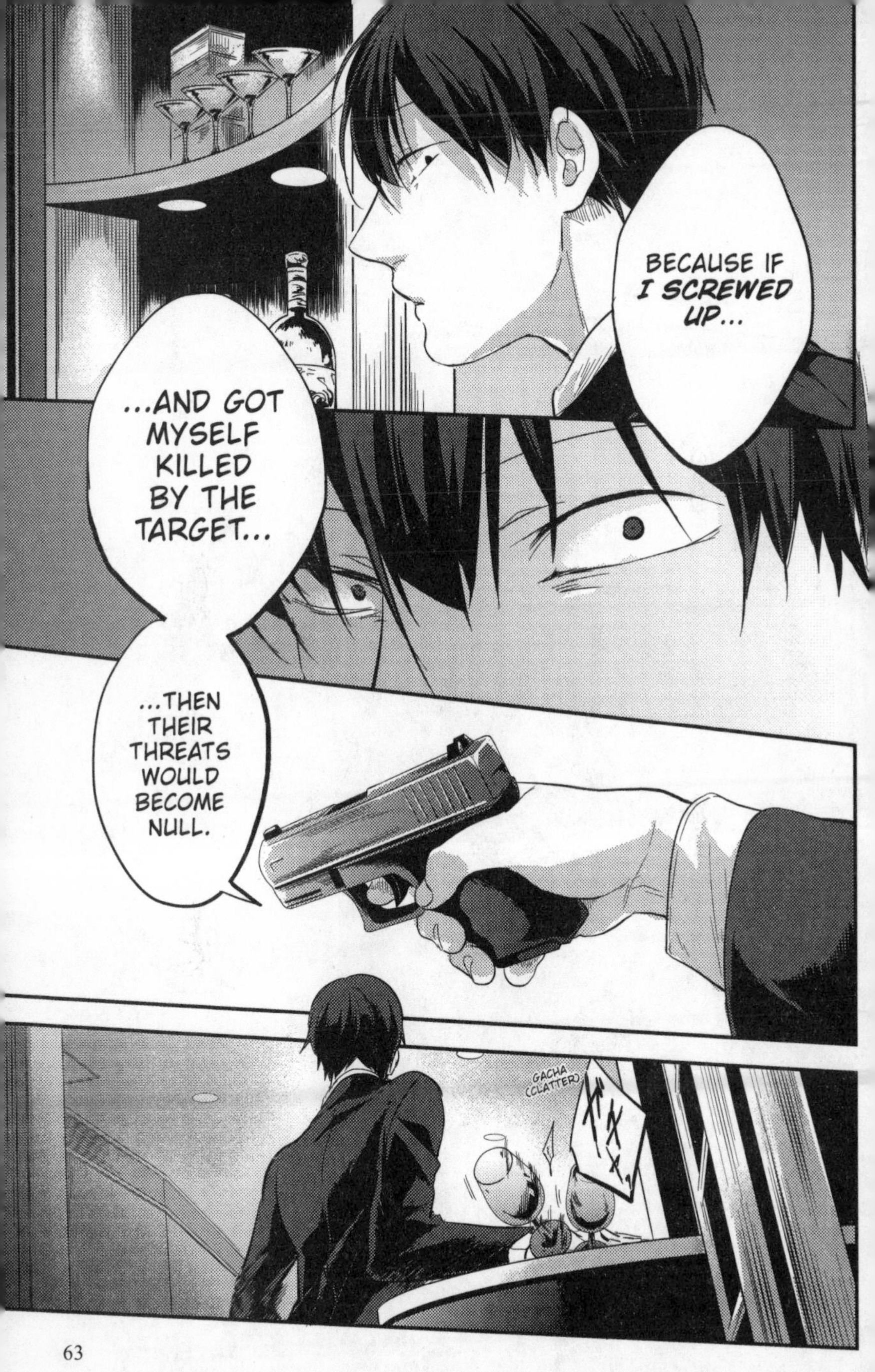
BECAUSE IF I SCREWED UP...
...AND GOT MYSELF KILLED BY THE TARGET...
...THEN THEIR THREATS WOULD BECOME NULL.
GACHA (CLATTER)

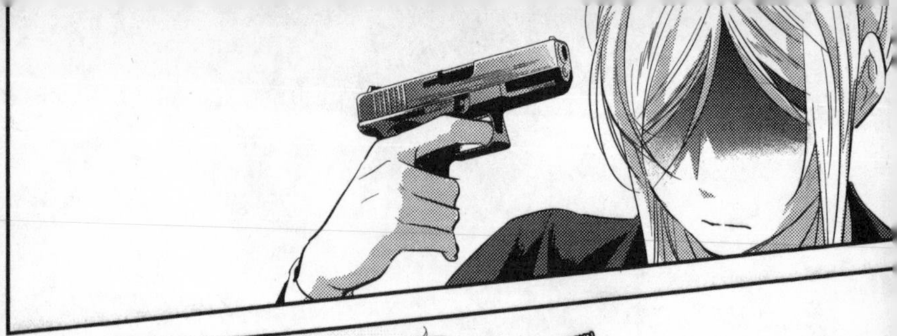

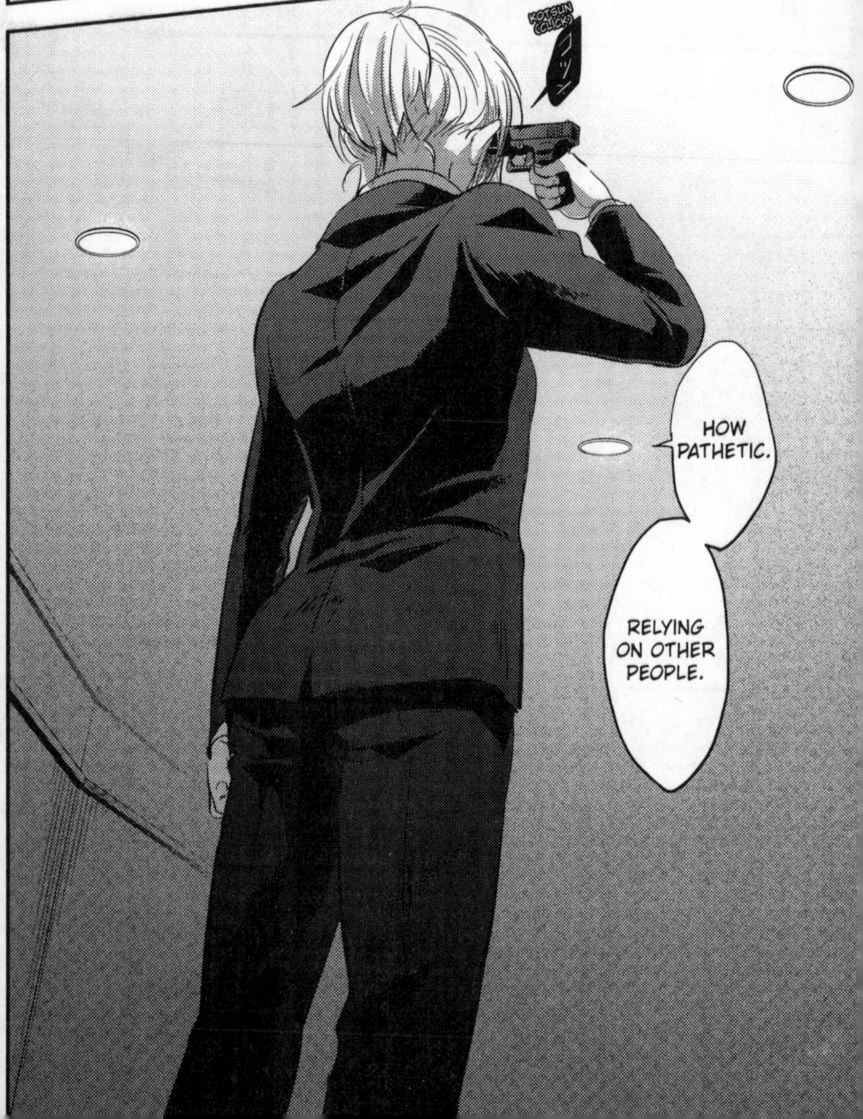
コツン
KOTSUN (CLICK)
HOW PATHETIC.
RELYING ON OTHER PEOPLE.

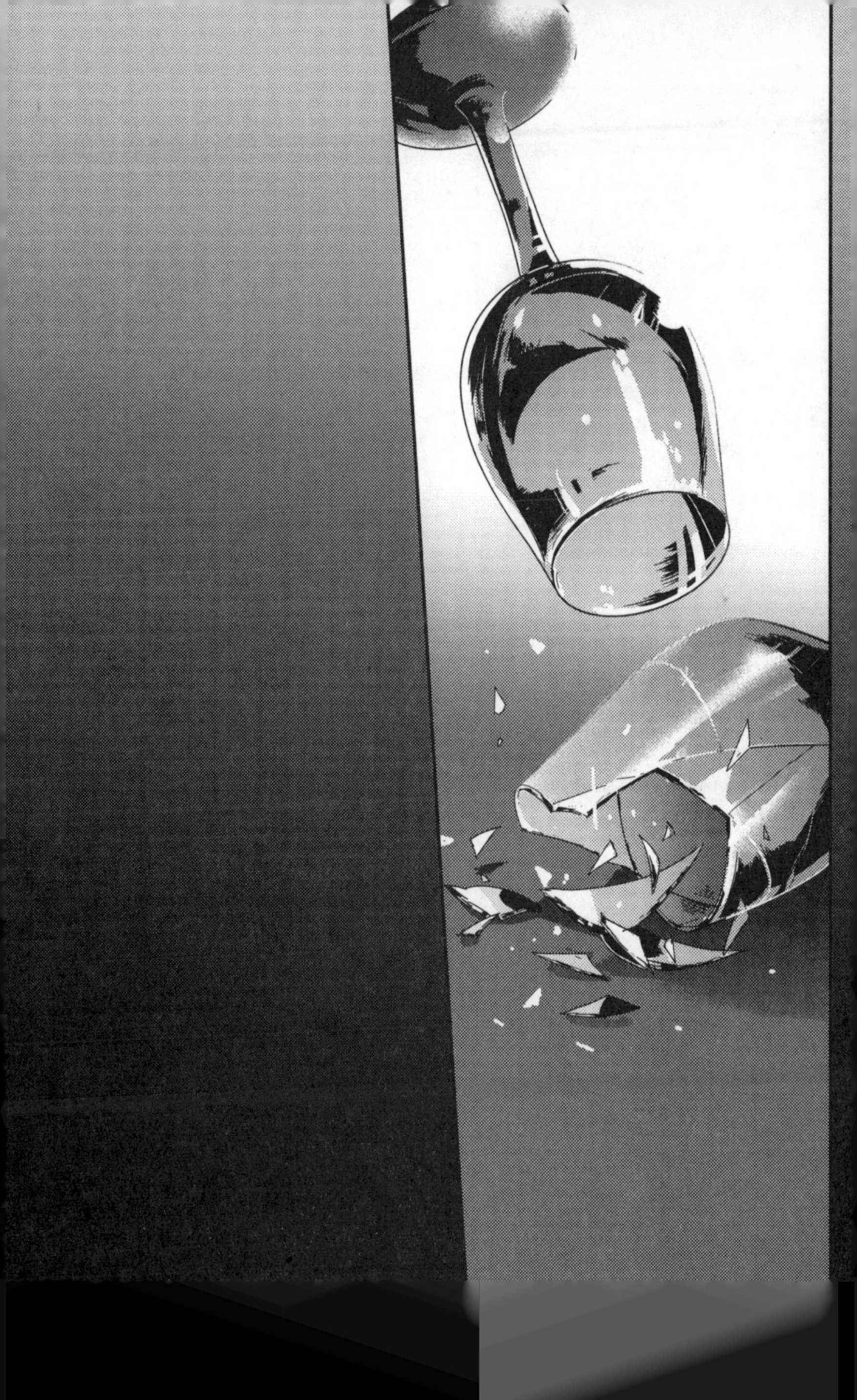

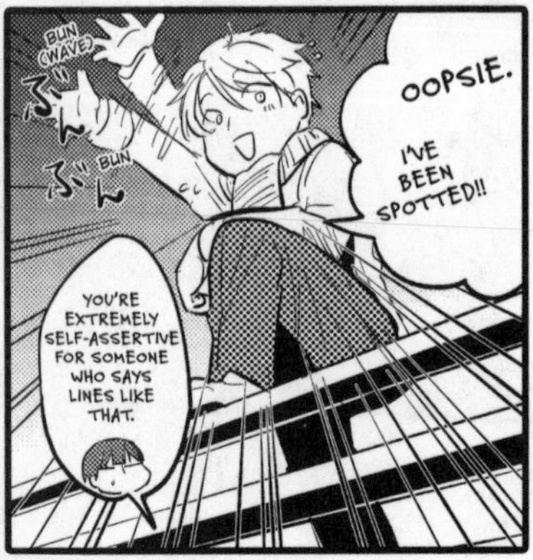
OOPSIE.
I'VE BEEN SPOTTED!!
BUN (WAVE)
ふん
ふん
BUN
YOU'RE EXTREMELY SELF-ASSERTIVE FOR SOMEONE WHO SAYS LINES LIKE THAT.

FILE 19: URGENT

THIS GUY ONLY POPPED UP FOR EXTREMELY SIGNIFICANT MOMENTS BEFORE, 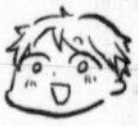 ← BUT HE FINALLY GOT SOME REAL SCREEN TIME HERE. I PICTURE HIM BEING LIKE A SMALL DOG WANDERING AROUND. POSSIBLY BECAUSE OF THE WIDE EYES, FOR A SHORT WHILE AFTER HIS FIRST APPEARANCE, MY EDITOR CALLED HIM MR. PSYCHOPATH, LOL...

FILE 20: UPSET

I FEEL LIKE I CAN HEAR EVERYONE COMING TO SCOLD ME, "HOW IS THE BOSS STILL ALIVE!?" ABOUT THAT... UM...I'M SORRY...THE CLIFF-HANGER I USED FOR THE ENDING OF VOLUME 3 TURNED OUT TO BE A SPECTACULAR DEATH FAKE-OUT, LOL. I DON'T REALLY KNOW IF HE WOULD BE OKAY AFTER BEING STABBED CLEAN THROUGH THE NECK IN THAT SPOT, BUT...UHH... THIS IS A WORK OF FICTION, SO...FORGIVE ME...?

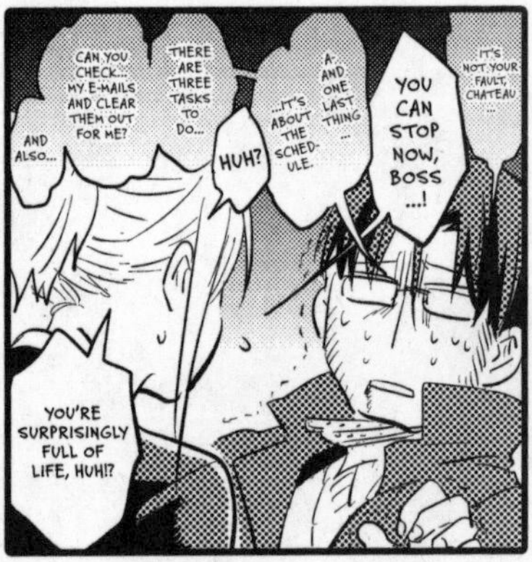
IT'S NOT YOUR FAULT, CHATEAU...
YOU CAN STOP NOW, BOSS...!
A-AND ONE LAST THING...
...IT'S ABOUT THE SCHED-ULE.
HUH?
THERE ARE THREE TASKS TO DO...
CAN YOU CHECK... MY E-MAILS AND CLEAR THEM OUT FOR ME?
AND ALSO...
YOU'RE SURPRISINGLY FULL OF LIFE, HUH!?

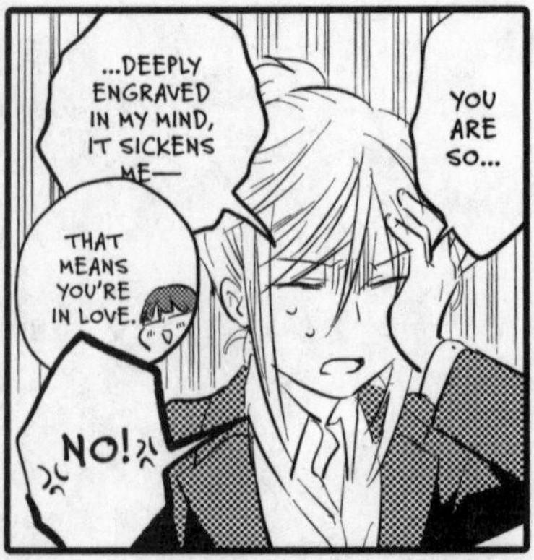
YOU ARE SO...
...DEEPLY ENGRAVED IN MY MIND, IT SICKENS ME—
THAT MEANS YOU'RE IN LOVE.
NO!

FILE 21: BULLET

I FEEL LIKE I HAD A VERY HARD TIME WRITING THIS PART OF THE STORY... IT WAS TOUGH...CHATEAU HAS STARTED SAYING EXTRAORDINARILY DIFFICULT THINGS RECENTLY, LOL...THIS WAS PROBABLY THE FIRST SCENE WHERE CHATEAU EXPRESSES HER FEELINGS, AND I STRUGGLED A LOT WITH CHOOS-ING HER WORDS...

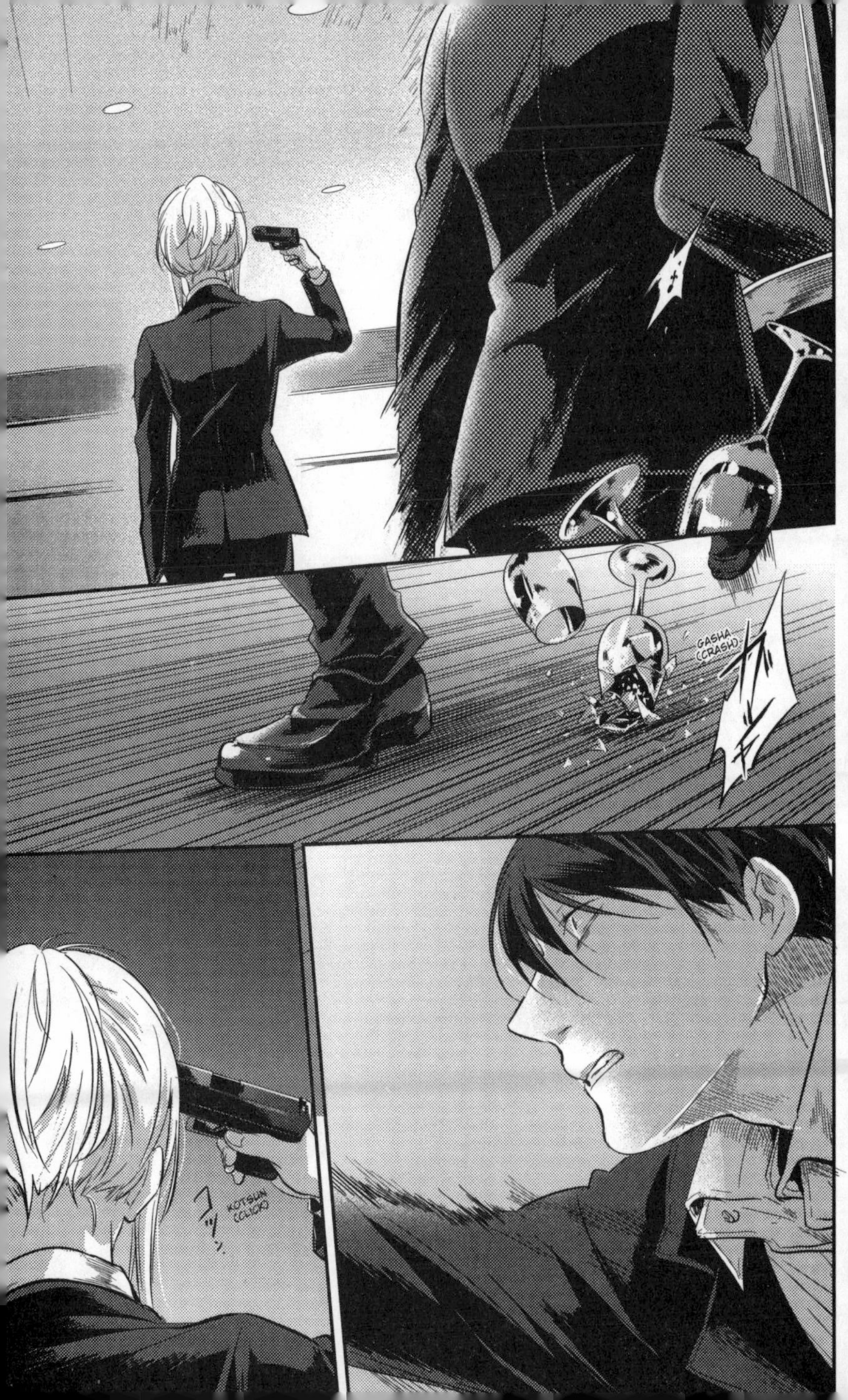
GASHA (CRASH)
KOTSUN (CLICK)

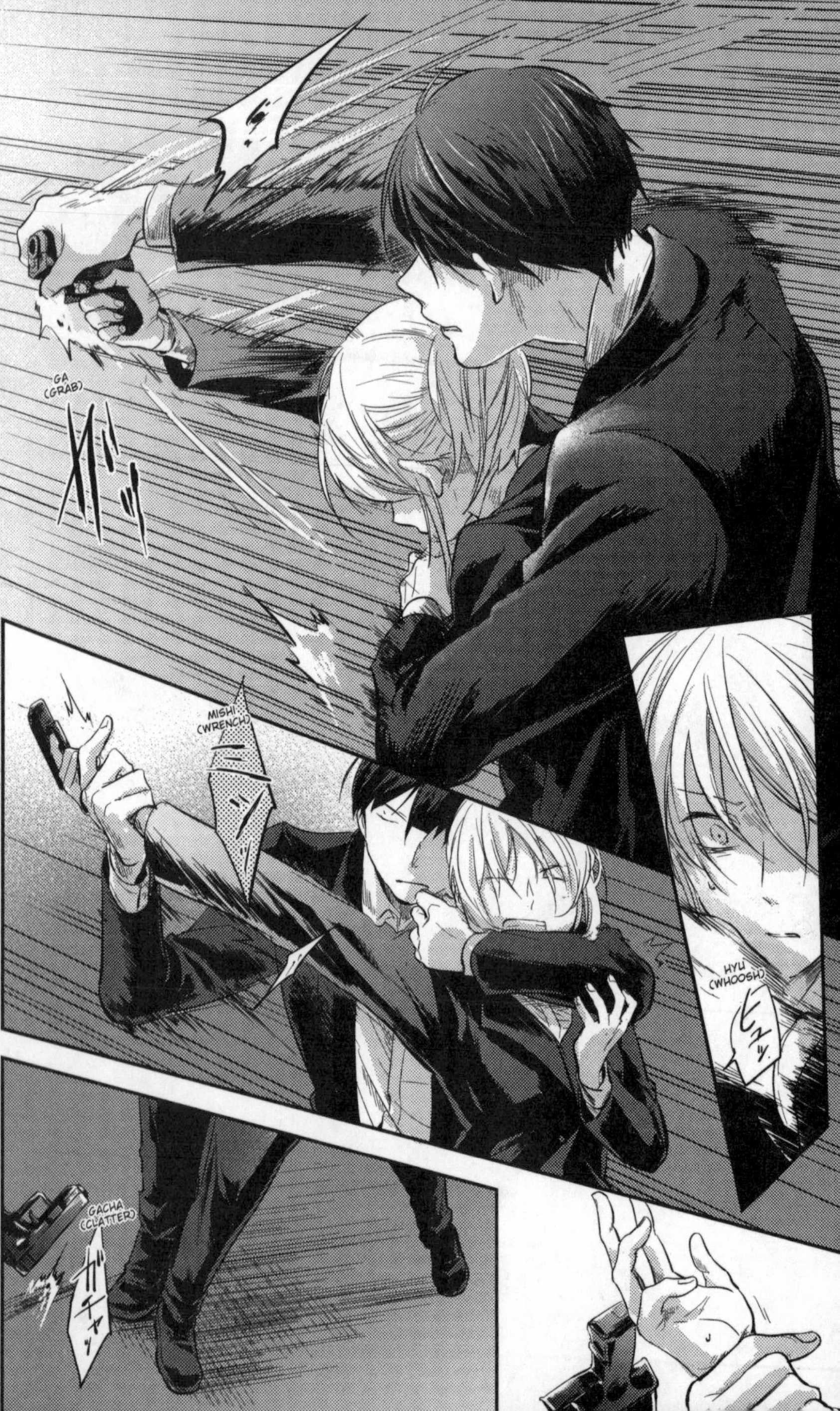
GA
(GRAB)
ガッ
HYU
(WHOOSH)
ヒュッ
MISHI
(WRENCH)
GACHA
(CLATTER)
ガチャッ

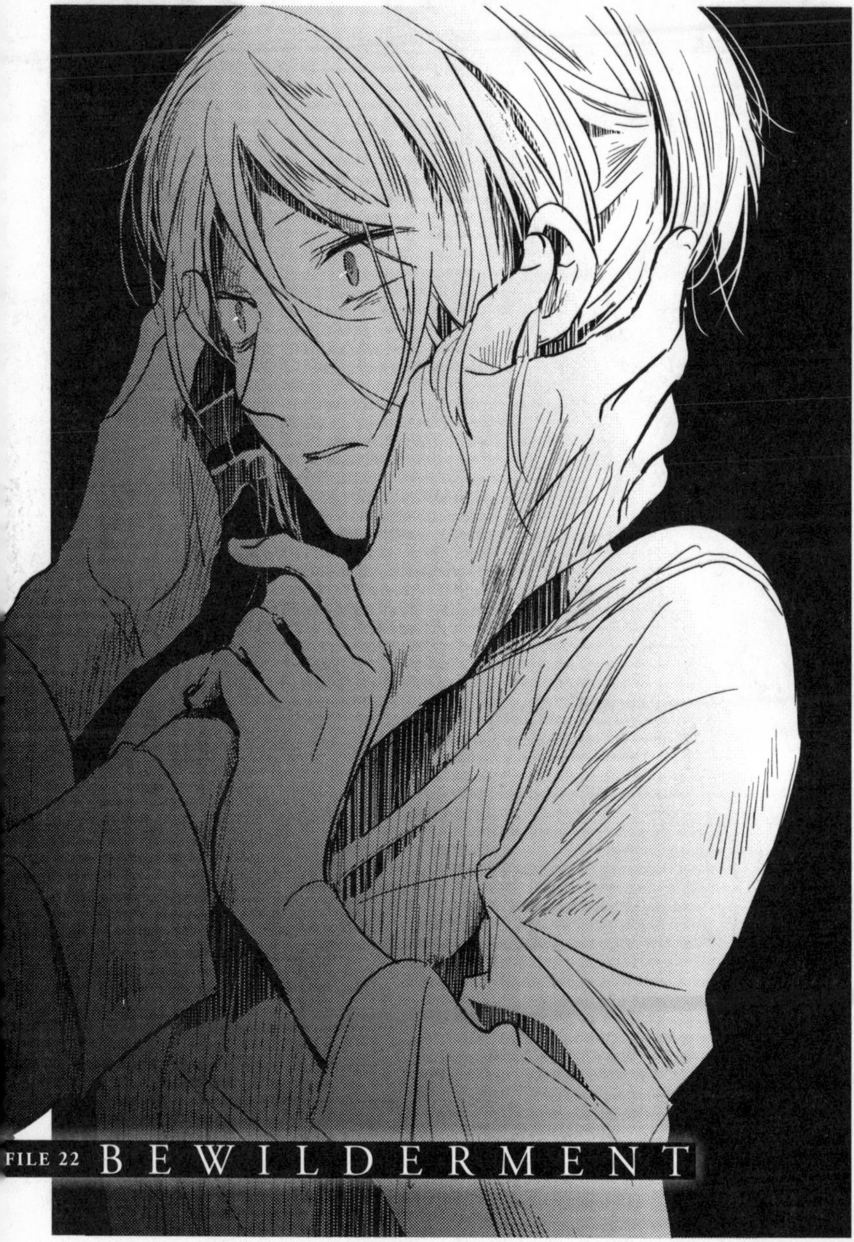
FILE 22 BEWILDERMENT

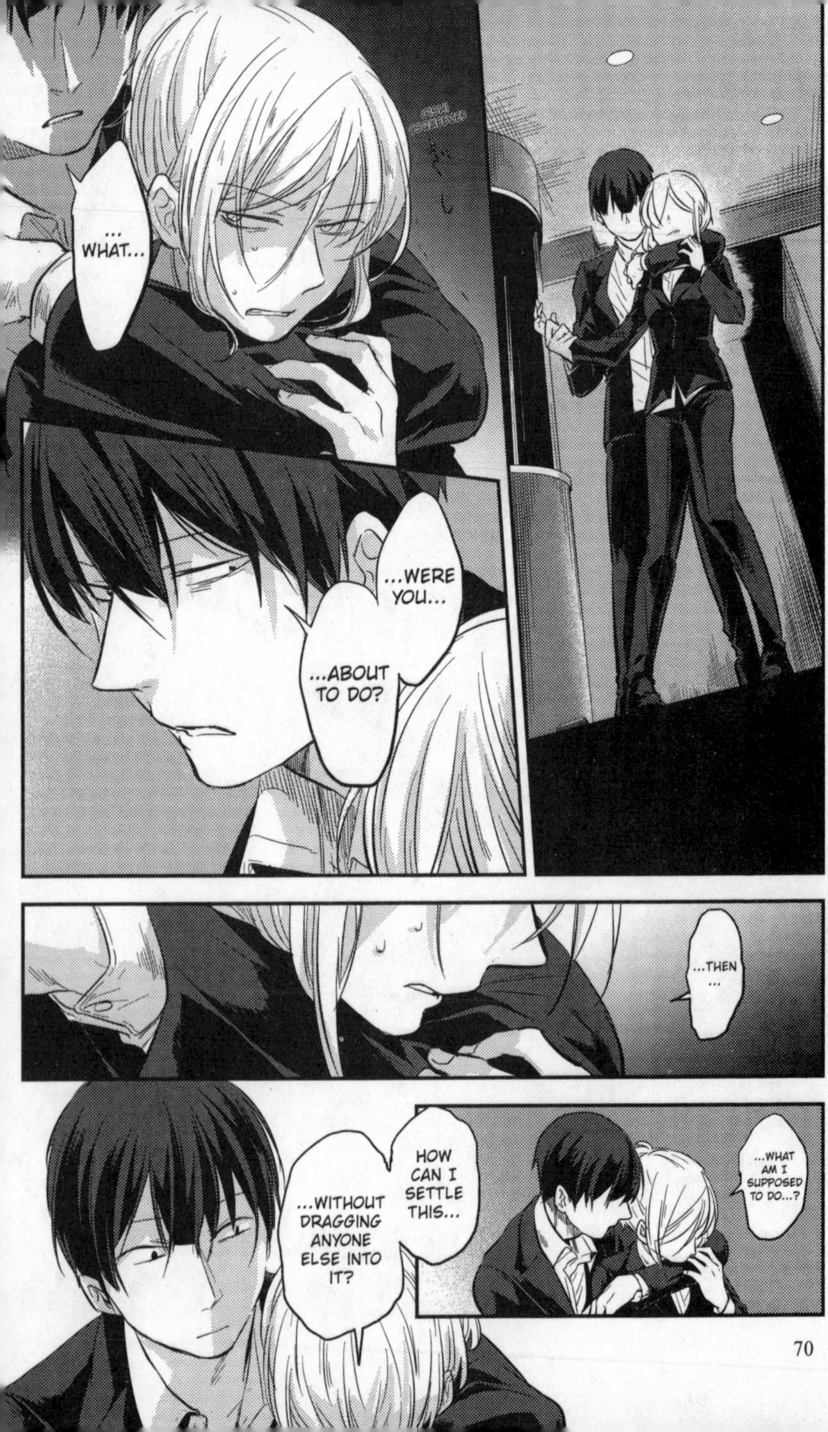
GISHI (SQUEEZE)
... WHAT...
...WERE YOU...
...ABOUT TO DO?
...THEN ...
...WHAT AM I SUPPOSED TO DO...?
HOW CAN I SETTLE THIS...
...WITHOUT DRAGGING ANYONE ELSE INTO IT?

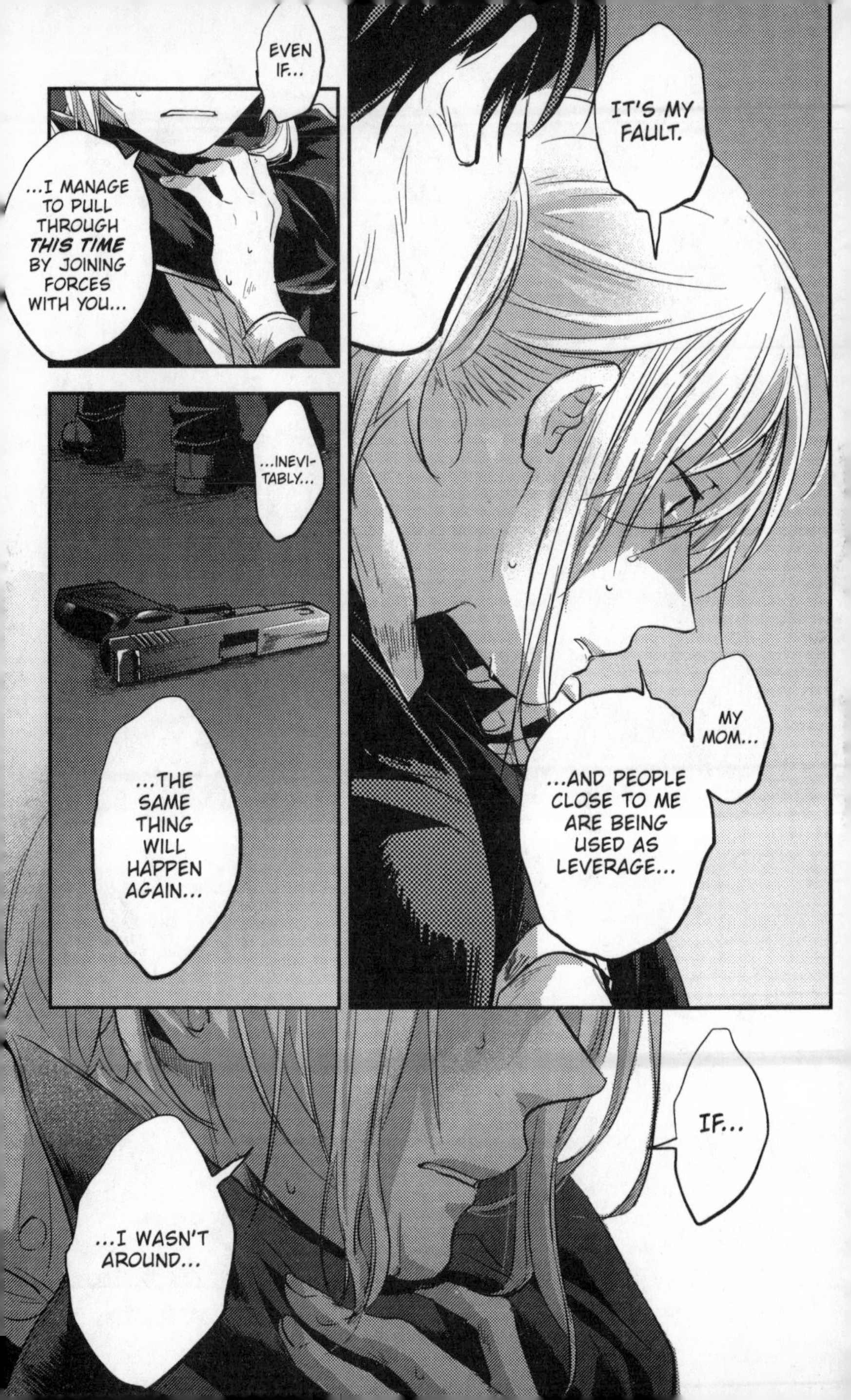
IT'S MY FAULT.
MY MOM...
...AND PEOPLE CLOSE TO ME ARE BEING USED AS LEVERAGE...
EVEN IF...
...I MANAGE TO PULL THROUGH *THIS TIME* BY JOINING FORCES WITH YOU...
...INEVITABLY...
...THE SAME THING WILL HAPPEN AGAIN...
IF...
...I WASN'T AROUND...

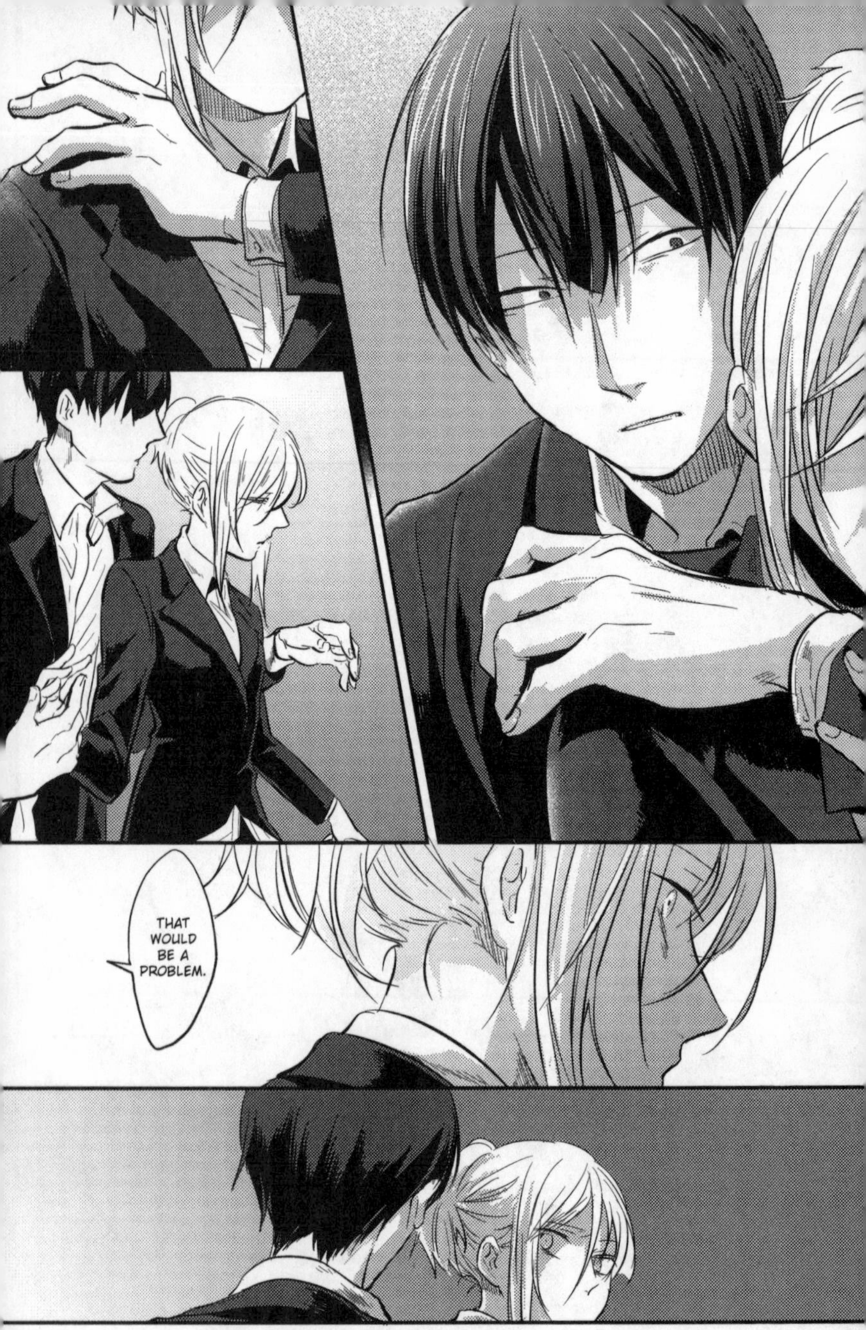
THAT WOULD BE A PROBLEM.

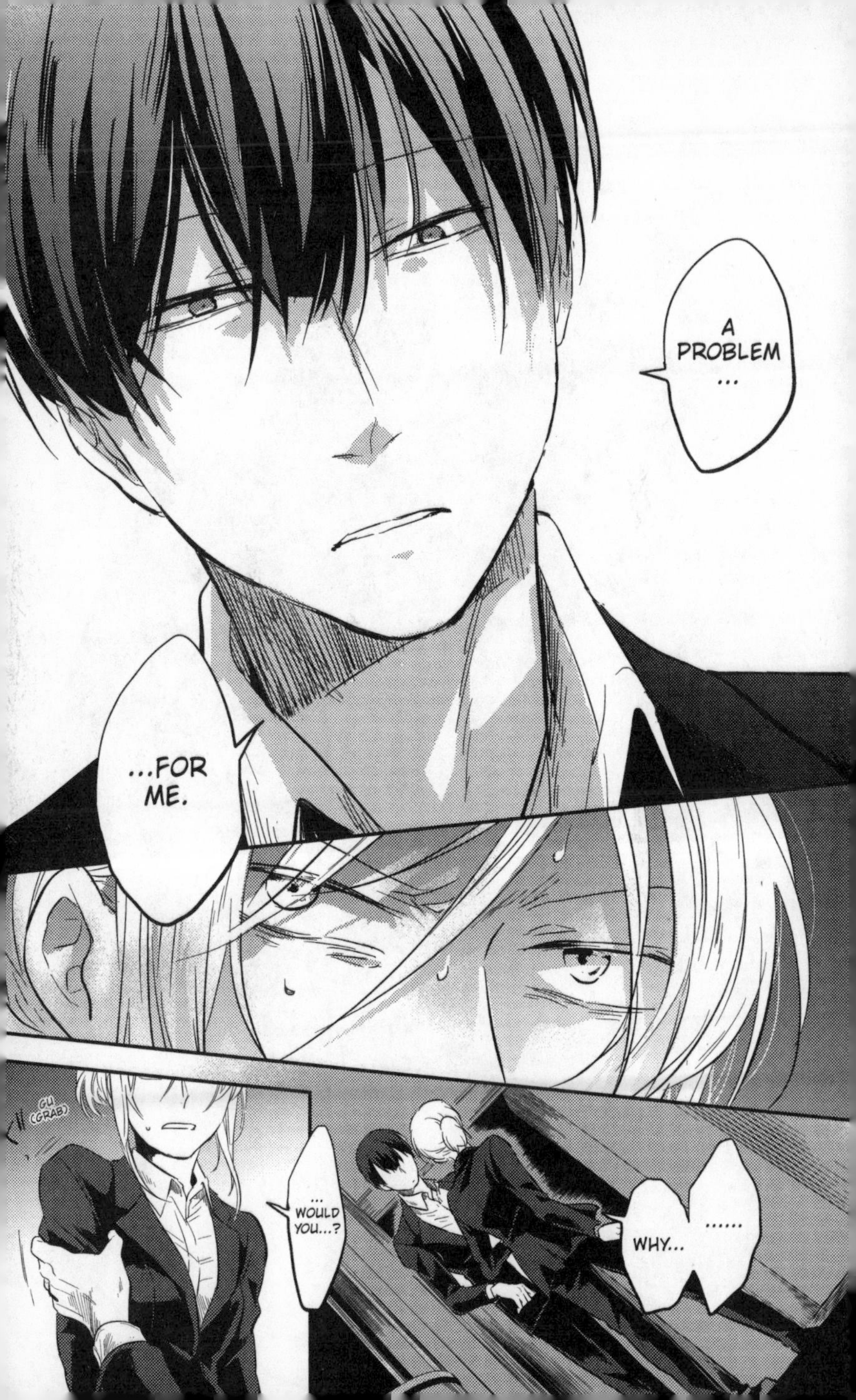
A PROBLEM ...
...FOR ME.
......
WHY...
... WOULD YOU...?
GU (GRAB)

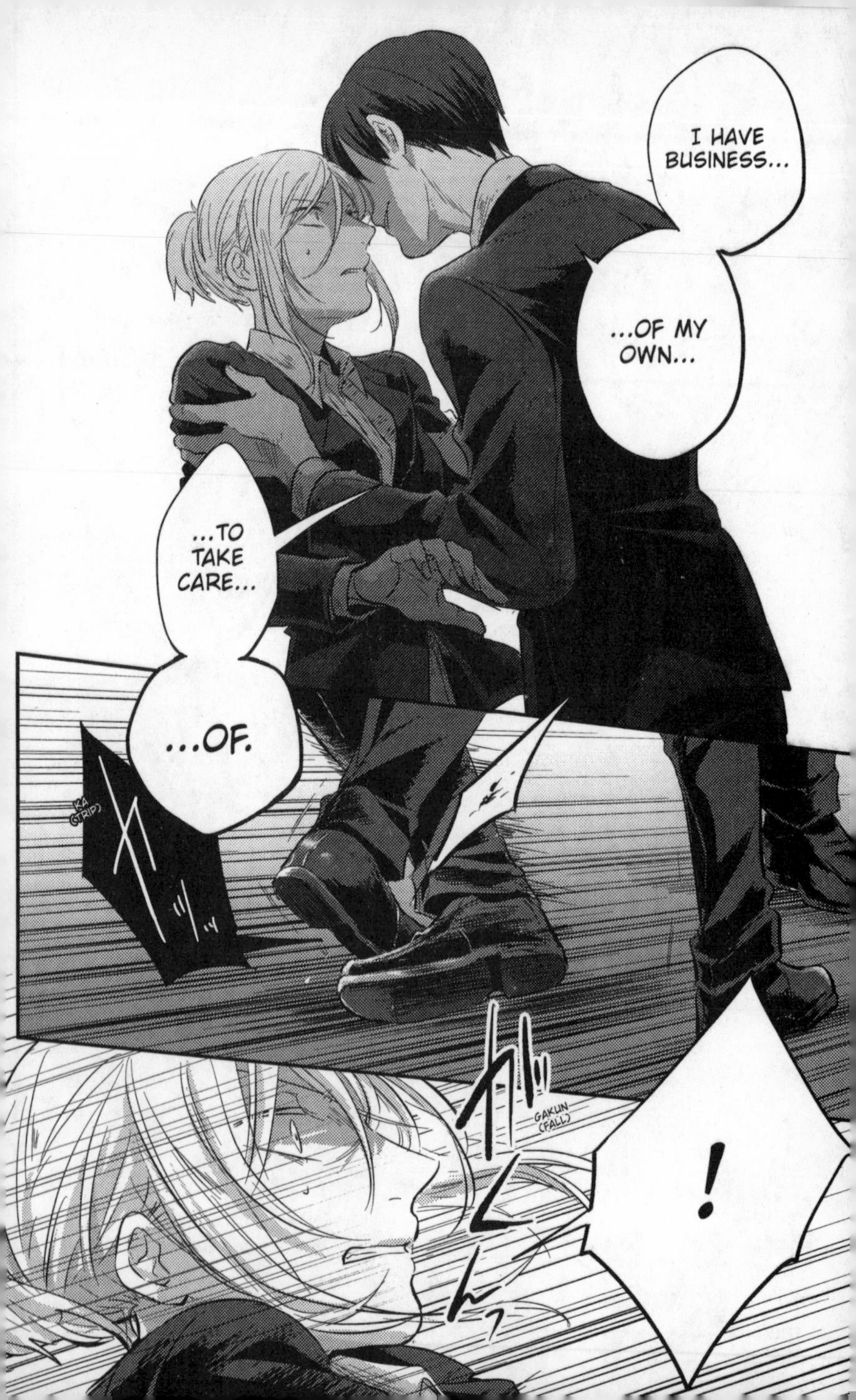
I HAVE BUSINESS...
...OF MY OWN...
...TO TAKE CARE...
...OF.
KA (TRIP)
GAKUN (FALL)
!

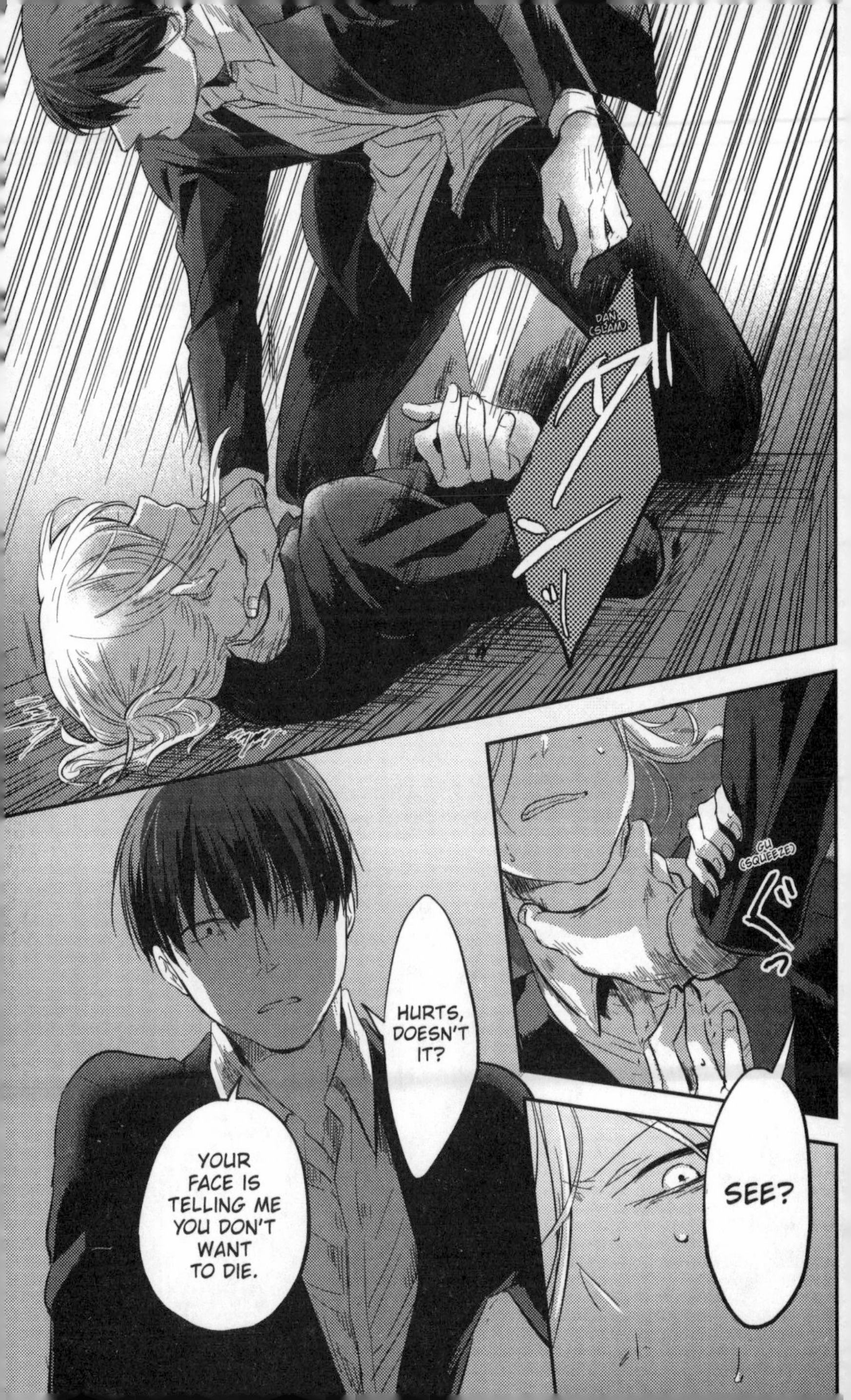
DAN (SLAM)
GU (SQUEEZE)
SEE?
HURTS, DOESN'T IT?
YOUR FACE IS TELLING ME YOU DON'T WANT TO DIE.

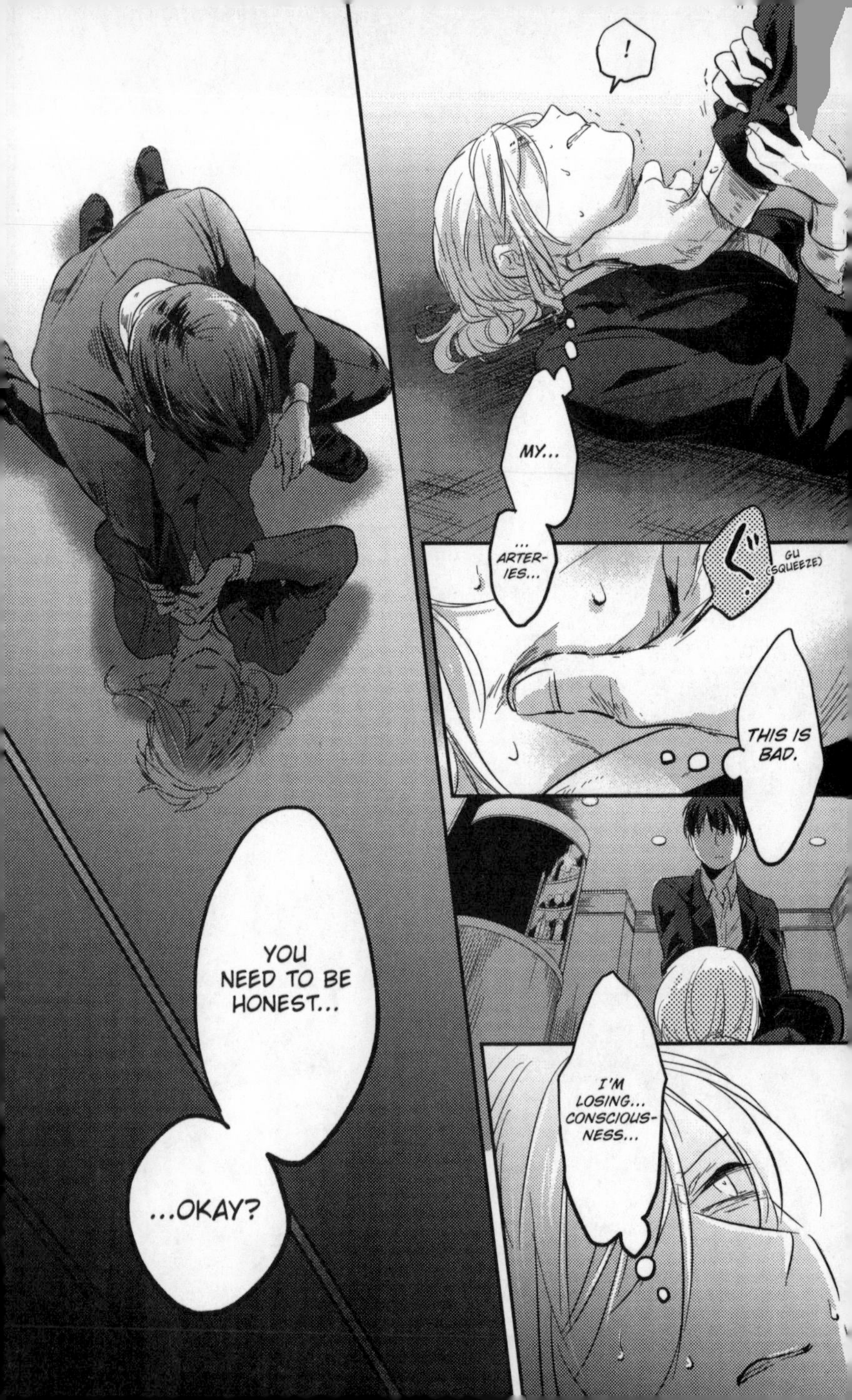
!
MY...
...ARTER-IES...
GU (SQUEEZE)
THIS IS BAD.
I'M LOSING... CONSCIOUS-NESS...
YOU NEED TO BE HONEST...
...OKAY?

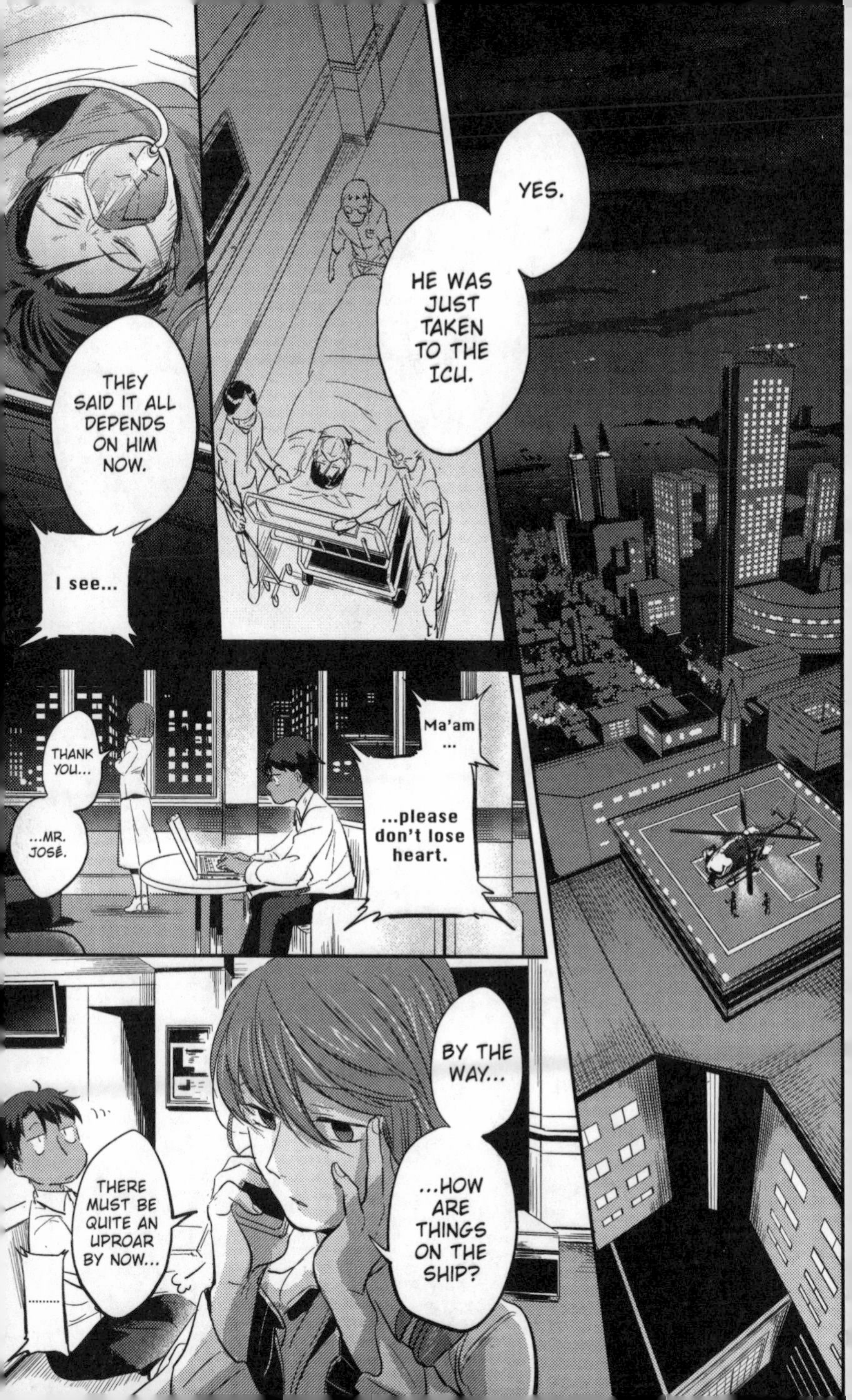
YES.
HE WAS JUST TAKEN TO THE ICU.
THEY SAID IT ALL DEPENDS ON HIM NOW.
I see...
Ma'am ...
...please don't lose heart.
THANK YOU...
...MR. JOSÉ.
BY THE WAY...
...HOW ARE THINGS ON THE SHIP?
THERE MUST BE QUITE AN UPROAR BY NOW...
....

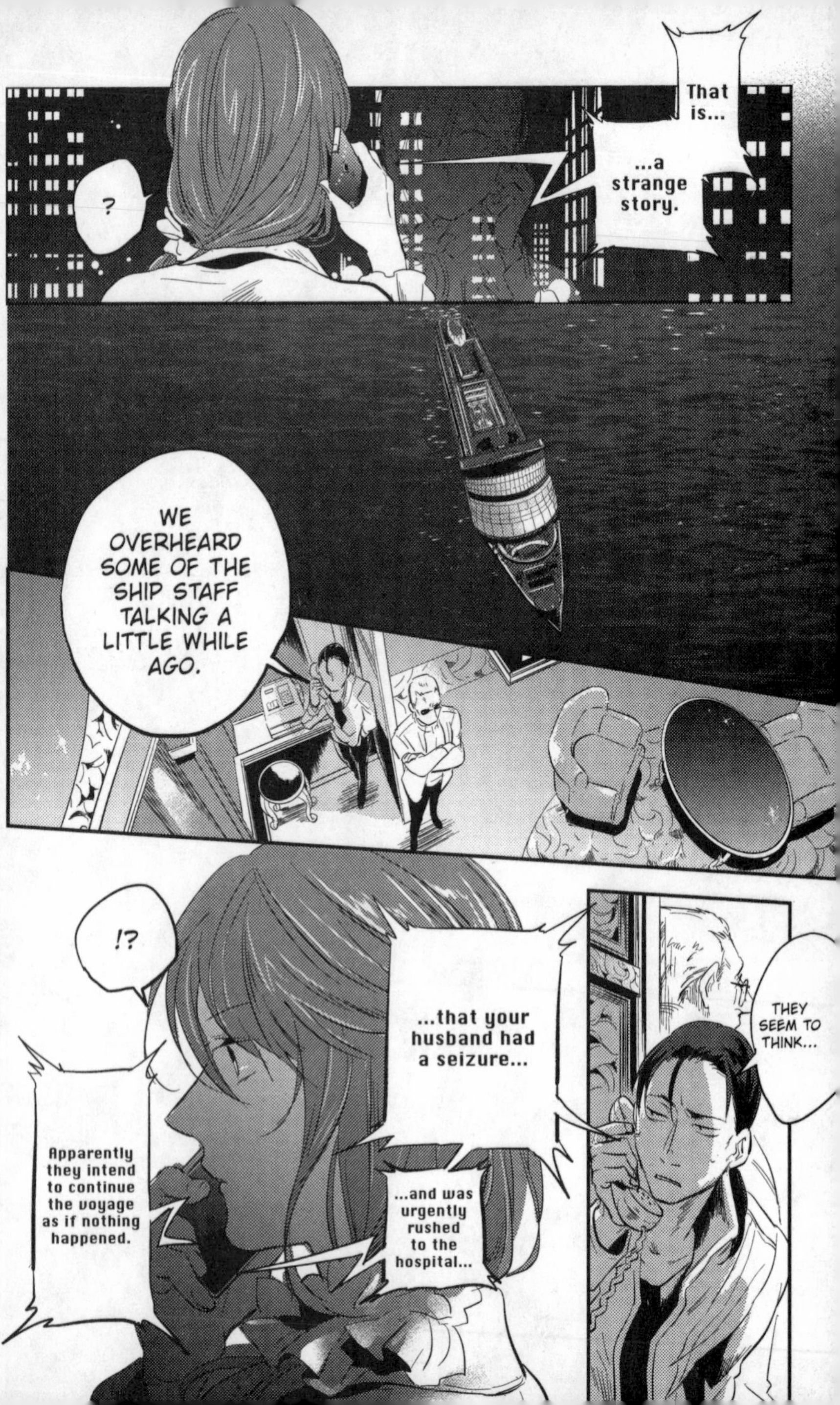
That is...
...a strange story.
?
WE OVERHEARD SOME OF THE SHIP STAFF TALKING A LITTLE WHILE AGO.
THEY SEEM TO THINK...
...that your husband had a seizure...
...and was urgently rushed to the hospital...
!?
Apparently they intend to continue the voyage as if nothing happened.

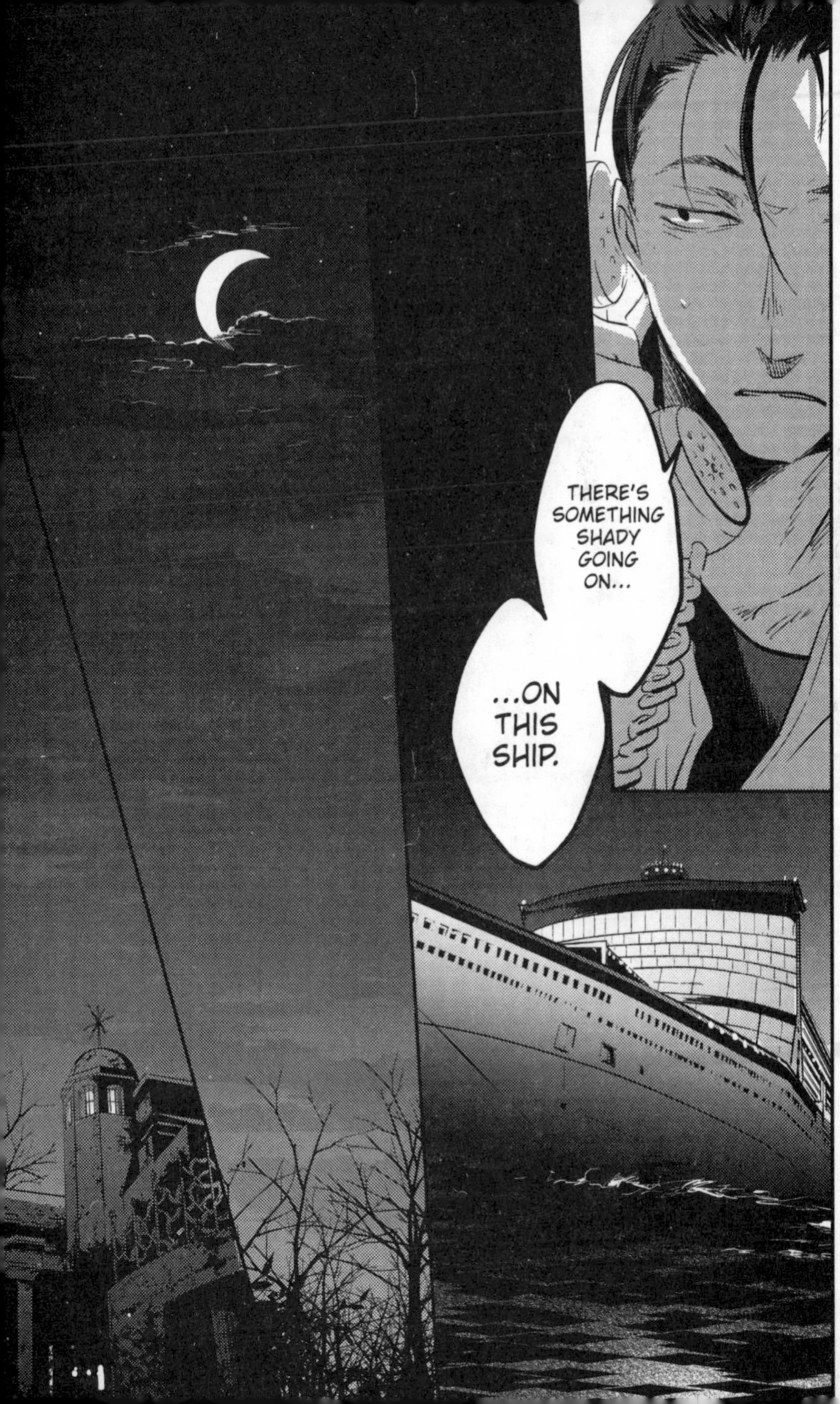
THERE'S SOMETHING SHADY GOING ON...
...ON THIS SHIP.

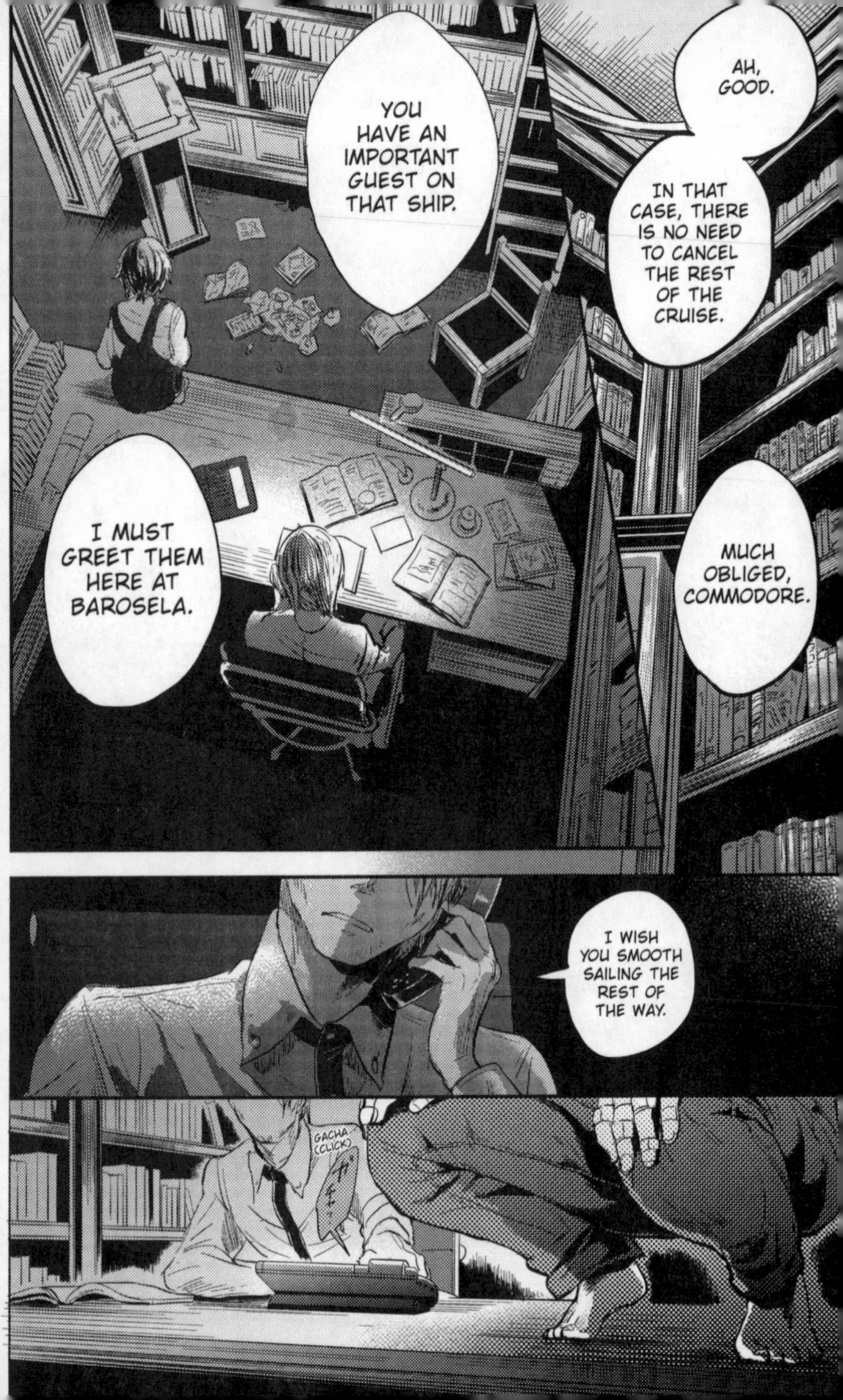
AH, GOOD.
YOU HAVE AN IMPORTANT GUEST ON THAT SHIP.
IN THAT CASE, THERE IS NO NEED TO CANCEL THE REST OF THE CRUISE.
MUCH OBLIGED, COMMODORE.
I MUST GREET THEM HERE AT BAROSELA.
I WISH YOU SMOOTH SAILING THE REST OF THE WAY.
GACHA (CLICK)

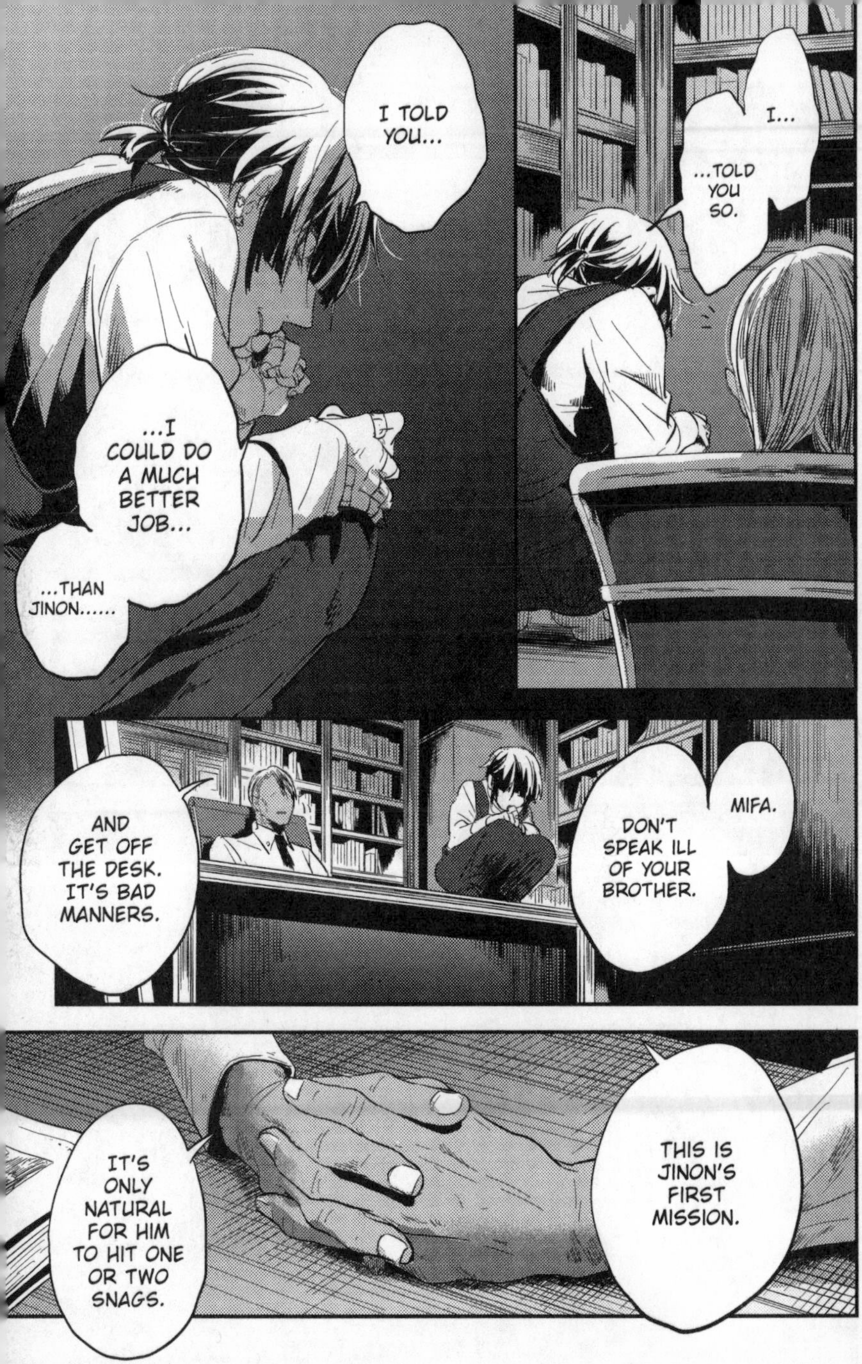
I...
...TOLD YOU SO.
I TOLD YOU...
...I COULD DO A MUCH BETTER JOB...
...THAN JINON......
MIFA.
DON'T SPEAK ILL OF YOUR BROTHER.
AND GET OFF THE DESK. IT'S BAD MANNERS.
THIS IS JINON'S FIRST MISSION.
IT'S ONLY NATURAL FOR HIM TO HIT ONE OR TWO SNAGS.

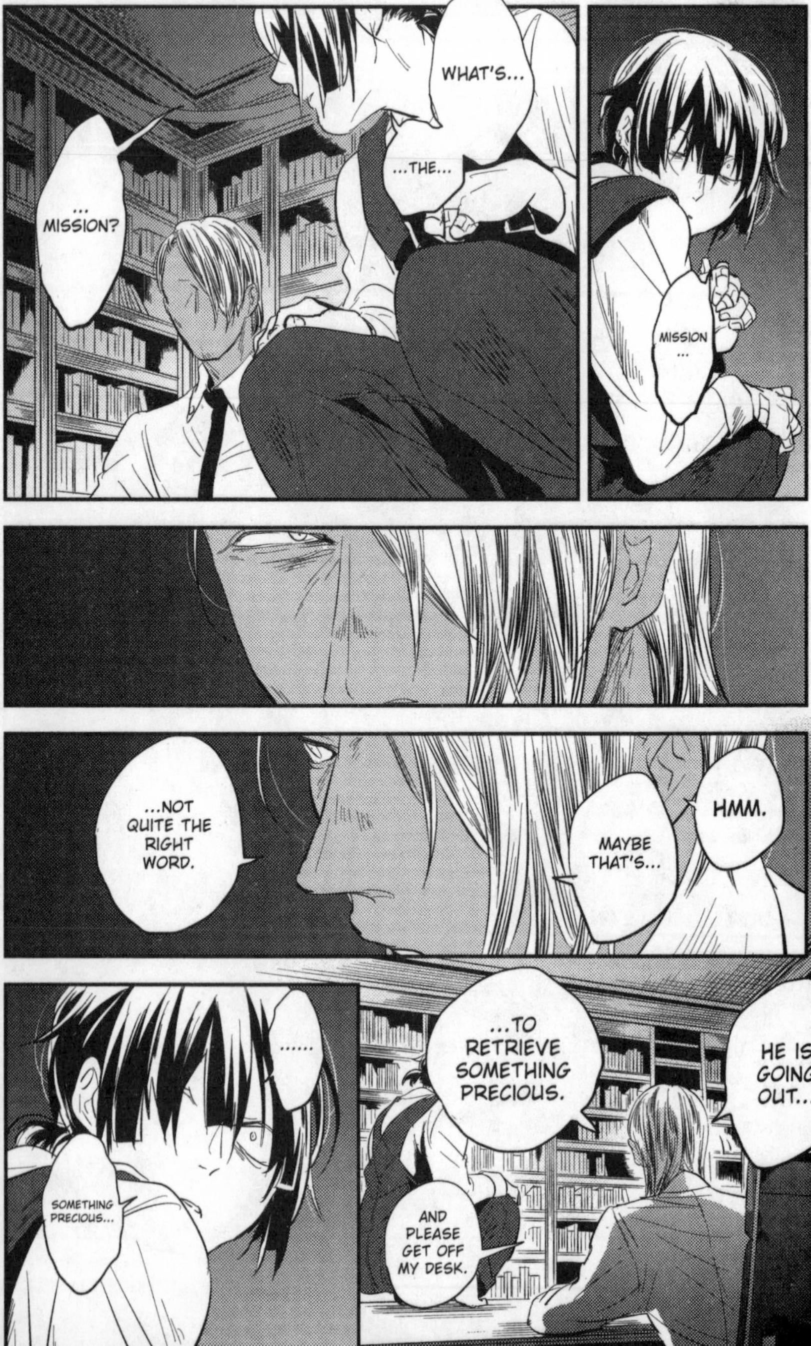
MISSION...
WHAT'S...
...THE...
... MISSION?
HMM.
MAYBE THAT'S...
...NOT QUITE THE RIGHT WORD.
HE IS GOING OUT...
...TO RETRIEVE SOMETHING PRECIOUS.
AND PLEASE GET OFF MY DESK.
......
SOMETHING PRECIOUS...

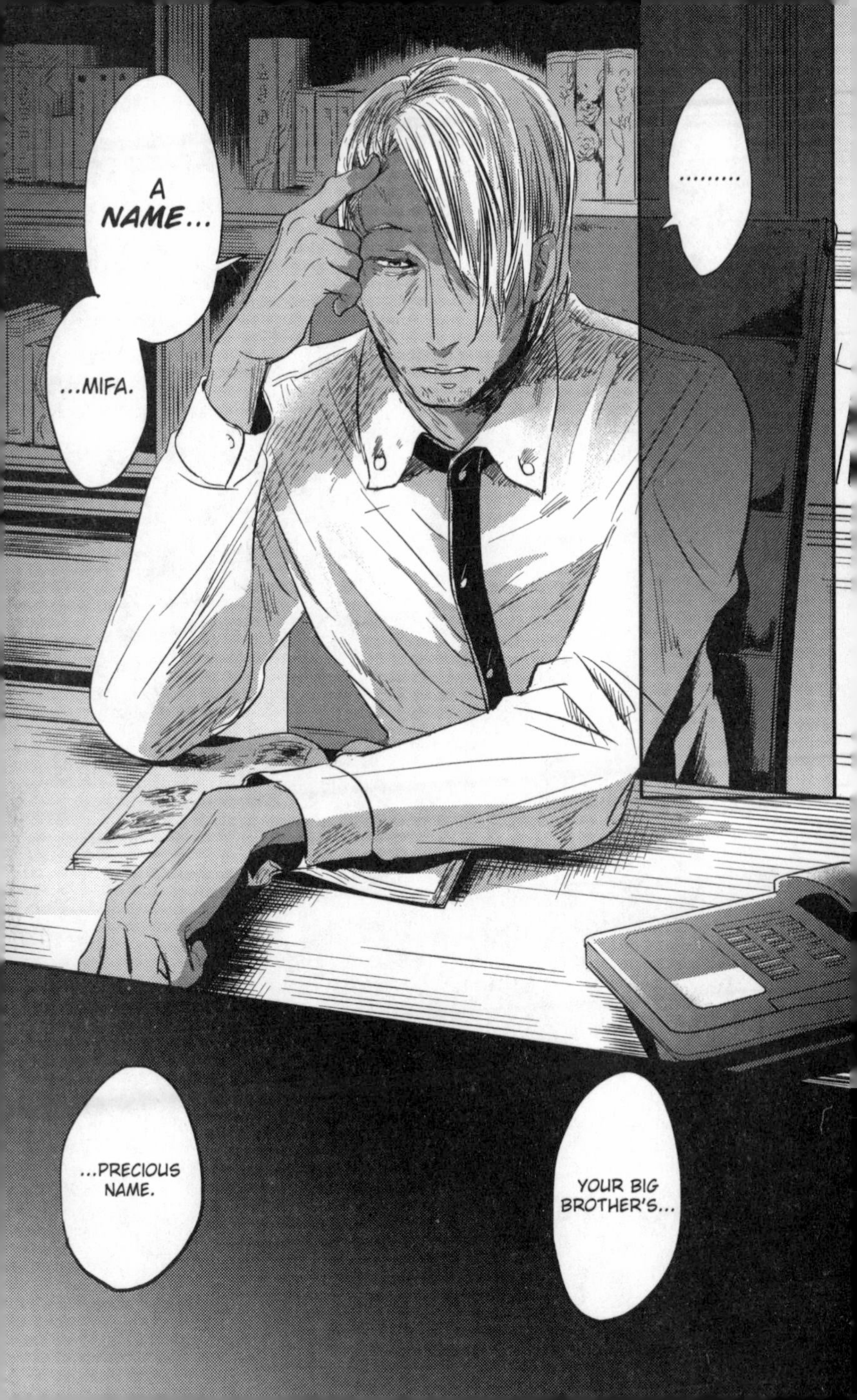
....
A NAME...
...MIFA.
YOUR BIG BROTHER'S...
...PRECIOUS NAME.

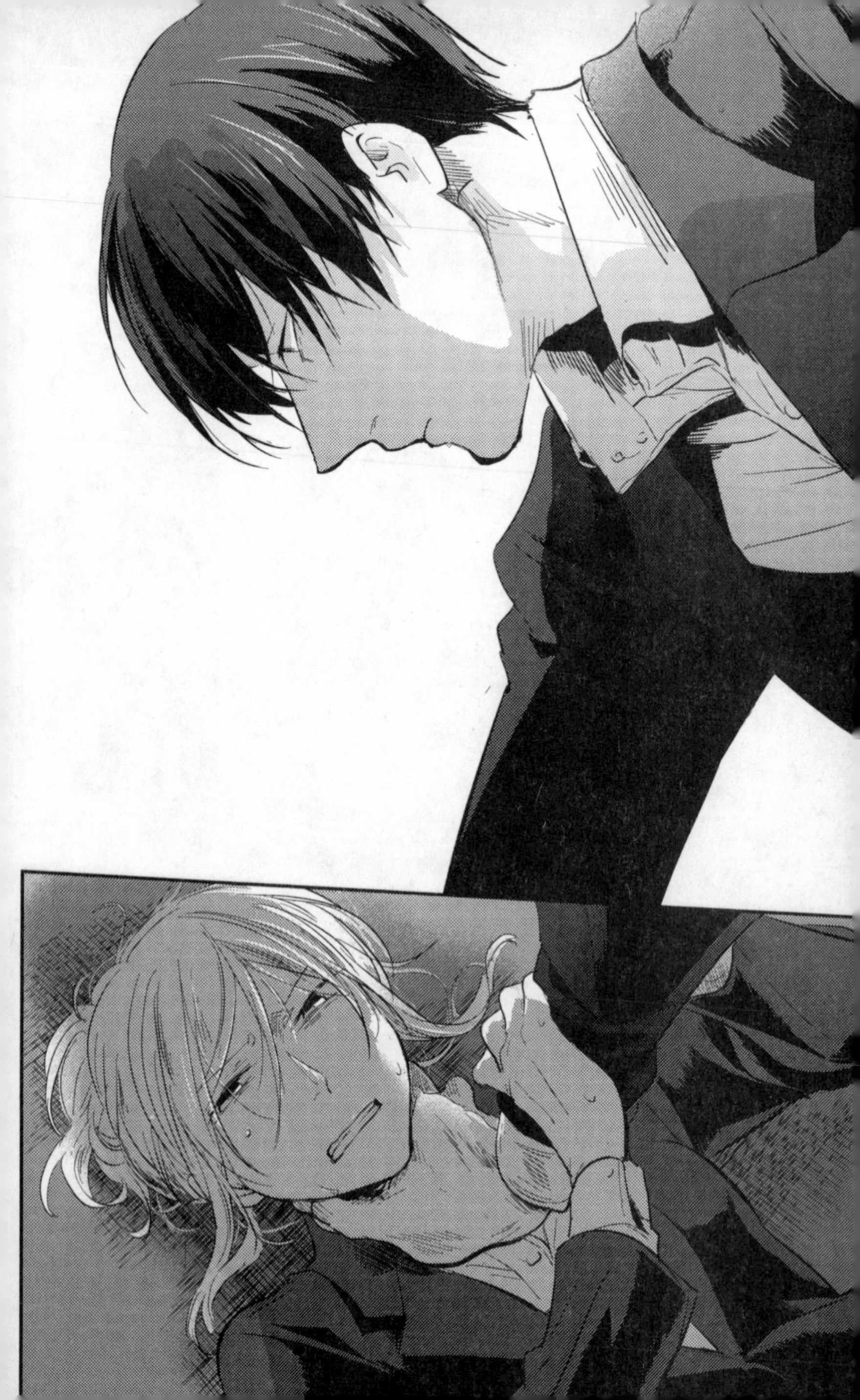

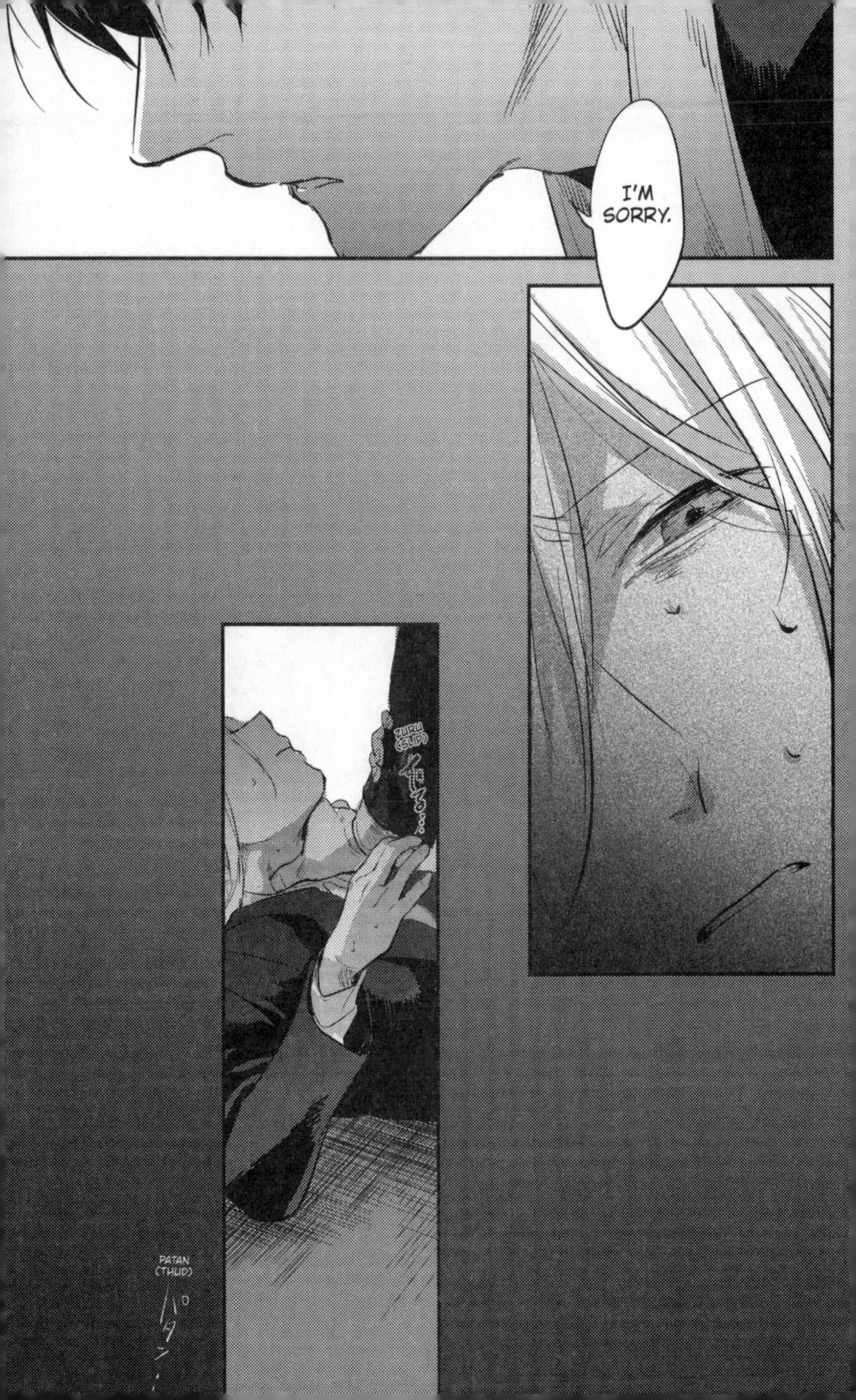
I'M SORRY.
ZURU (SLIP)
PATAN (THUD)

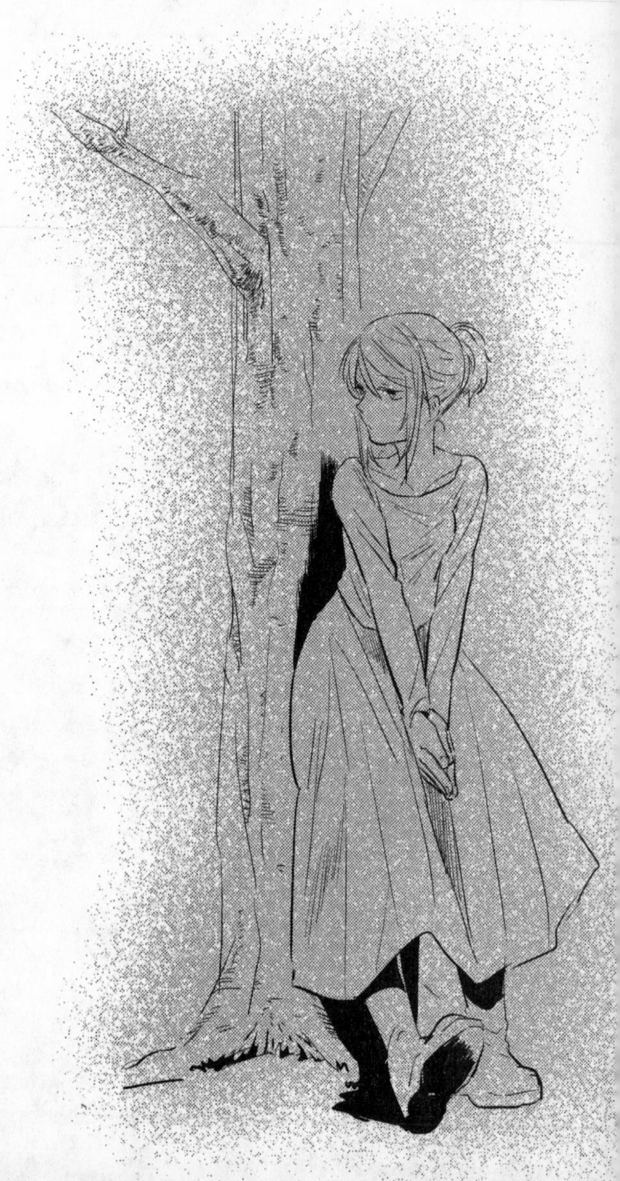

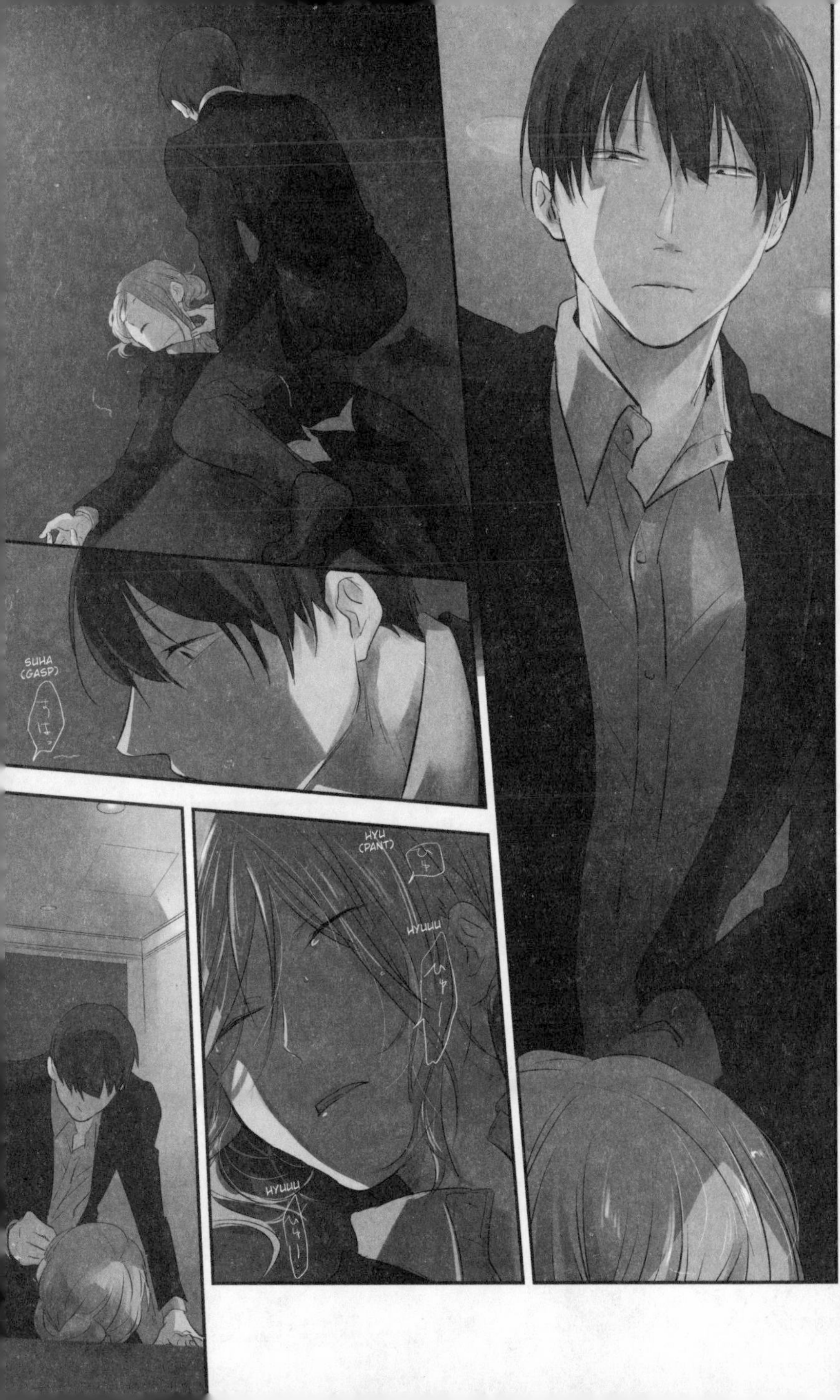
SUHA (GASP)
HYU (PANT)
HYUUU
HYUUU

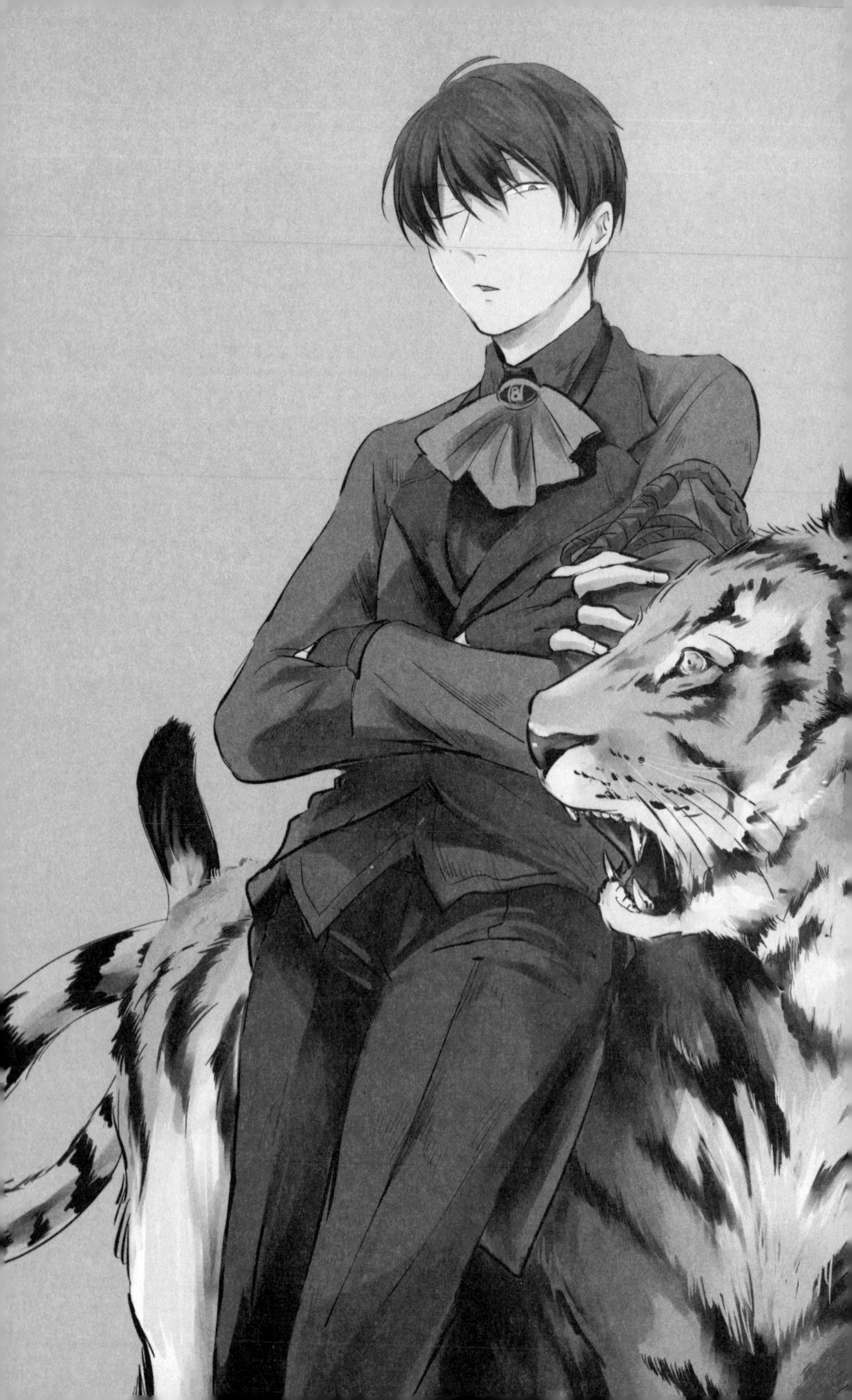

FILE 23 FAMILY

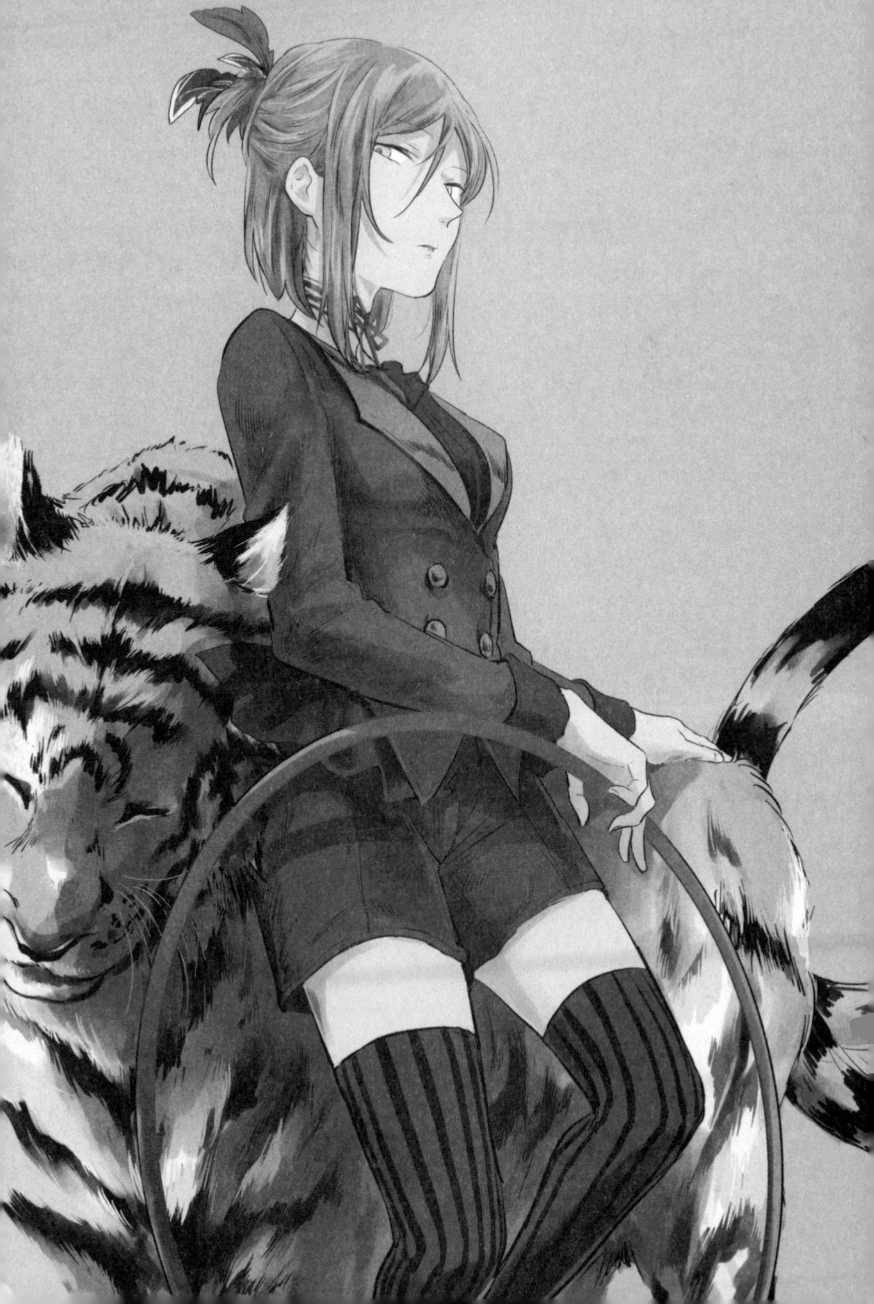

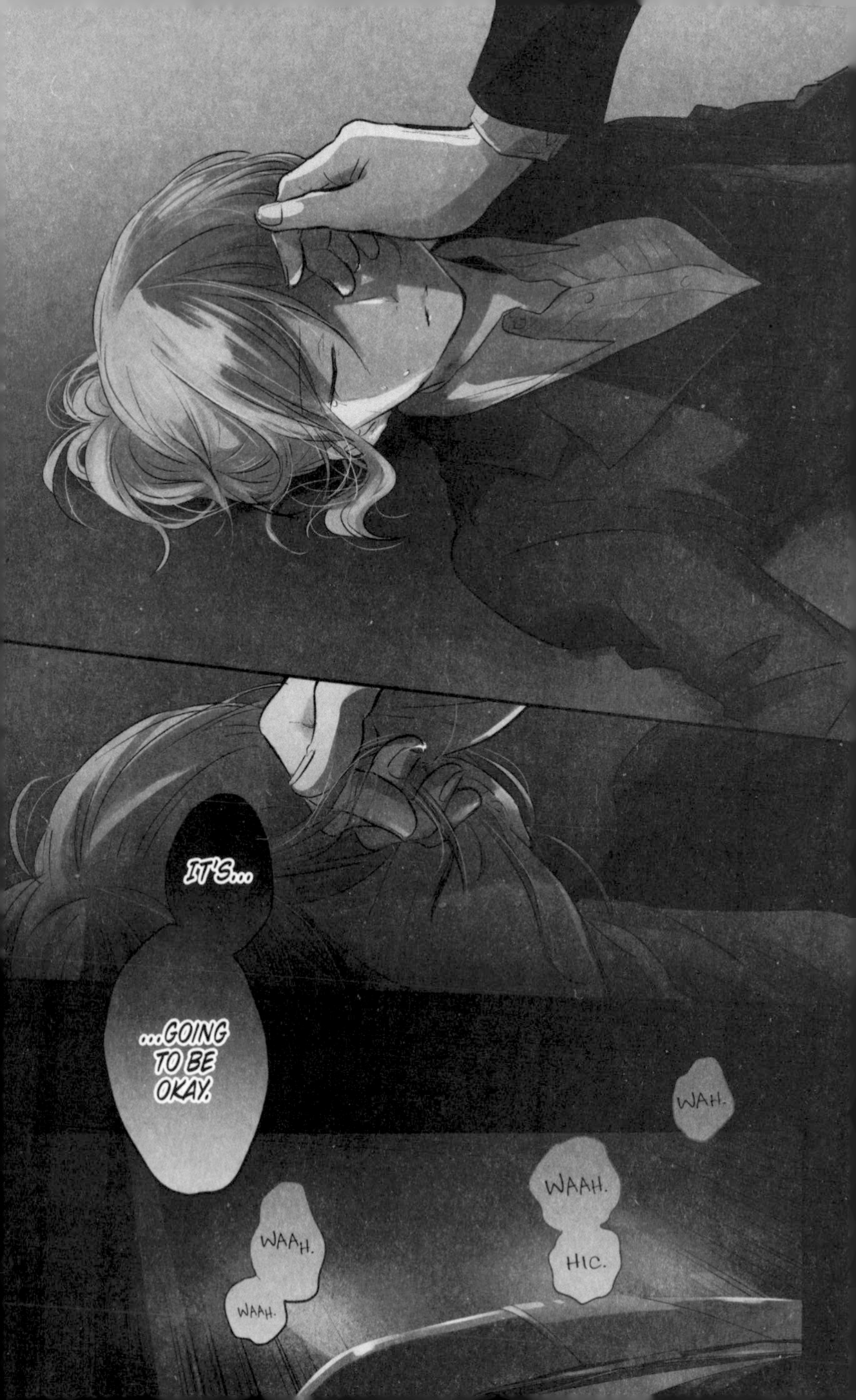
IT'S...
...GOING TO BE OKAY.
WAH.
WAAH.
HIC.
WAAH.
WAAH.

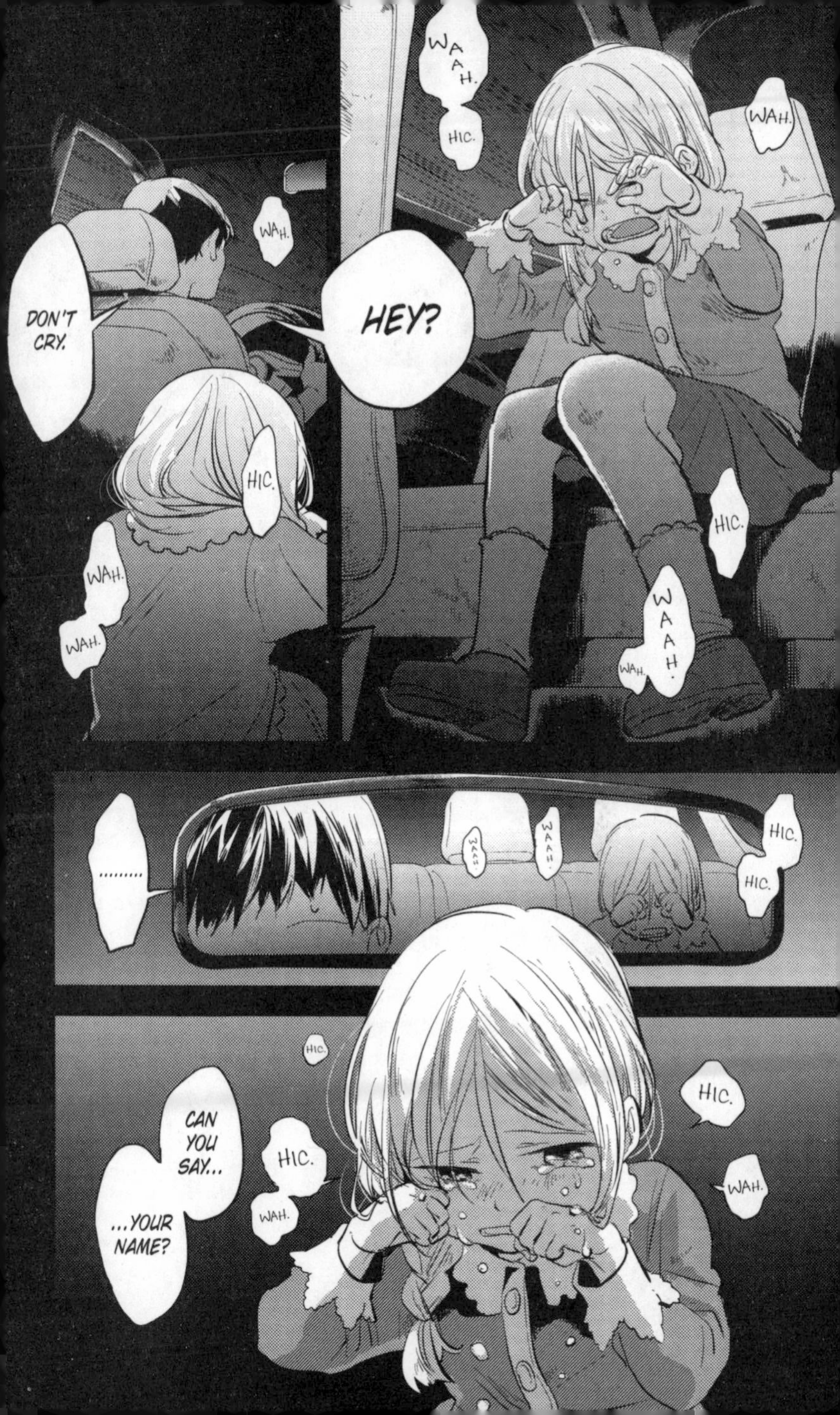
WAH.
WAAH.
HIC.
HEY?
HIC.
WAAH.
WAH.
WAH.
DON'T CRY.
HIC.
WAH.
WAH.
HIC.
HIC.
WAAH.
WAAH.
....
HIC.
HIC.
WAH.
CAN YOU SAY...
HIC.
WAH.
...YOUR NAME?

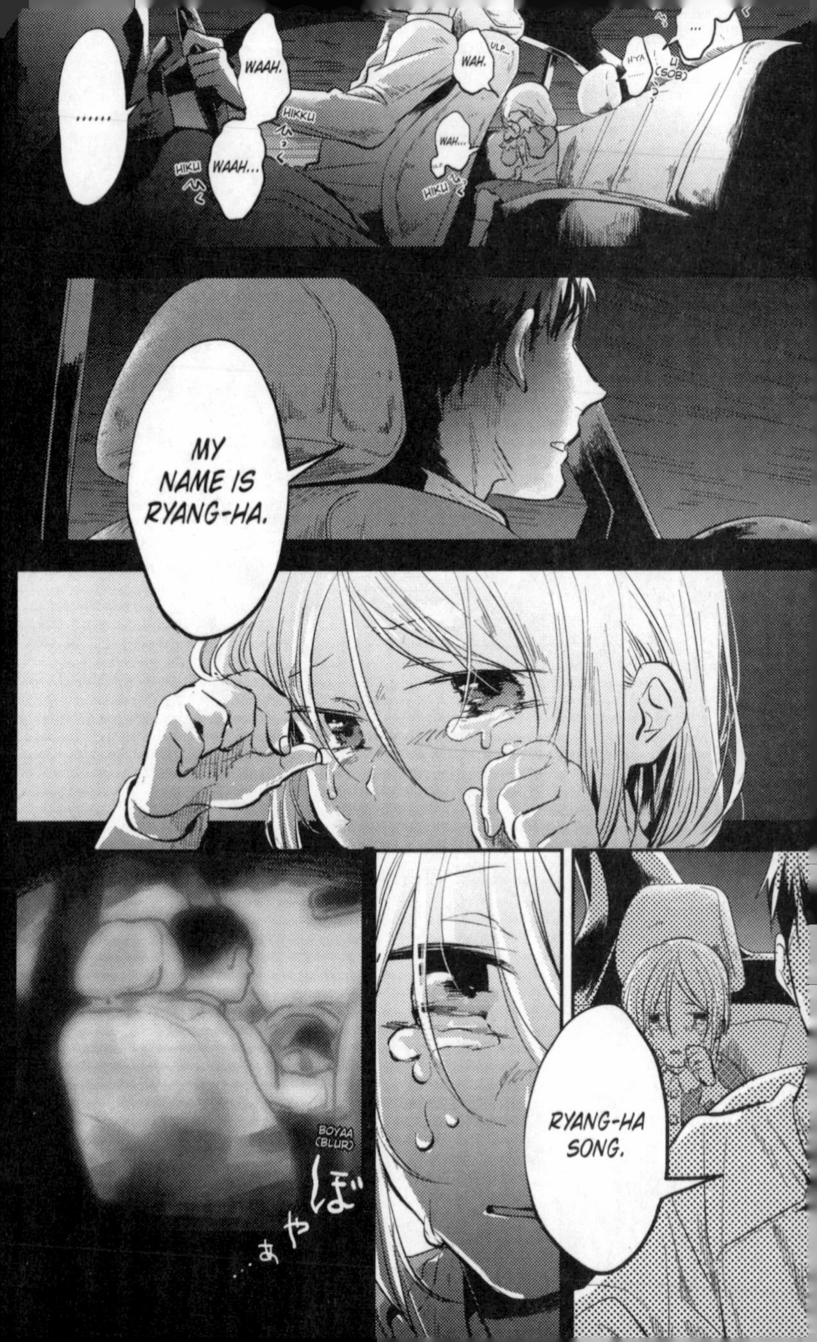
...
HYA ......
U (SOB)
WAH.
ULP...
WAH...
HIKU
HIKKU
WAAH.
WAAH...
HIKU
......
MY NAME IS RYANG-HA.
RYANG-HA SONG.
BOYAA (BLUR)

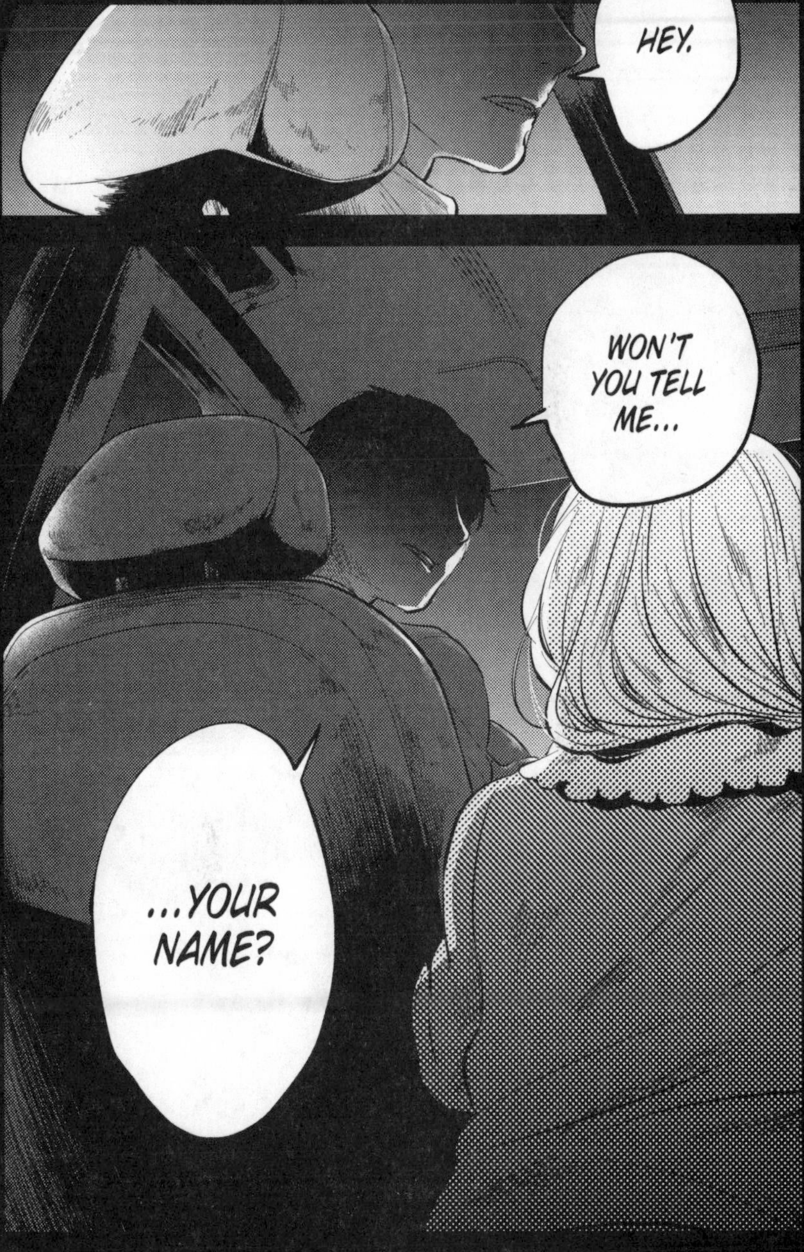
HEY.
WON'T YOU TELL ME...
...YOUR NAME?

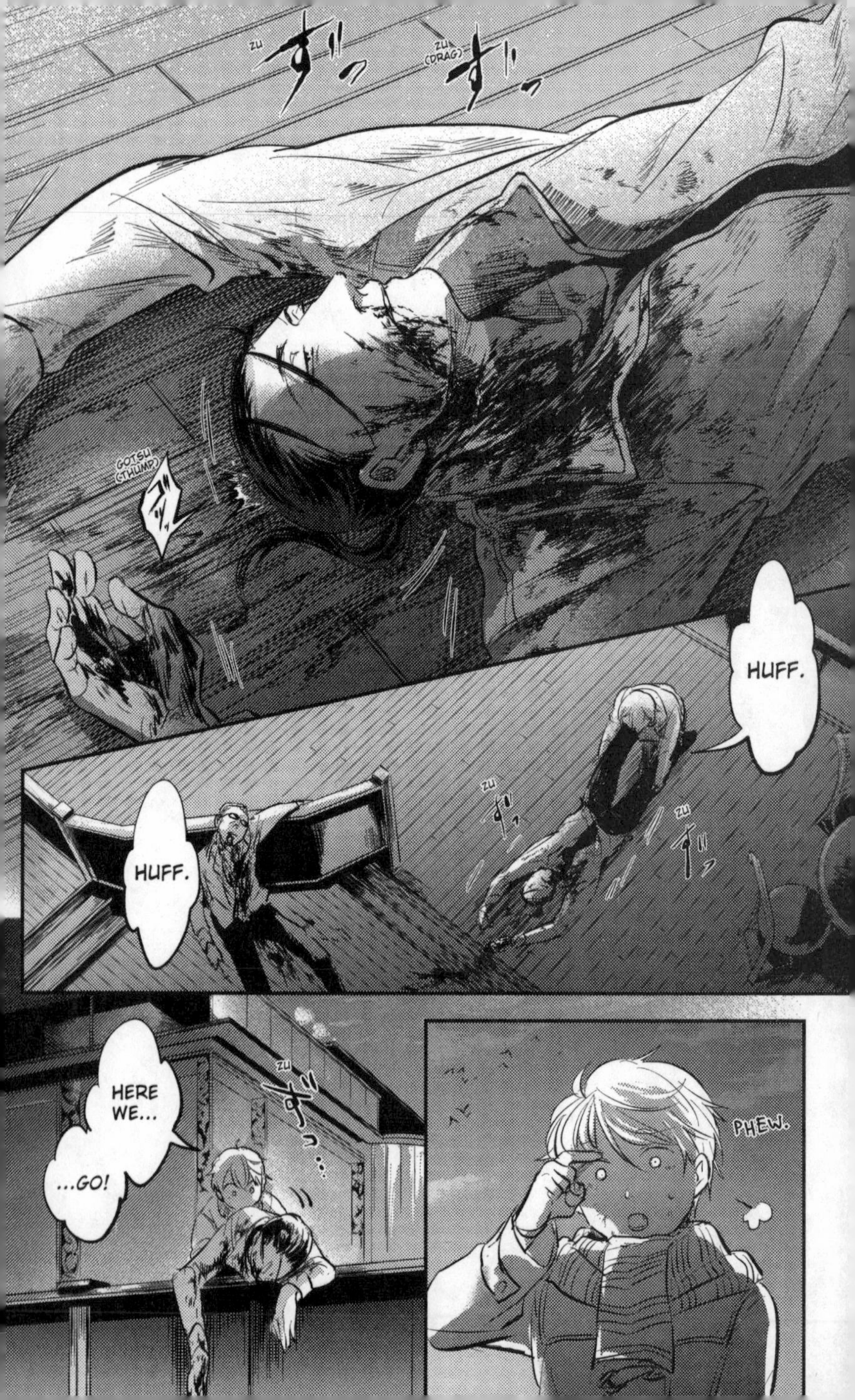
ZU (DRAG)
ZU
GOTSU (THUMP)
HUFF.
ZU
ZU
HUFF.
PHEW.
HERE WE...
...GO!
ZU

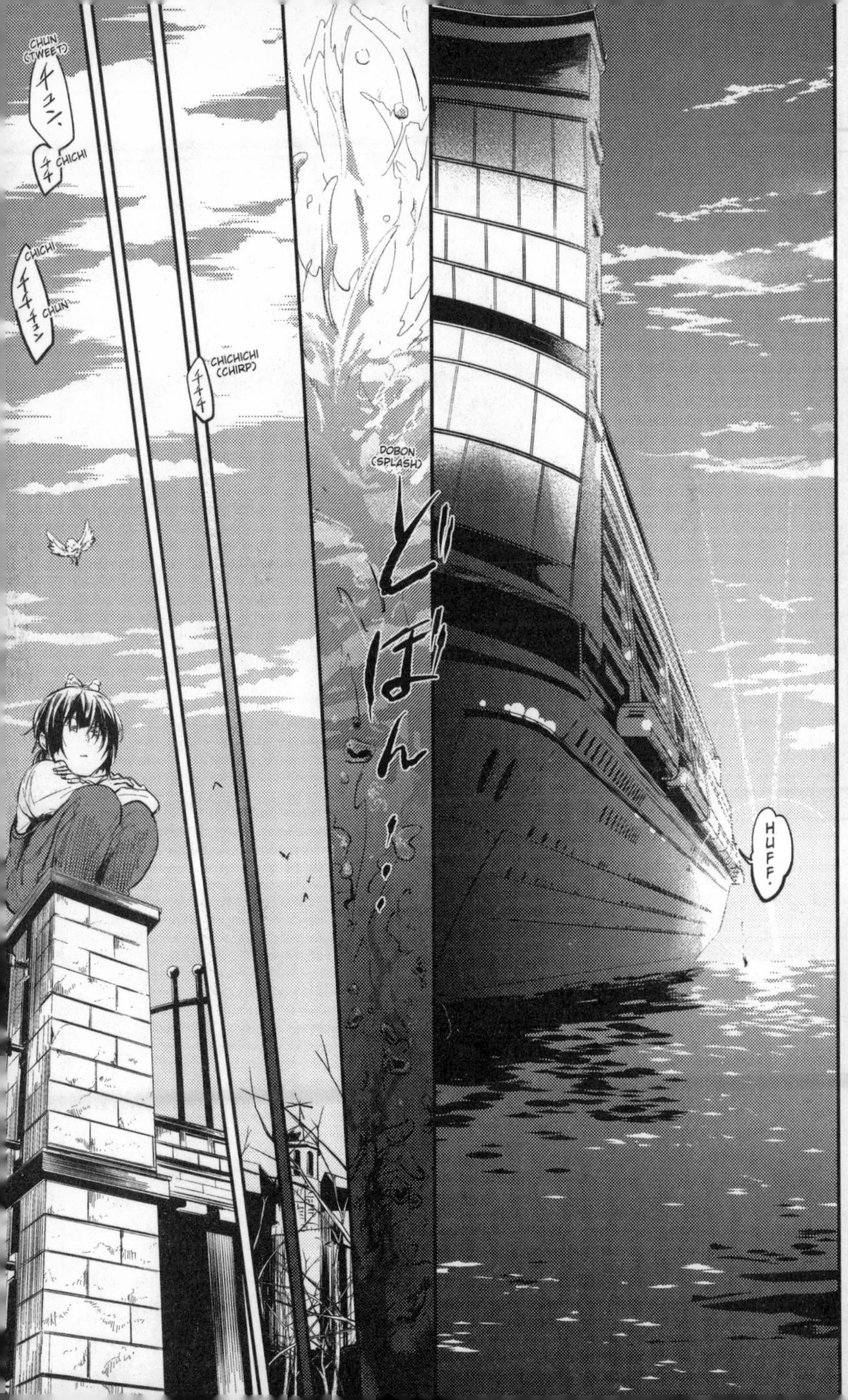
HUFF.
DOBON (SPLASH)
どぼん…
CHICHICHI (CHIRP)
チチチ
CHUN (TWEET)
チュン、
CHICHI
チチ
CHICHI CHUN
チチチュン

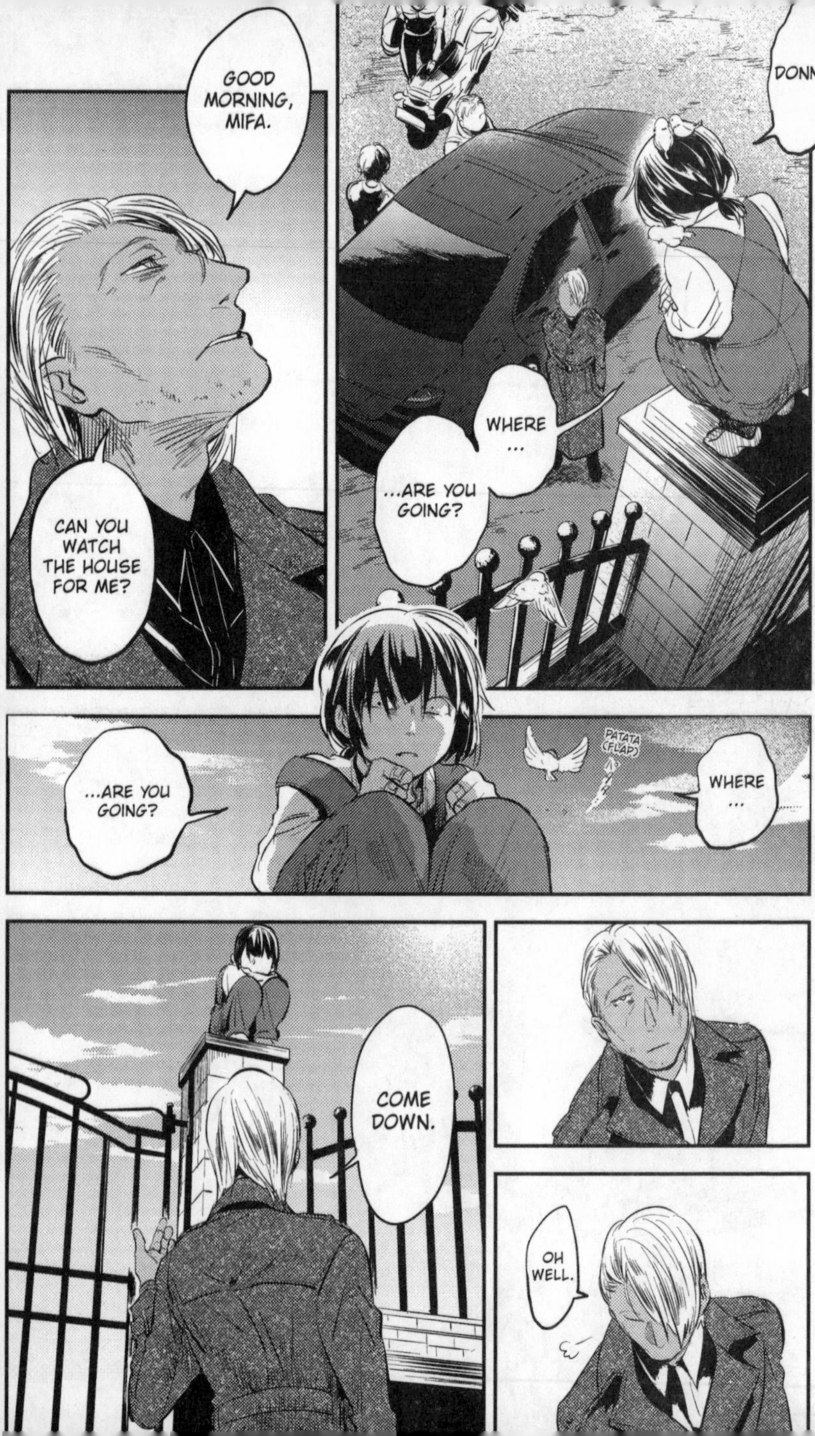
DONNY.
WHERE ...
...ARE YOU GOING?
GOOD MORNING, MIFA.
CAN YOU WATCH THE HOUSE FOR ME?
WHERE ...
PATATA (FLAP)
...ARE YOU GOING?
OH WELL.
COME DOWN.

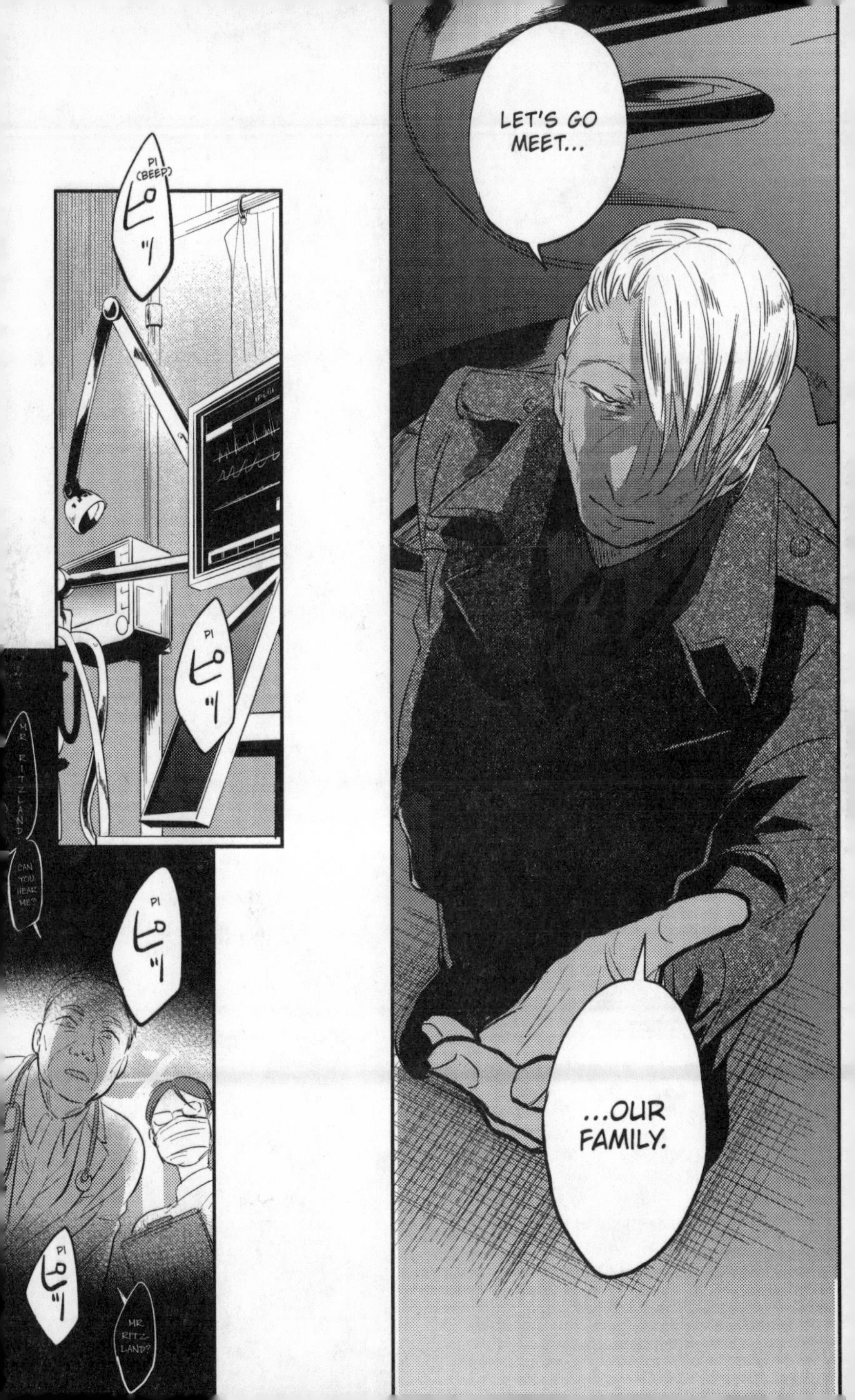
LET'S GO MEET...
...OUR FAMILY.
PI (BEEP) ピッ
PI ピッ
MR RITZLAND
CAN YOU HEAR ME?
PI ピッ
PI ピッ
MR RITZ-LAND?

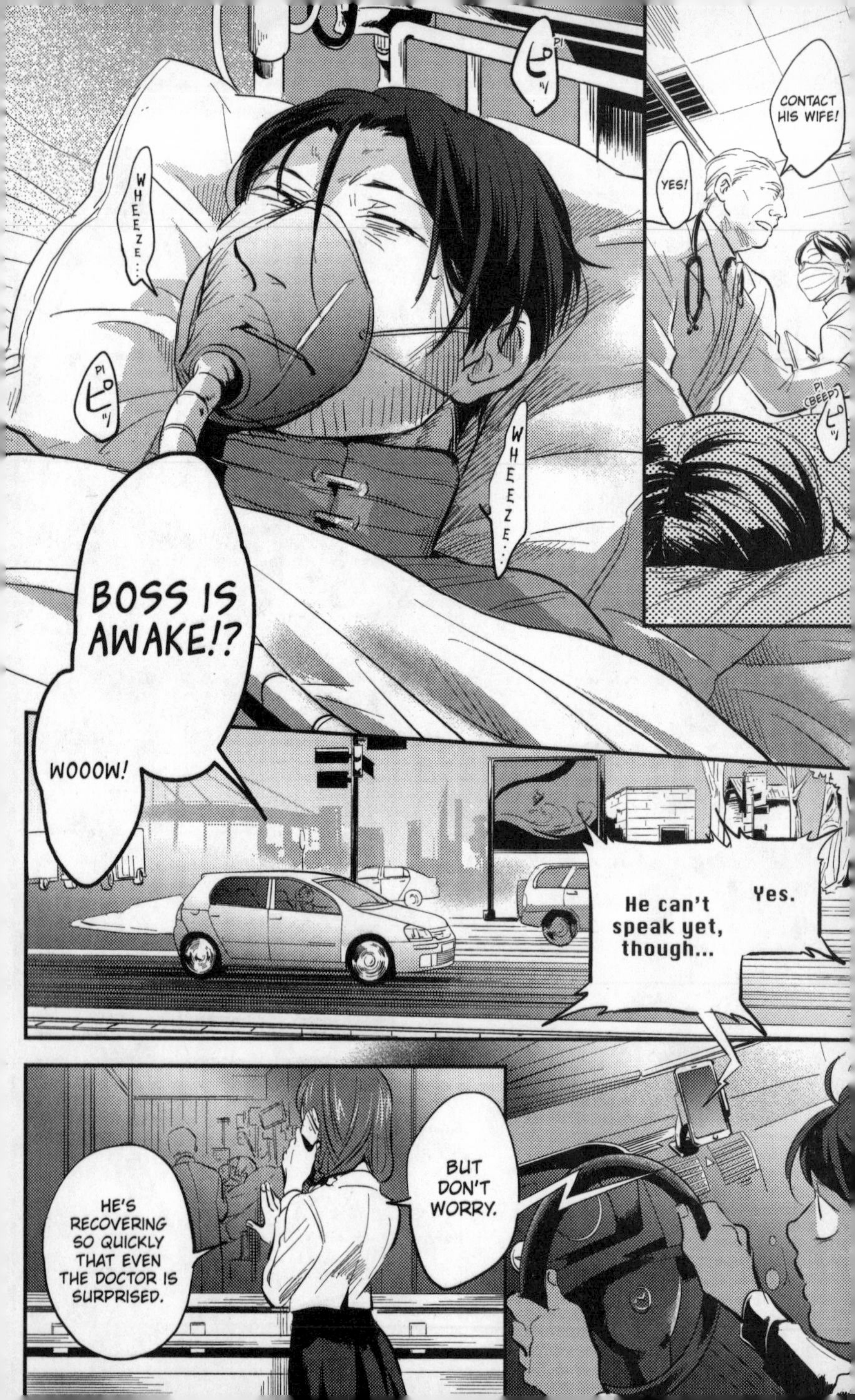
CONTACT HIS WIFE!
YES!
PI (BEEP) ピッ
ピッ PI
WHEEZE...
ピッ PI
WHEEZE...
BOSS IS AWAKE!?
WOOOW!
Yes.
He can't speak yet, though...
BUT DON'T WORRY.
HE'S RECOVERING SO QUICKLY THAT EVEN THE DOCTOR IS SURPRISED.

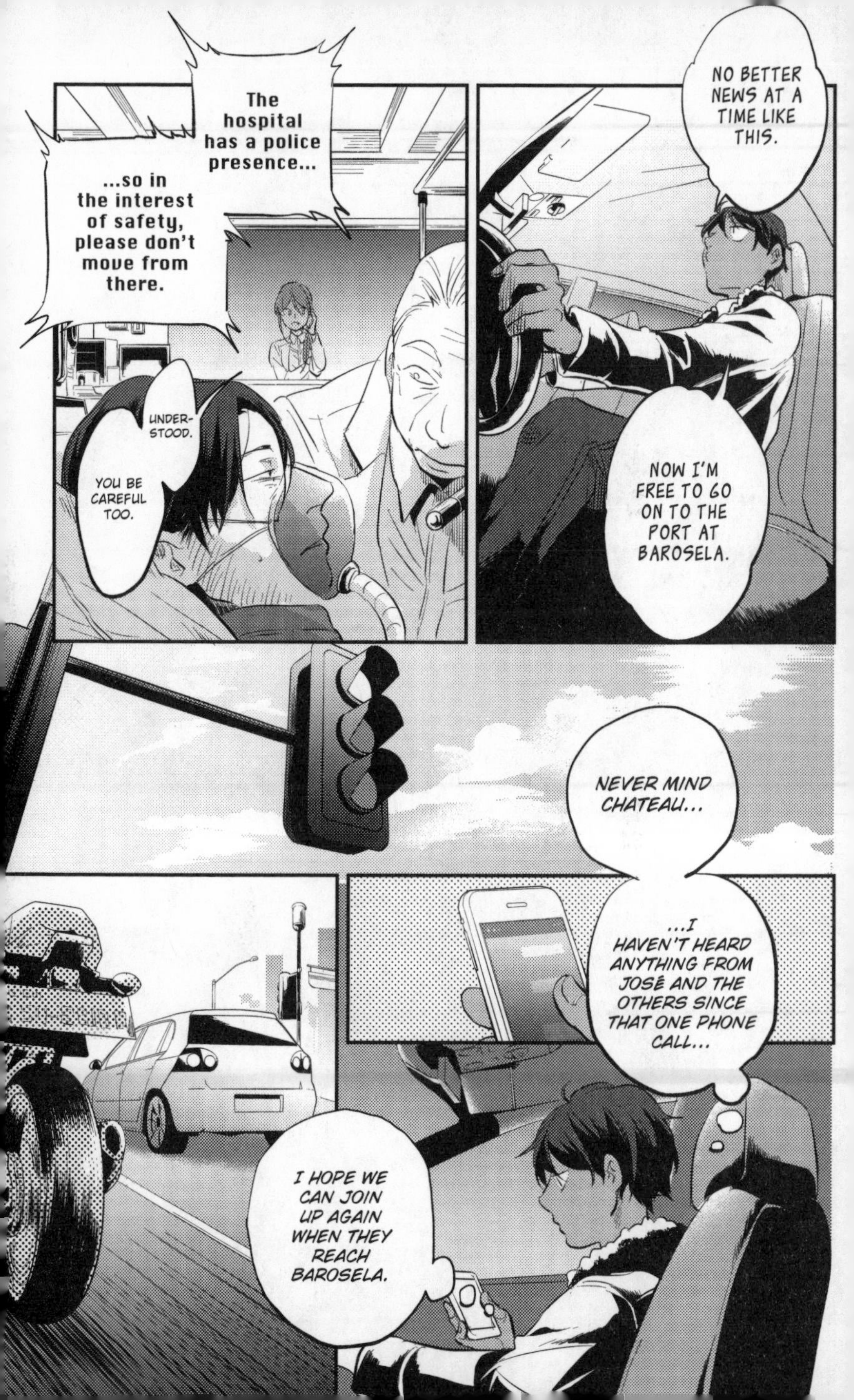
NO BETTER NEWS AT A TIME LIKE THIS.
NOW I'M FREE TO GO ON TO THE PORT AT BAROSELA.
The hospital has a police presence...
...so in the interest of safety, please don't move from there.
UNDER-STOOD.
YOU BE CAREFUL TOO.
NEVER MIND CHATEAU...
...I HAVEN'T HEARD ANYTHING FROM JOSÊ AND THE OTHERS SINCE THAT ONE PHONE CALL...
I HOPE WE CAN JOIN UP AGAIN WHEN THEY REACH BAROSELA.

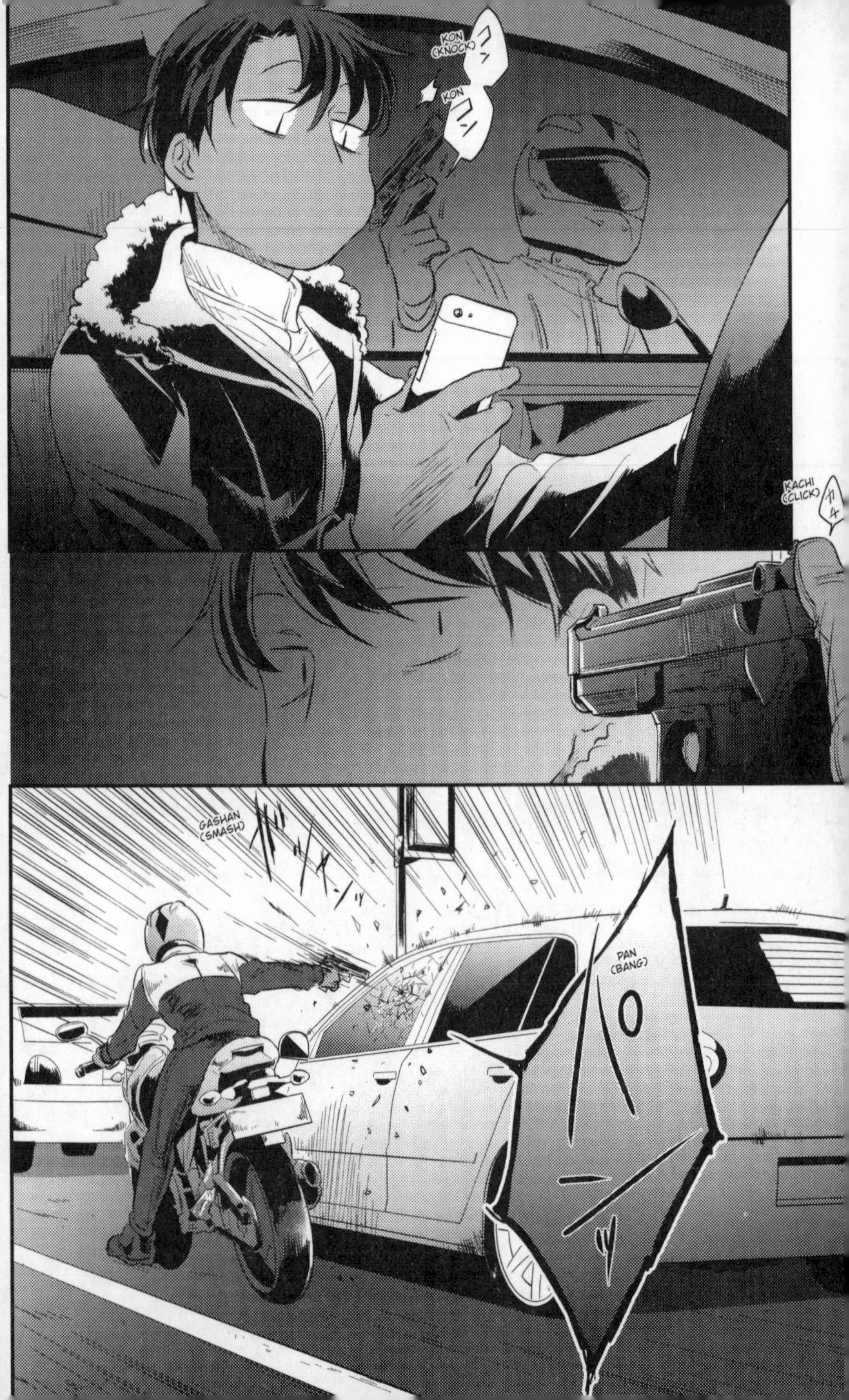
KON (KNOCK)
KON
KACHI (CLICK)
PAN (BANG)
GASHAN (SMASH)

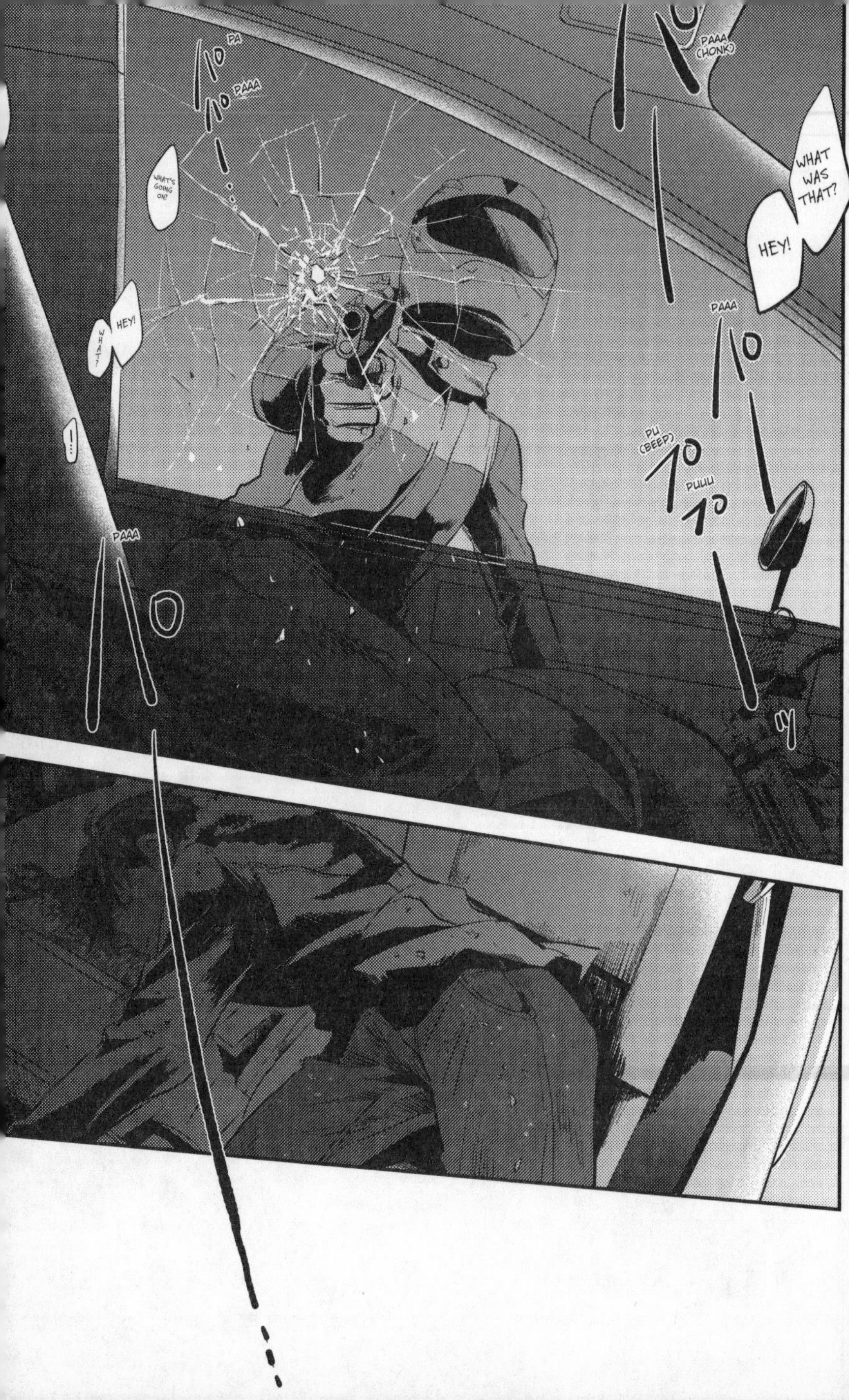
PAAA (CHONK)
WHAT WAS THAT?
HEY!
PAAA
PU (BEEP)
PUUU
PA
PAAA
WHAT'S GOING ON?
HEY!
WHAT?
!
PAAA

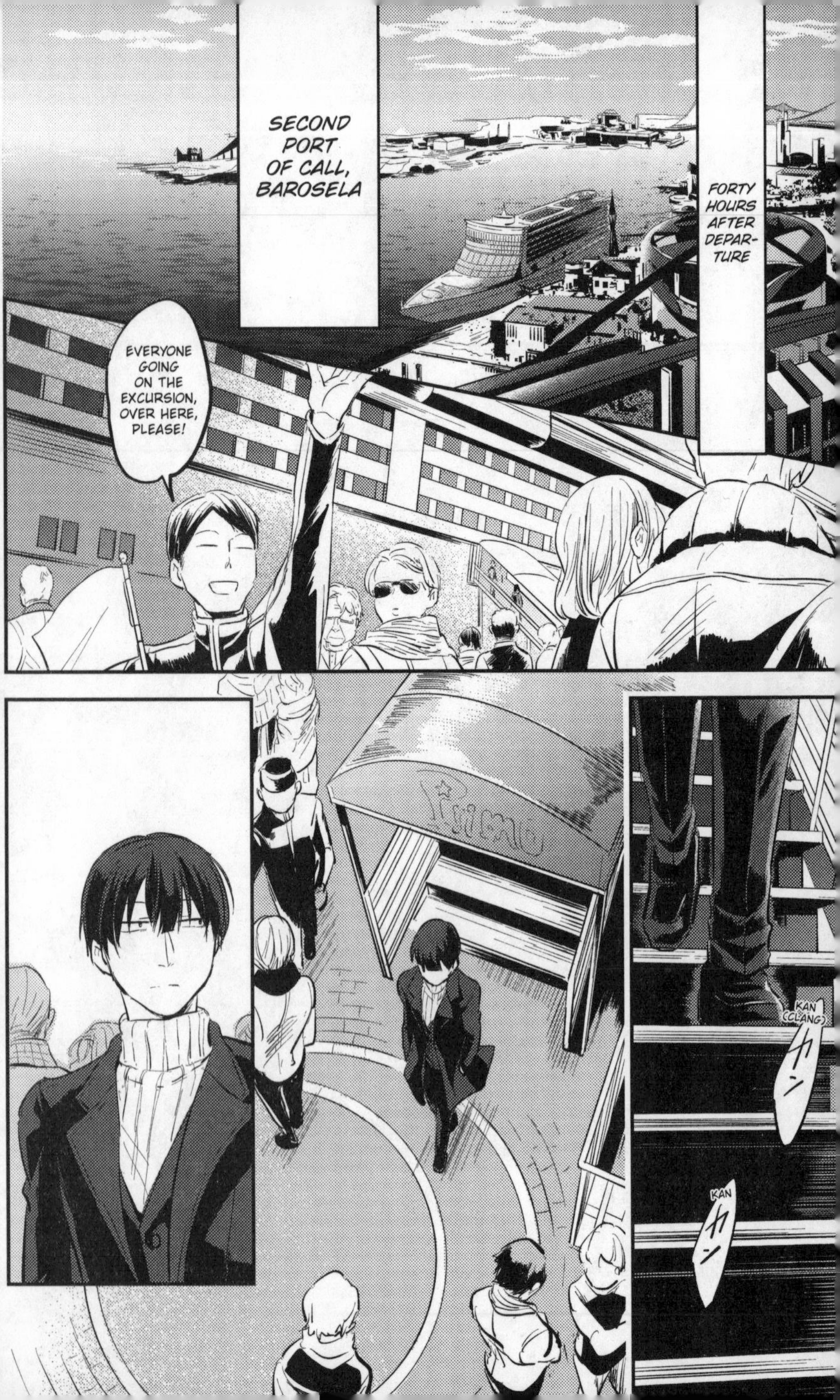
FORTY HOURS AFTER DEPARTURE
SECOND PORT OF CALL, BAROSELA
EVERYONE GOING ON THE EXCURSION, OVER HERE, PLEASE!
KAN (CLANG)
KAN

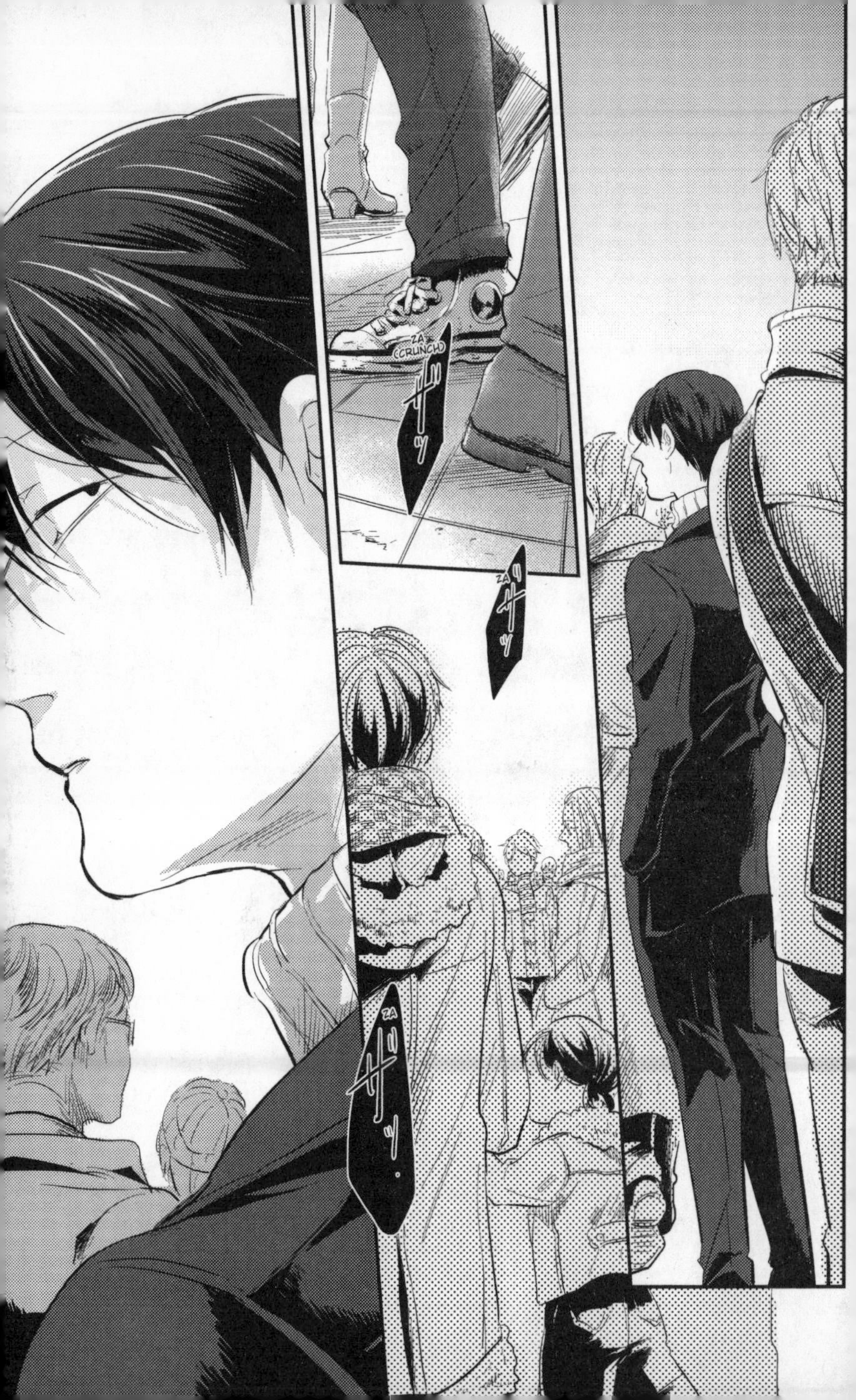
ZA (CRUNCH)
ZA
ZA

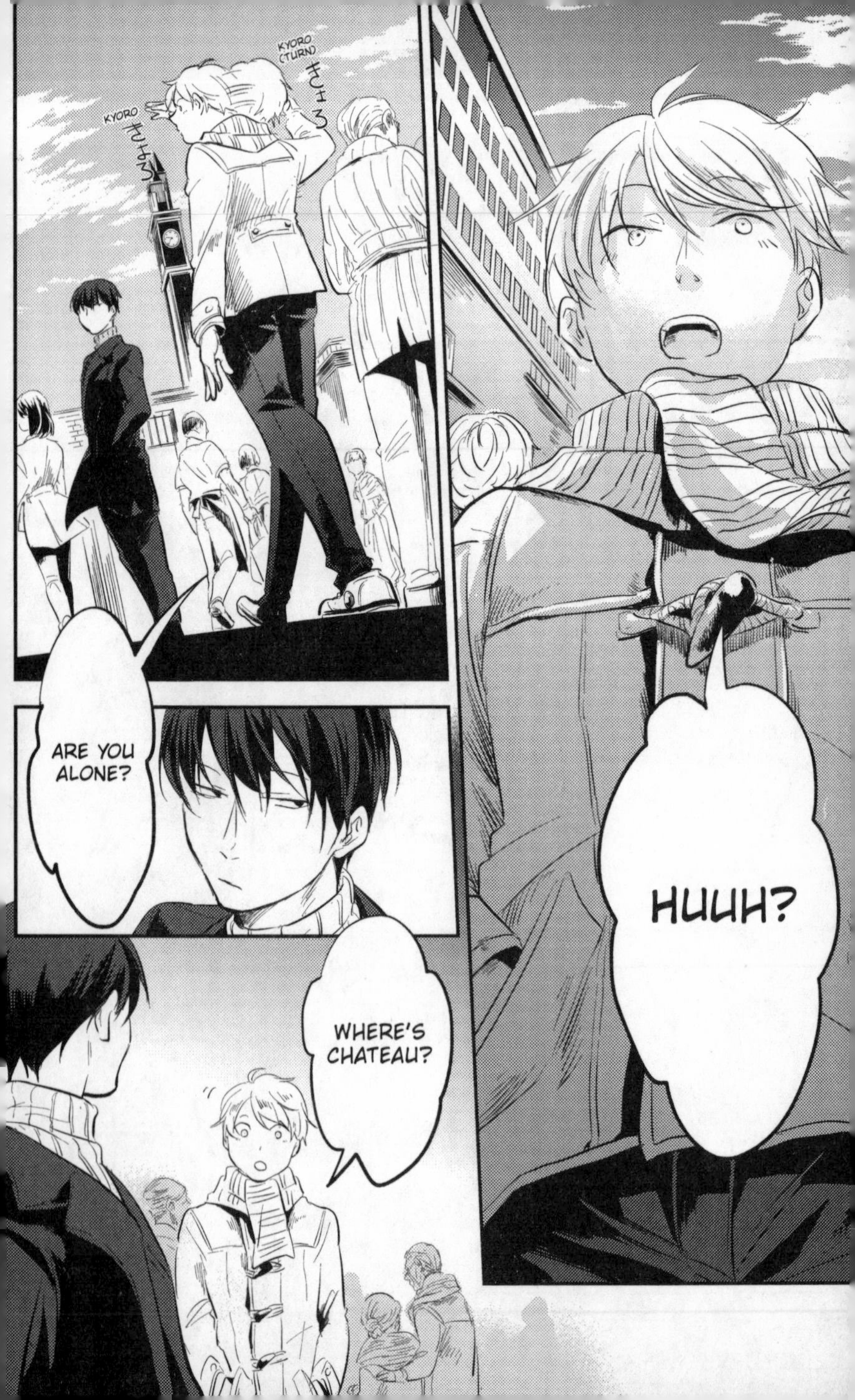
HUUH?
KYORO (TURN)
KYORO
ARE YOU ALONE?
WHERE'S CHATEAU?

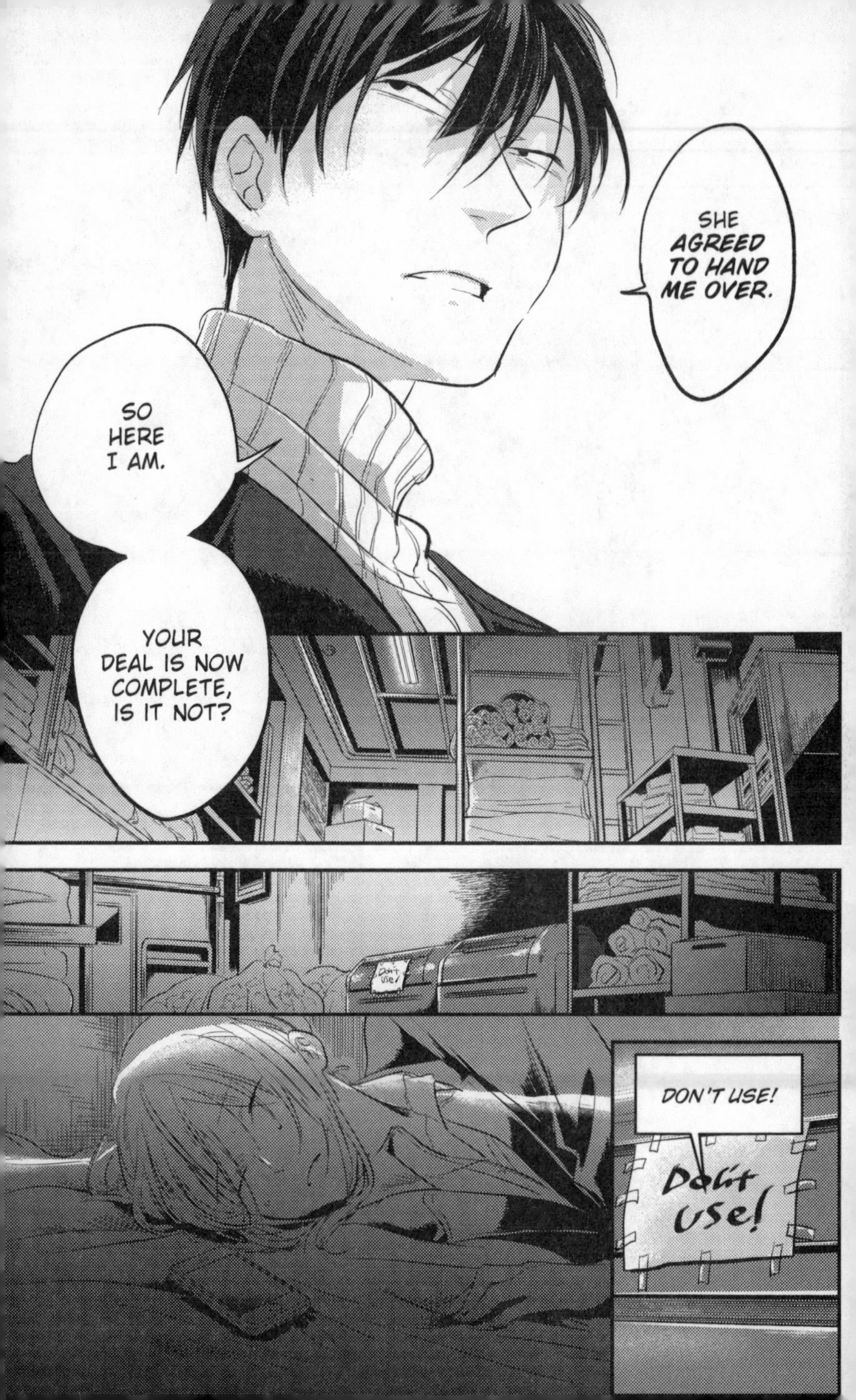
SHE AGREED TO HAND ME OVER.
SO HERE I AM.
YOUR DEAL IS NOW COMPLETE, IS IT NOT?
Don't use!
DON'T USE!
Don't use!

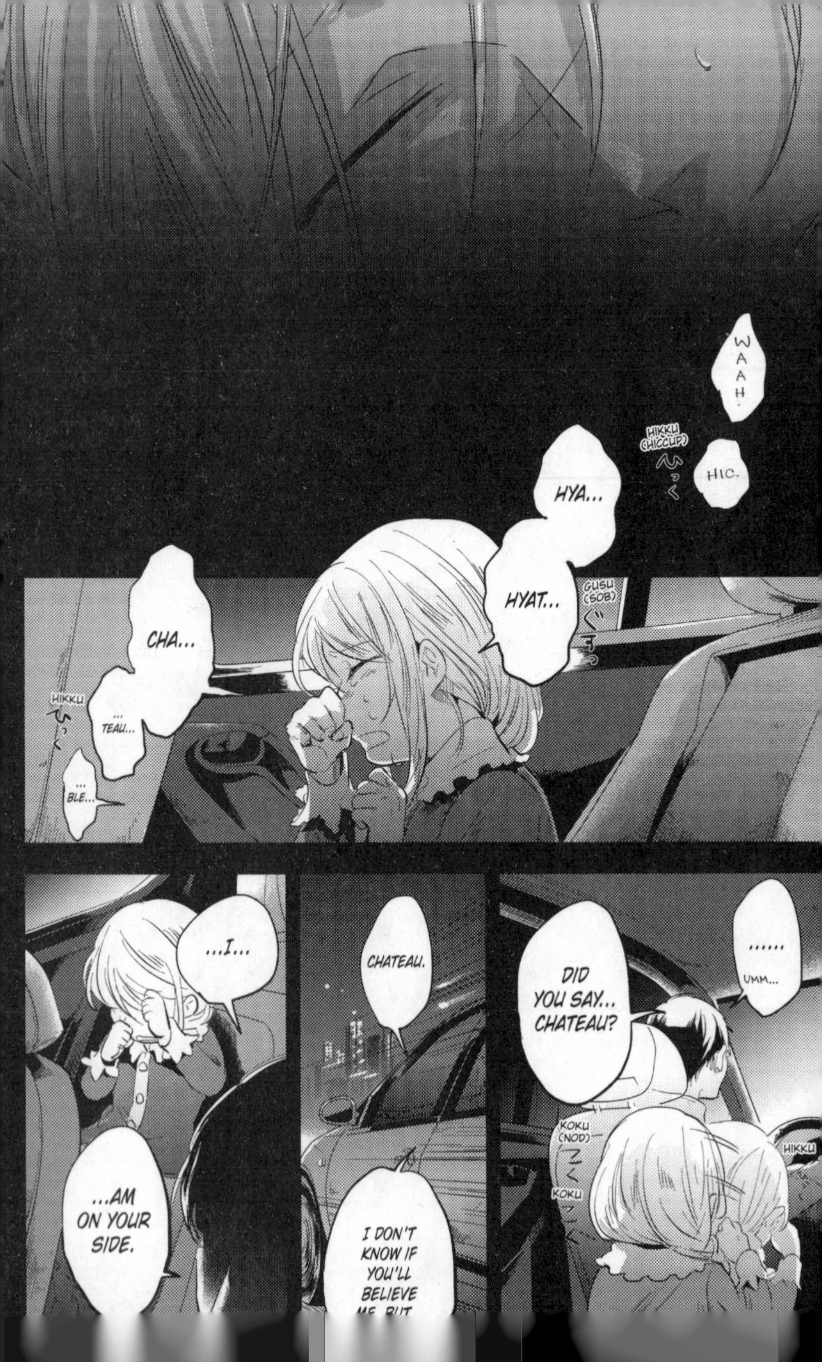
WAAH.
HIKKU (HICCUP)
HIC.
HYA...
GUSU (SOB)
HYAT...
CHA...
HIKKU
...TEAU...
...BLE...
......
UMM...
DID YOU SAY... CHATEAU?
HIKKU
KOKU (NOD)
KOKU
CHATEAU.
I DON'T KNOW IF YOU'LL BELIEVE ME, BUT
...I...
...AM ON YOUR SIDE.

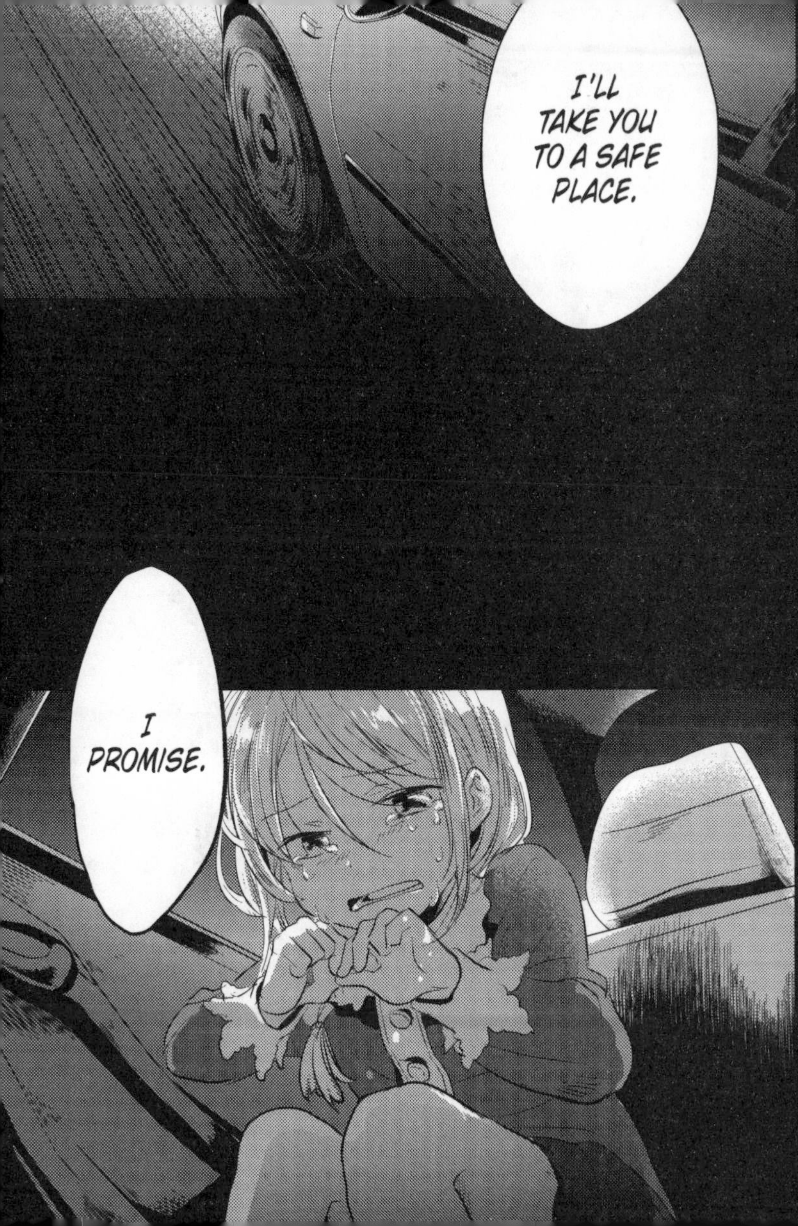
I'LL TAKE YOU TO A SAFE PLACE.
I PROMISE.

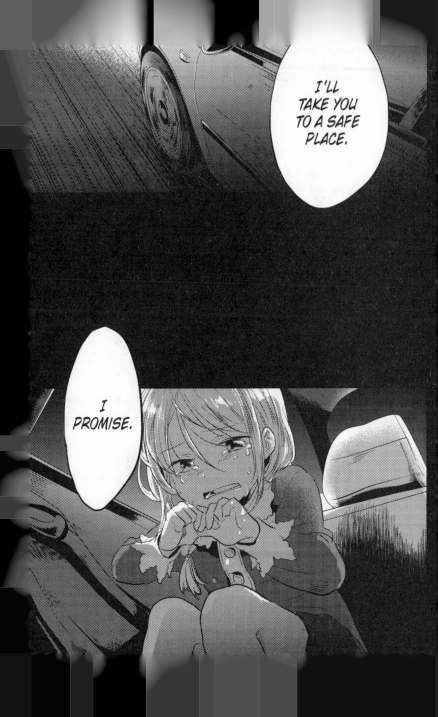

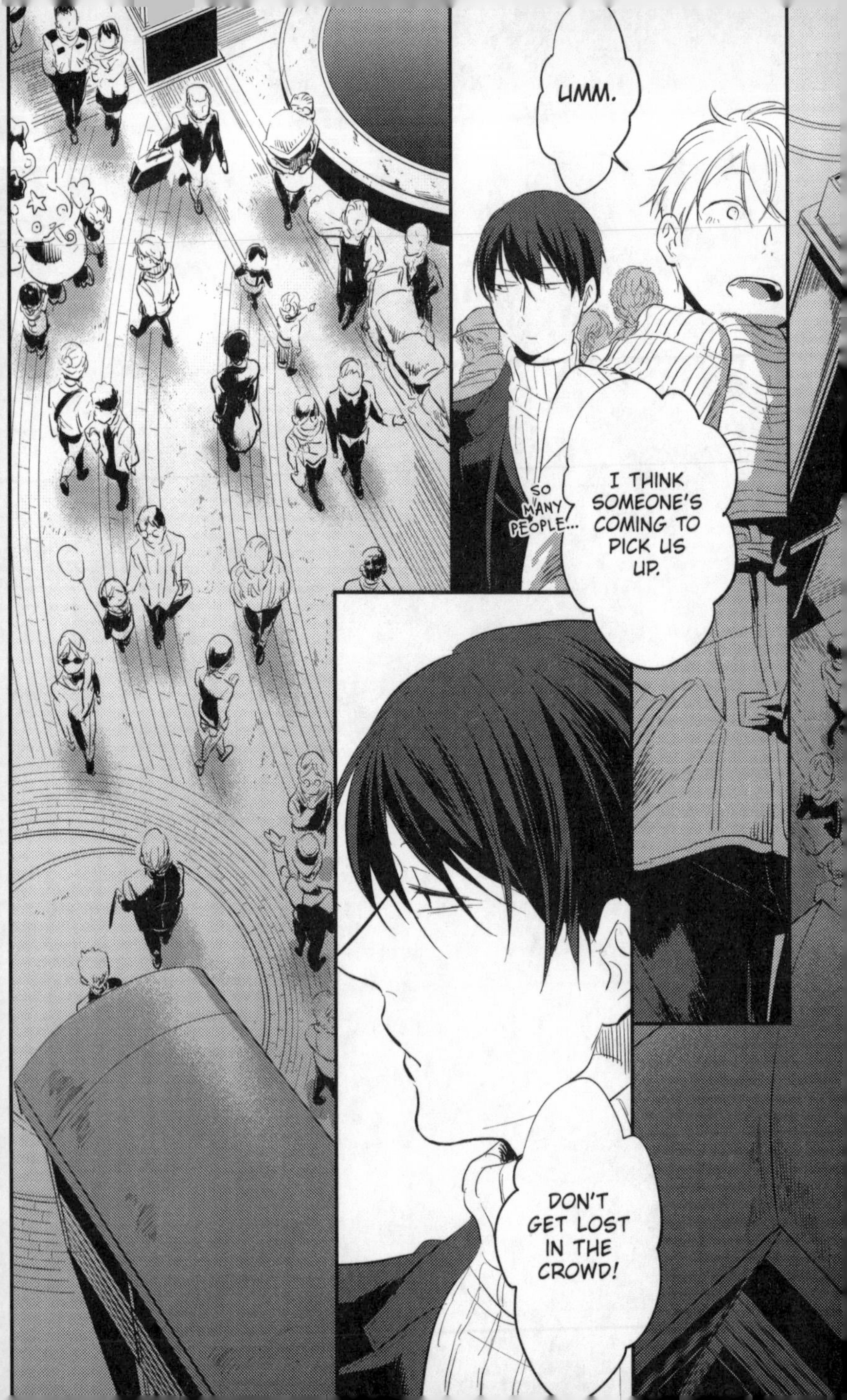
UMM.
I THINK SOMEONE'S COMING TO PICK US UP.
SO MANY PEOPLE...
DON'T GET LOST IN THE CROWD!

FILE 22: BEWILDERMENT

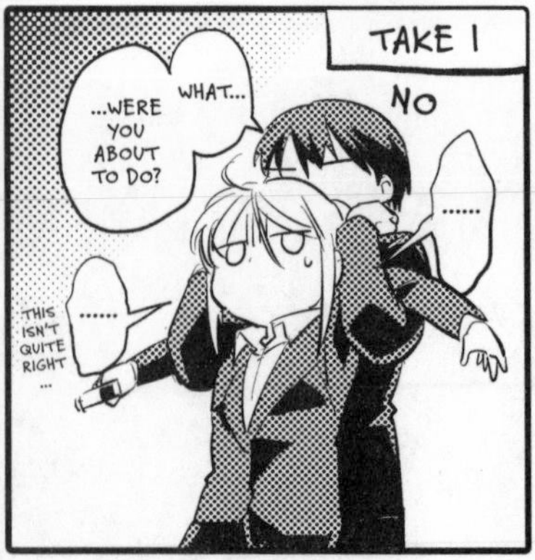
TAKE 1
NO
WHAT... ...WERE YOU ABOUT TO DO?
......
......
THIS ISN'T QUITE RIGHT...

WHICH IS PROBABLY BELOW MIDDLE SCHOOL LEVEL...

THESE CHAPTER TITLES ARE ALWAYS A GOOD TEST OF MY ENGLISH KNOWLEDGE. (MY EDITOR COMES UP WITH THEM FOR ME.) BUT THIS TIME, I HAD ABSOLUTELY NO IDEA, LOL. I AM TOLD IT MEANS CONFUSION OR PERPLEXITY. SEEING AS IT STARTS WITH "BE WILD," I THOUGHT IT WAS A TERM FOR SOMETHING TO DO WITH WILDNESS, BUT APPARENTLY NOT...

FILE 23: FAMILY

SO MANY THINGS HAPPEN ALL OVER THE PLACE IN THIS CHAPTER, MEANWHILE CHATEAU IS UNCONSCIOUS FOR THE THIRD TIME IN TOTAL, LOL...
I KNOW IT'S TOO LATE TO SAY THIS, BUT THIS GIRL GETS KNOCKED UNCONSCIOUS A BIT TOO OFTEN, LOL...
I WILL BE MORE CAREFUL IN THE FUTURE...
RYANG-HA HAD TO LEAVE THE SHIP BEFORE THE FORMAL NIGHT HE WAS SO EXCITED FOR. HE MUST HAVE BEEN RAGING INTERNALLY.

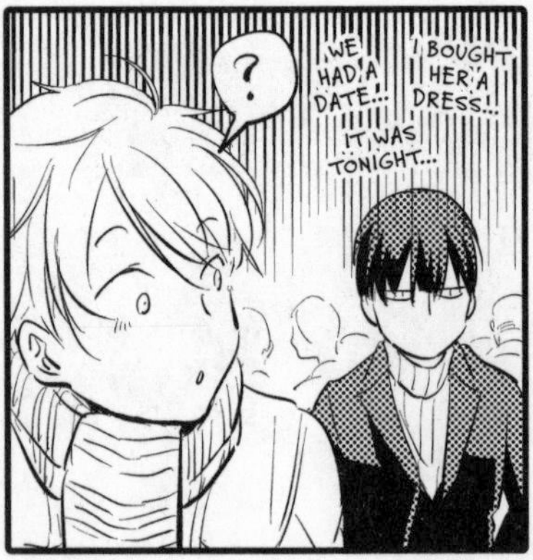
I BOUGHT HER A DRESS...!
WE HAD A DATE... IT WAS TONIGHT...
?

FILE 24: DONNY

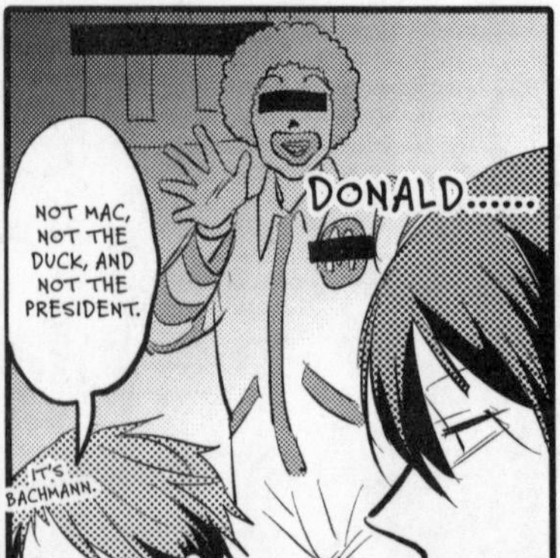
DONALD......
NOT MAC, NOT THE DUCK, AND NOT THE PRESIDENT.
IT'S BACHMANN.

THE ENEMY SIDE IS STEADILY TURNING INTO A LARGE FAMILY, LOL...
WITH DONNY, NIKKA, AND THE OTHERS, I WORRIED A LOT ABOUT THEIR APPEARANCES AND NAMES. I IMAGINE YOU CAN CLEARLY TELL I'M NOT USED TO DRAWING THEM, LOL...
I WANT TO WORK ON MY BASICS SO THAT I CAN DRAW MANY DIFFERENT CHARACTERS NATURALLY.

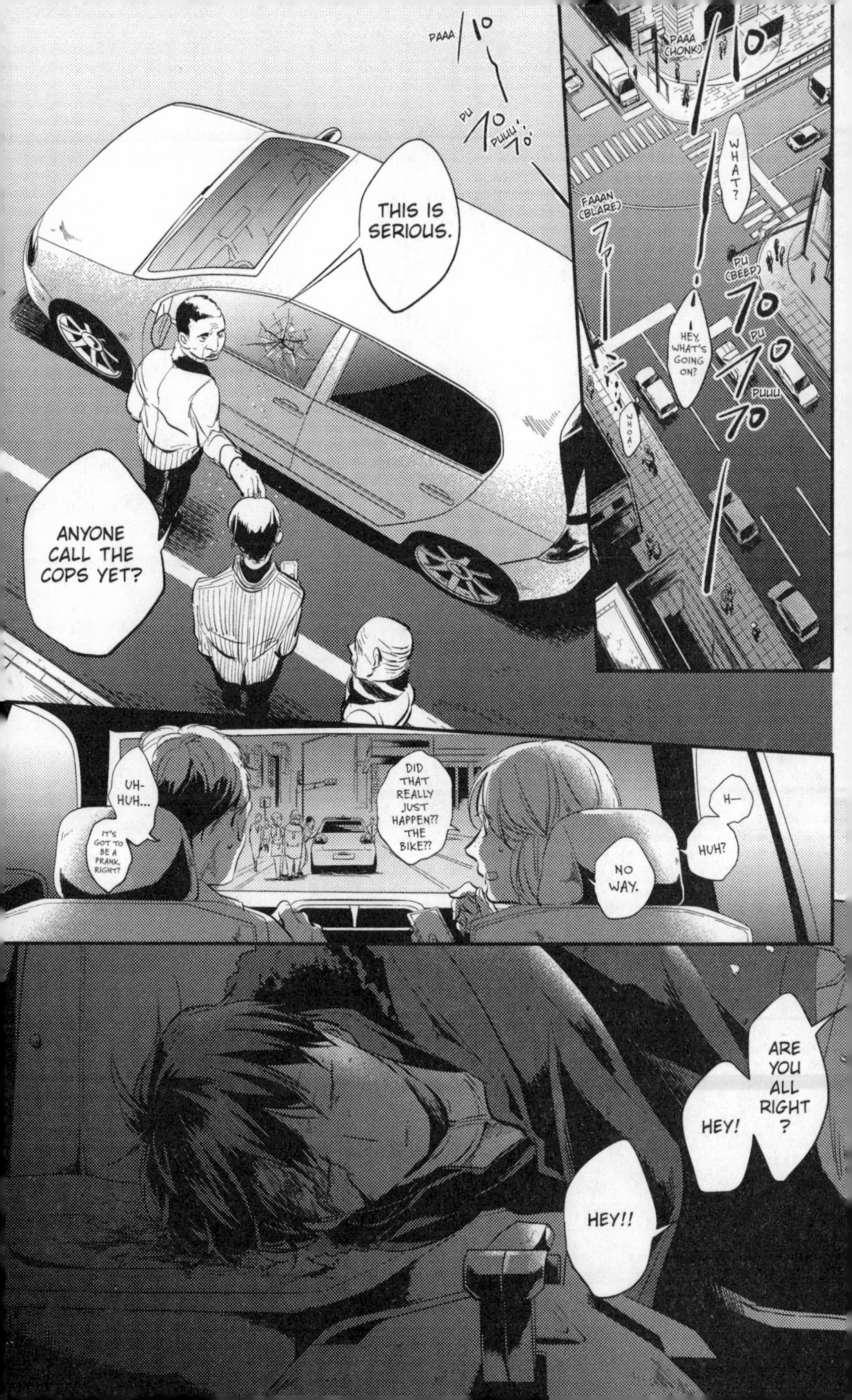
PAAA (HONK)
WHAT?
FAAAN (BLARE)
PU (BEEP)
PU
PUUU
HEY, WHAT'S GOING ON?
WHOA.
PAAA
PU
PUUU
THIS IS SERIOUS.
ANYONE CALL THE COPS YET?
H— HUH?
NO WAY.
DID THAT REALLY JUST HAPPEN?? THE BIKE??
UH-HUH...
IT'S GOT TO BE A PRANK, RIGHT?
ARE YOU ALL RIGHT?
HEY!
HEY!!

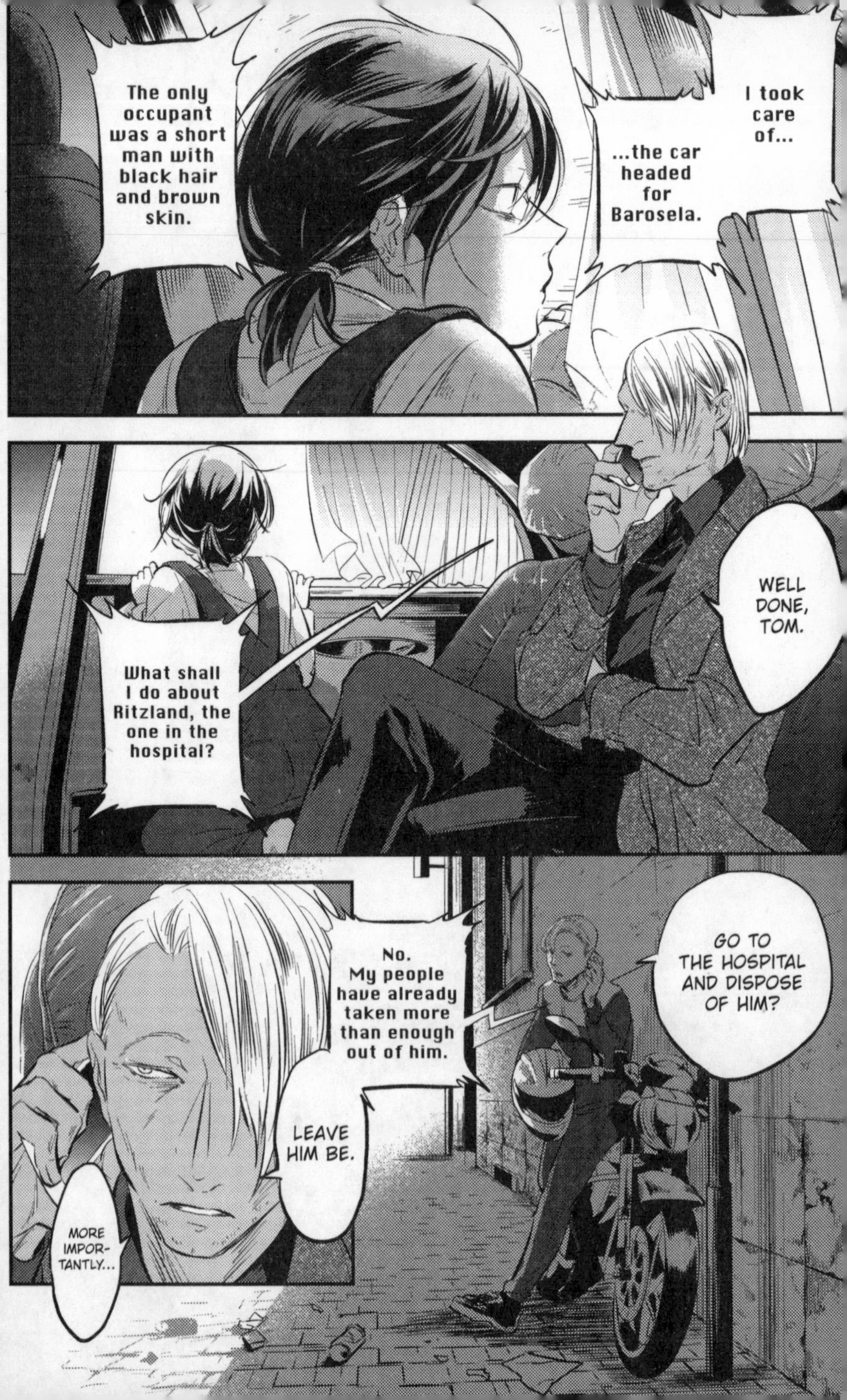
I took care of...
...the car headed for Barosela.
The only occupant was a short man with black hair and brown skin.
WELL DONE, TOM.
What shall I do about Ritzland, the one in the hospital?
GO TO THE HOSPITAL AND DISPOSE OF HIM?
No. My people have already taken more than enough out of him.
LEAVE HIM BE.
MORE IMPOR-TANTLY...

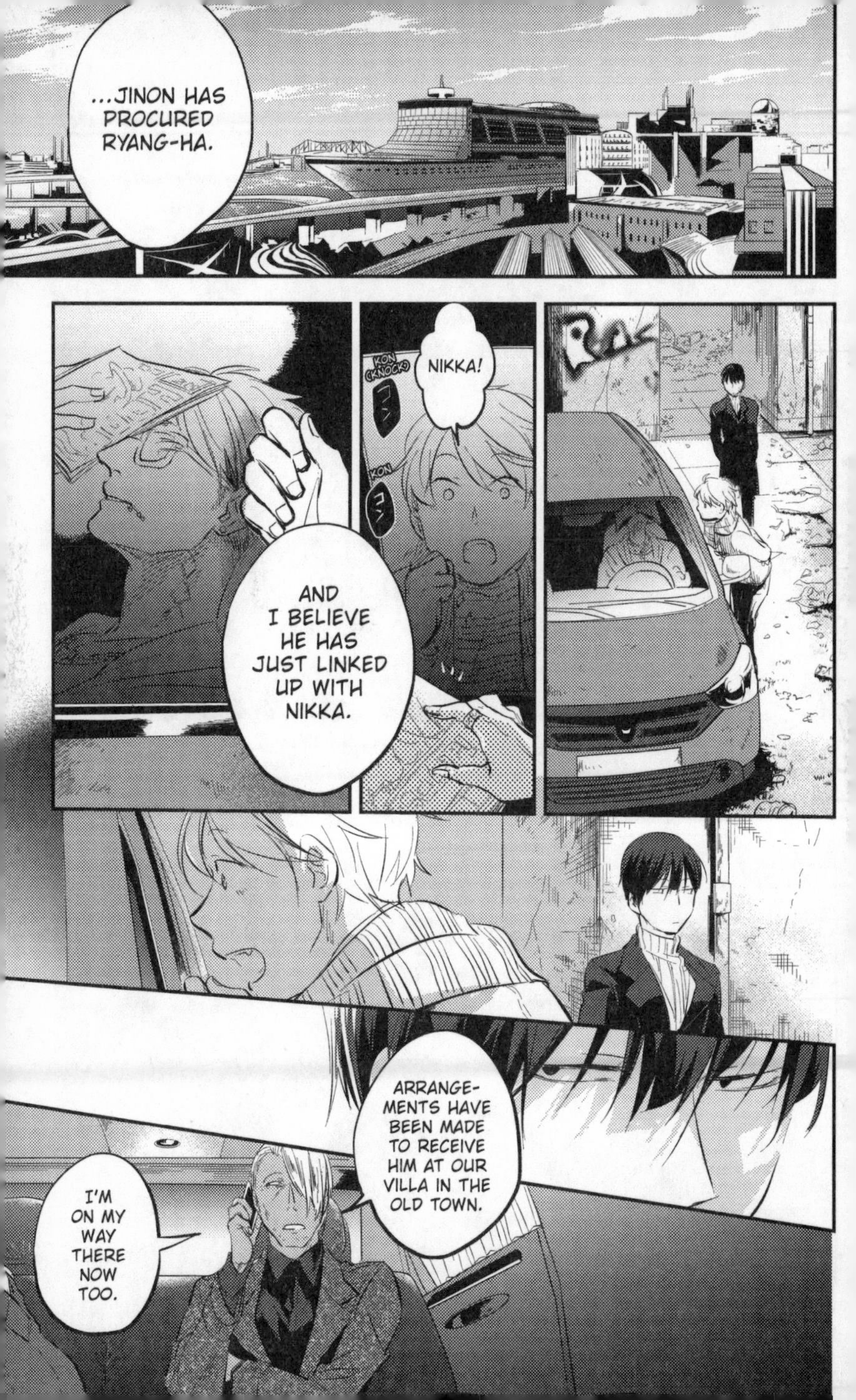
...JINON HAS PROCURED RYANG-HA.
NIKKA!
KON (KNOCK)
KON
AND I BELIEVE HE HAS JUST LINKED UP WITH NIKKA.
ARRANGE-MENTS HAVE BEEN MADE TO RECEIVE HIM AT OUR VILLA IN THE OLD TOWN.
I'M ON MY WAY THERE NOW TOO.

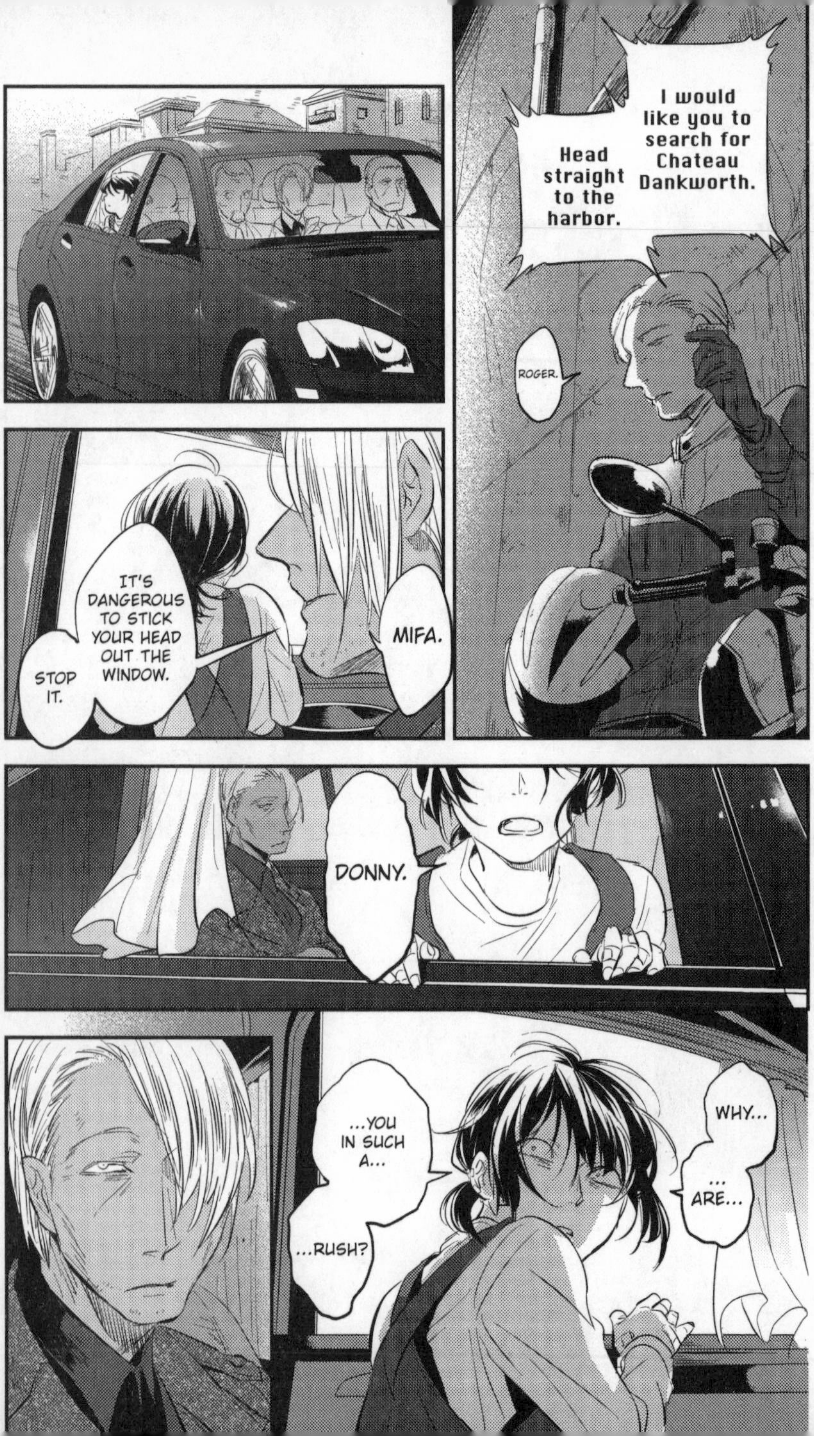
I would like you to search for Chateau Dankworth.
Head straight to the harbor.
ROGER.
MIFA.
IT'S DANGEROUS TO STICK YOUR HEAD OUT THE WINDOW.
STOP IT.
DONNY.
WHY...
... ARE...
...YOU IN SUCH A...
...RUSH?

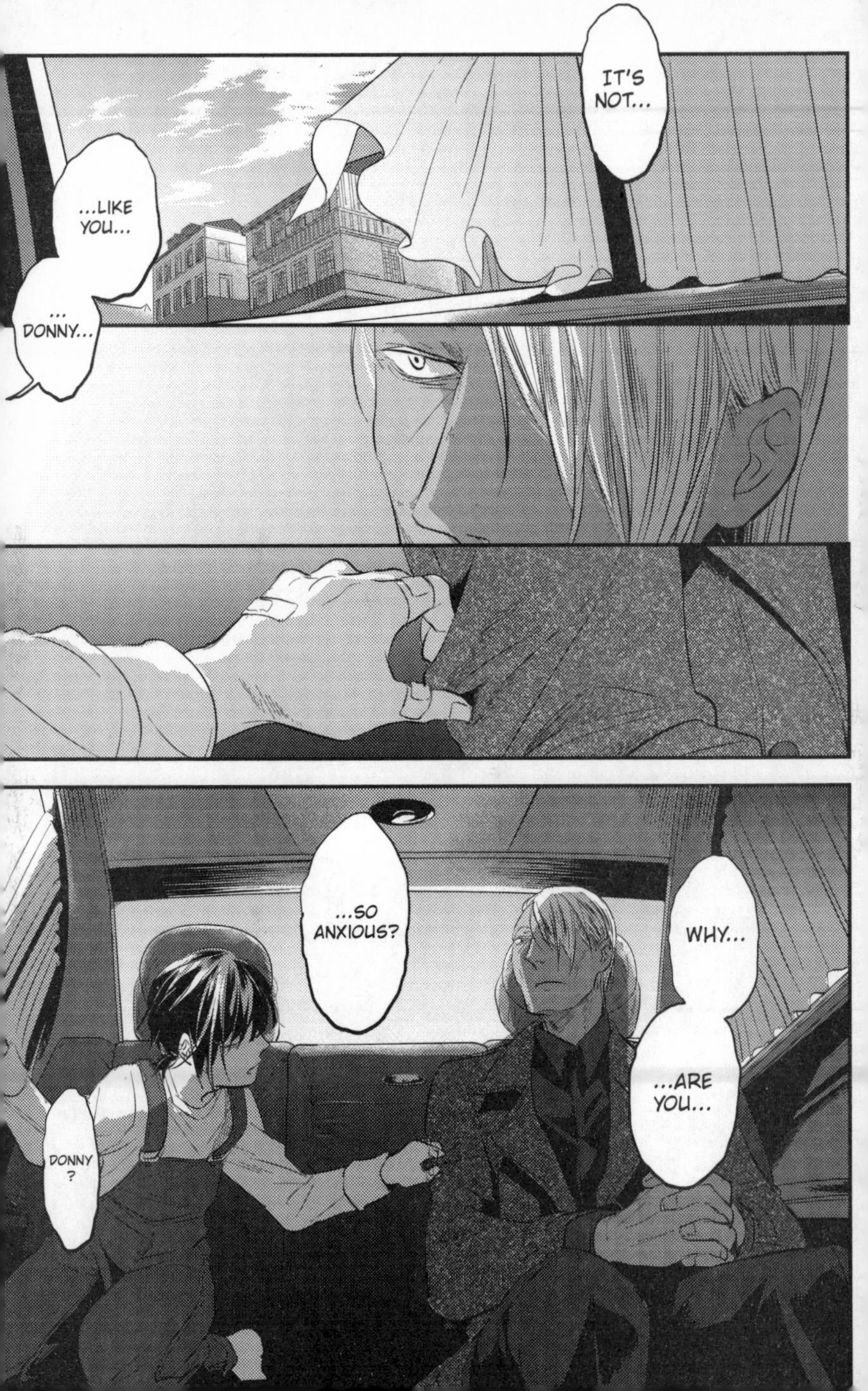
IT'S NOT...
...LIKE YOU...
... DONNY...
WHY...
...ARE YOU...
...SO ANXIOUS?
DONNY ?

FILE 24 DONNY

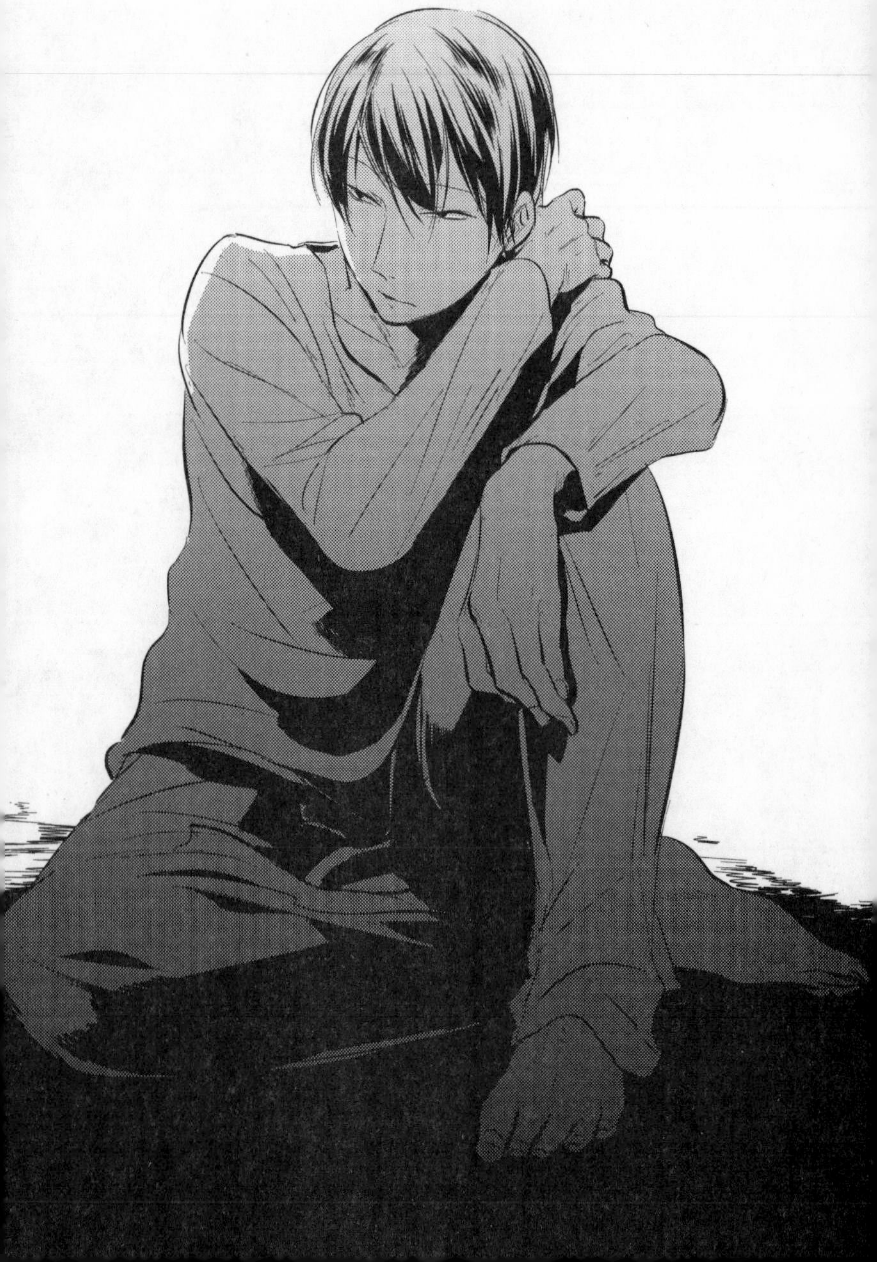

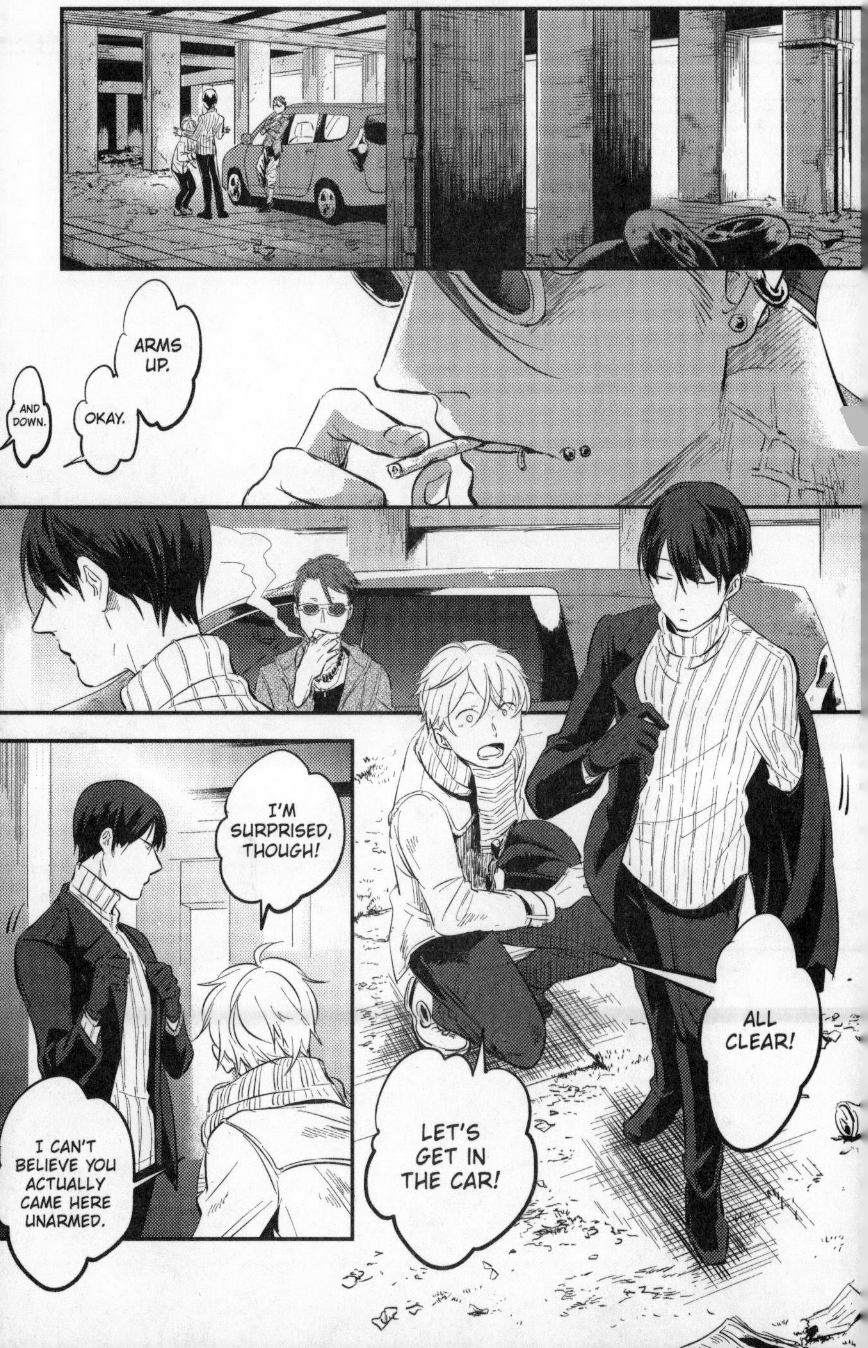
ARMS UP.
OKAY.
AND DOWN.
ALL CLEAR!
LET'S GET IN THE CAR!
I'M SURPRISED, THOUGH!
I CAN'T BELIEVE YOU ACTUALLY CAME HERE UNARMED.

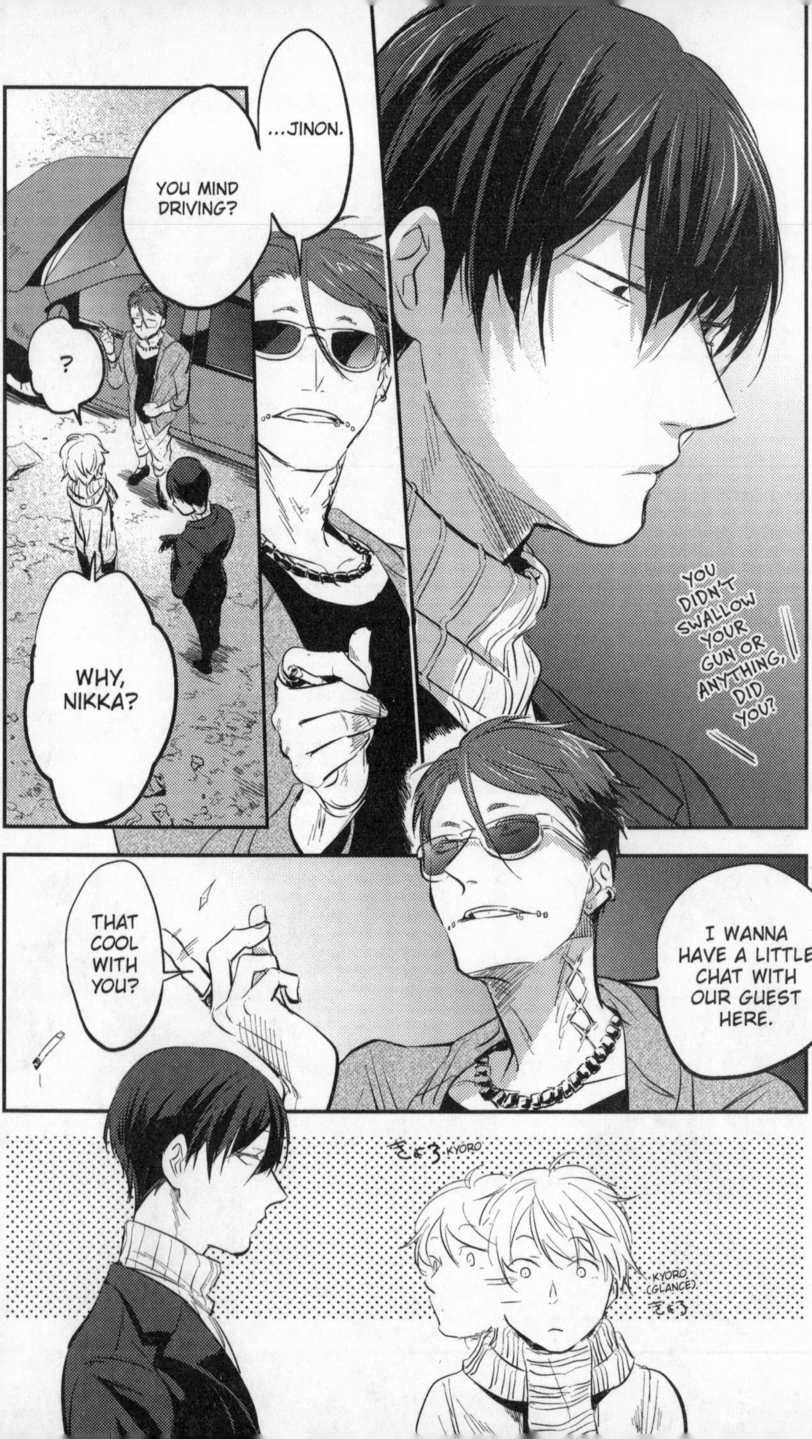
YOU DIDN'T SWALLOW YOUR GUN OR ANYTHING, DID YOU?
...JINON.
YOU MIND DRIVING?
?
WHY, NIKKA?
I WANNA HAVE A LITTLE CHAT WITH OUR GUEST HERE.
THAT COOL WITH YOU?
きょろ KYORO
KYORO (GLANCE) きょろ

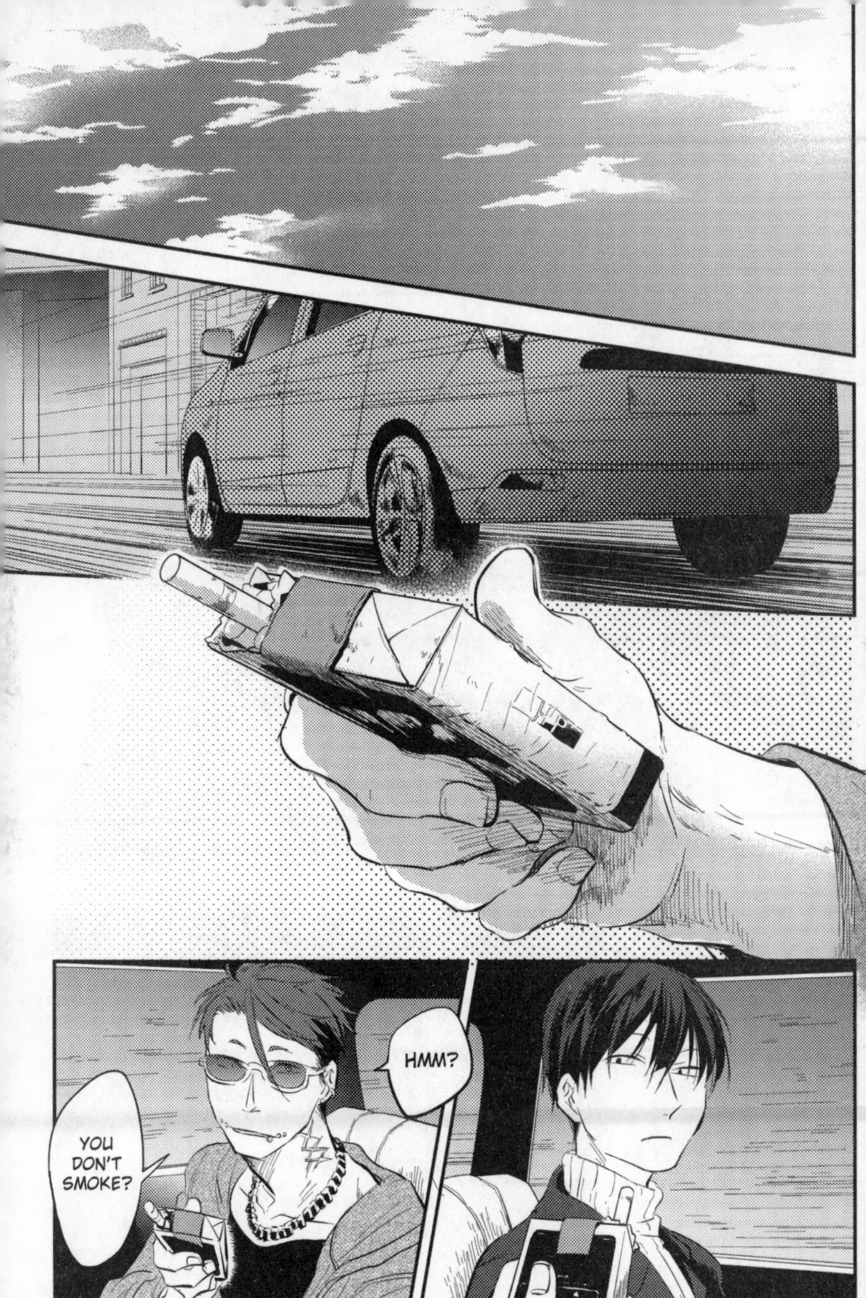
HMM?
YOU DON'T SMOKE?

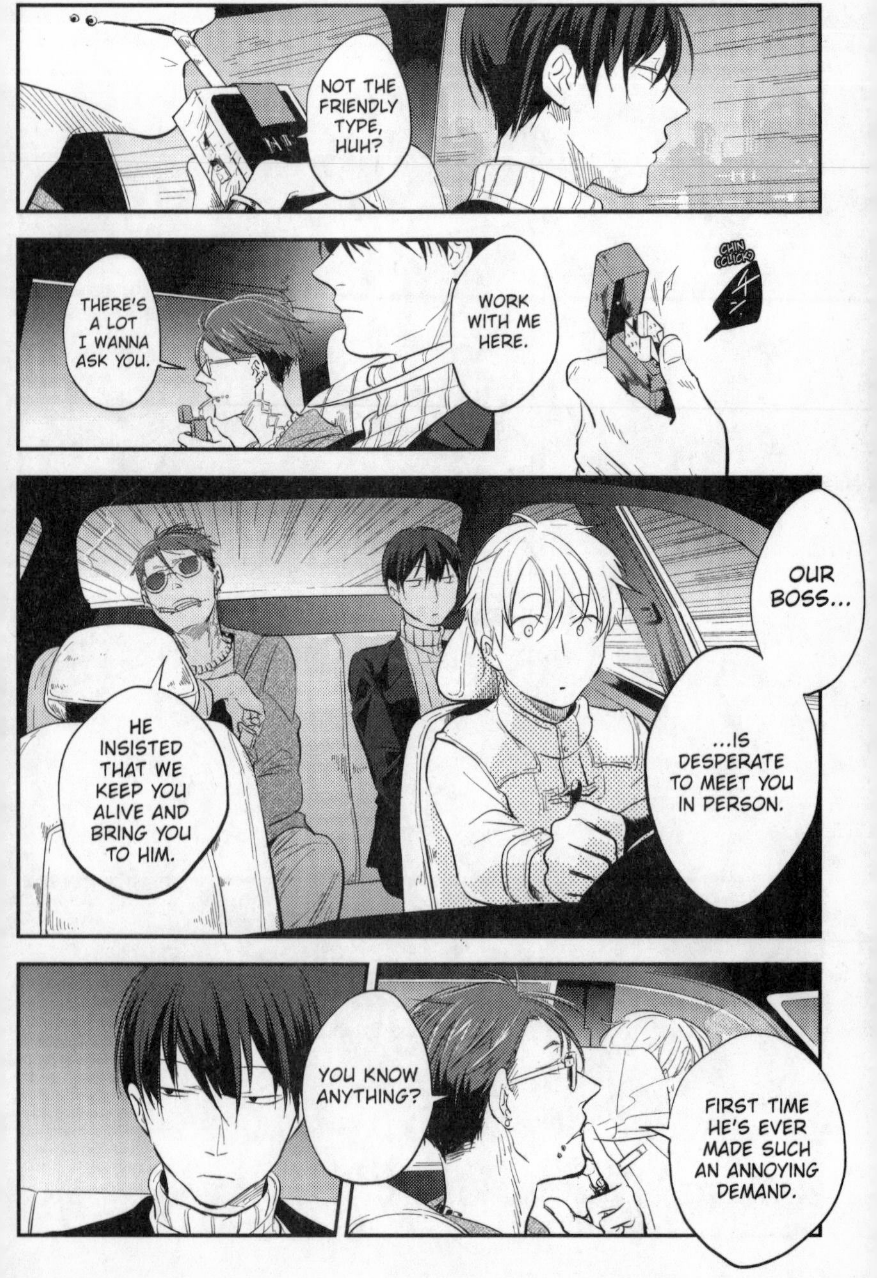
NOT THE FRIENDLY TYPE, HUH?
CHIN (CLICK)
WORK WITH ME HERE.
THERE'S A LOT I WANNA ASK YOU.
OUR BOSS...
...IS DESPERATE TO MEET YOU IN PERSON.
HE INSISTED THAT WE KEEP YOU ALIVE AND BRING YOU TO HIM.
FIRST TIME HE'S EVER MADE SUCH AN ANNOYING DEMAND.
YOU KNOW ANYTHING?

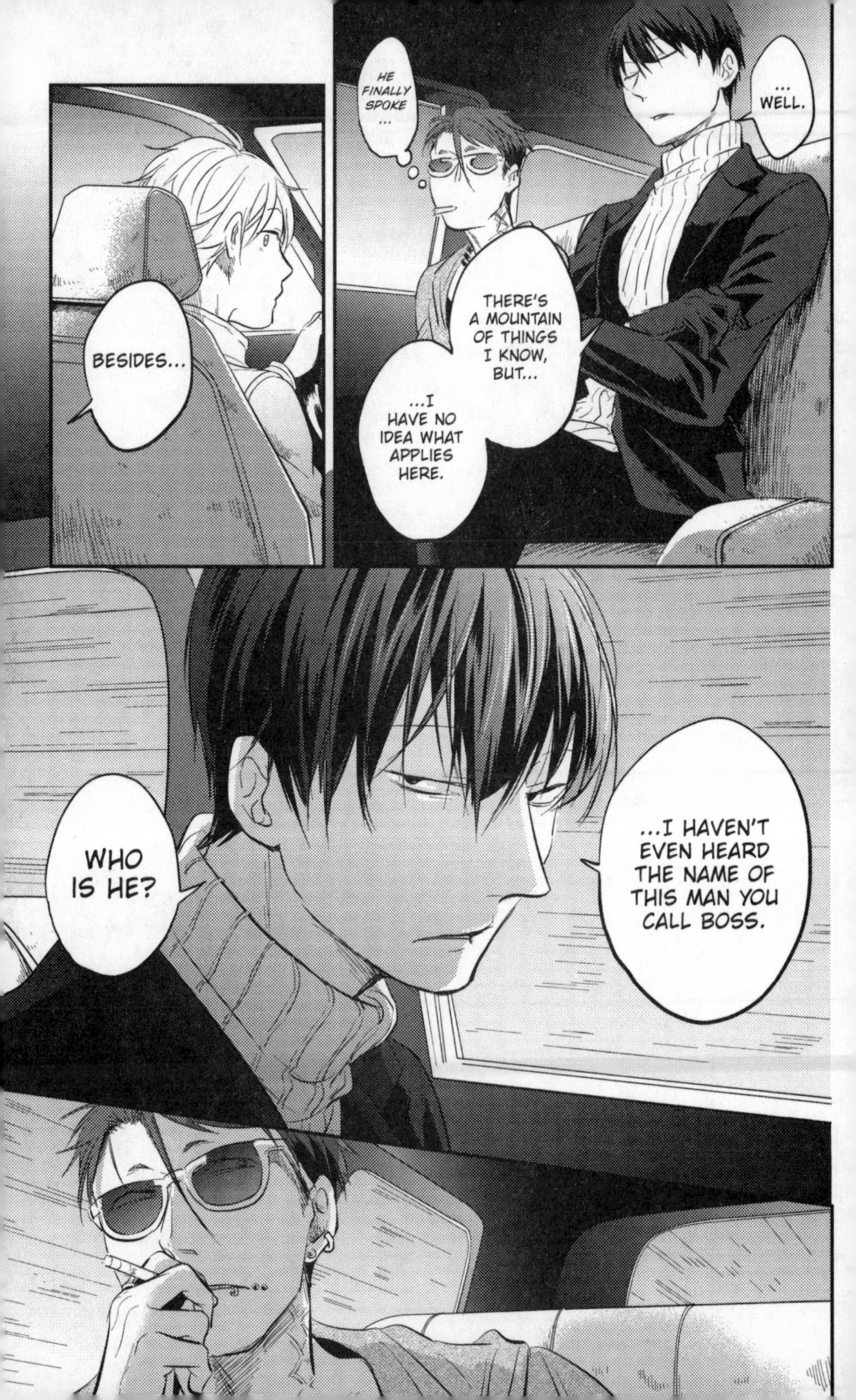
...WELL.
HE FINALLY SPOKE...
THERE'S A MOUNTAIN OF THINGS I KNOW, BUT...
...I HAVE NO IDEA WHAT APPLIES HERE.
BESIDES...
...I HAVEN'T EVEN HEARD THE NAME OF THIS MAN YOU CALL BOSS.
WHO IS HE?

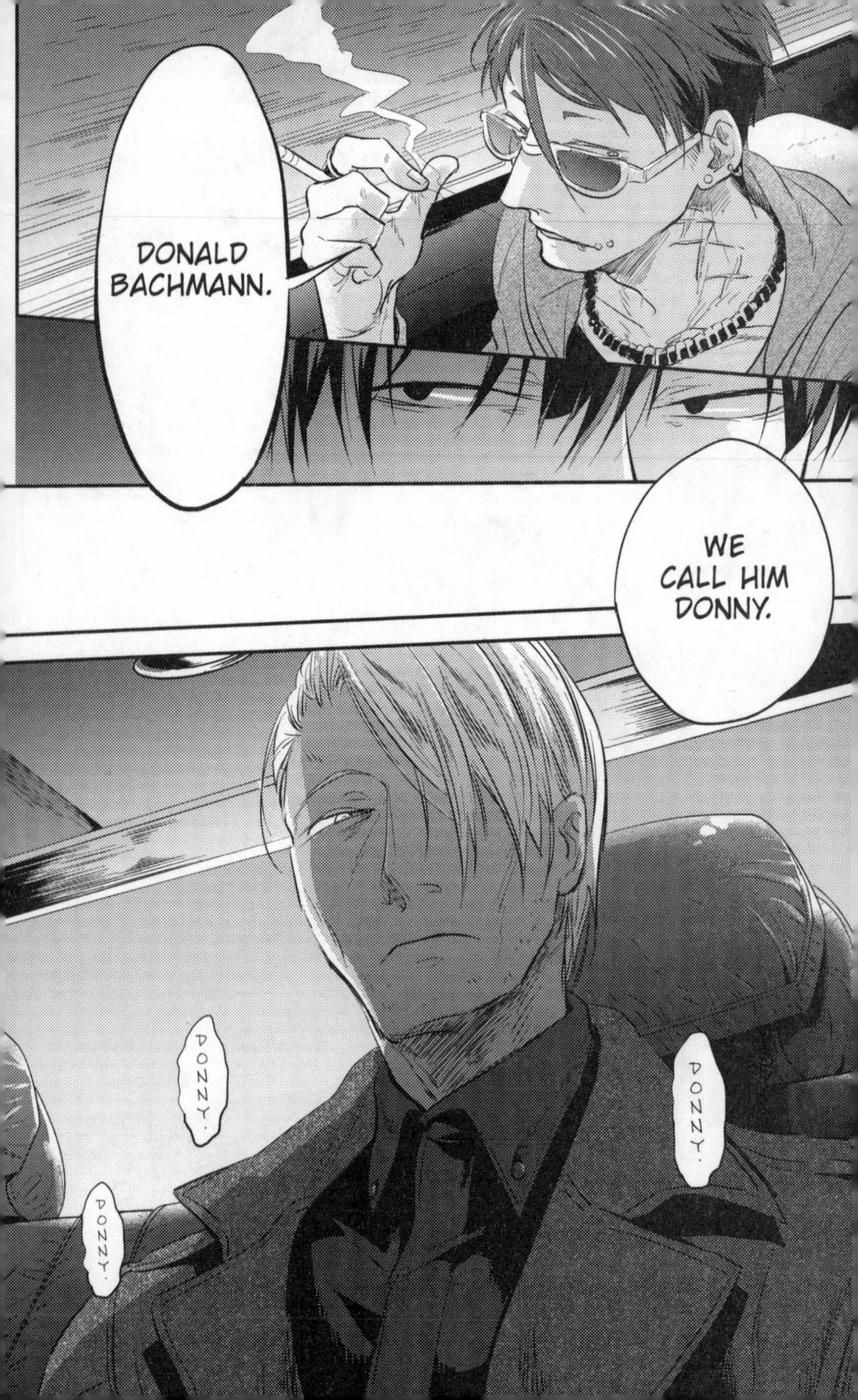
DONALD BACHMANN.
WE CALL HIM DONNY.
DONNY.
DONNY.
DONNY.

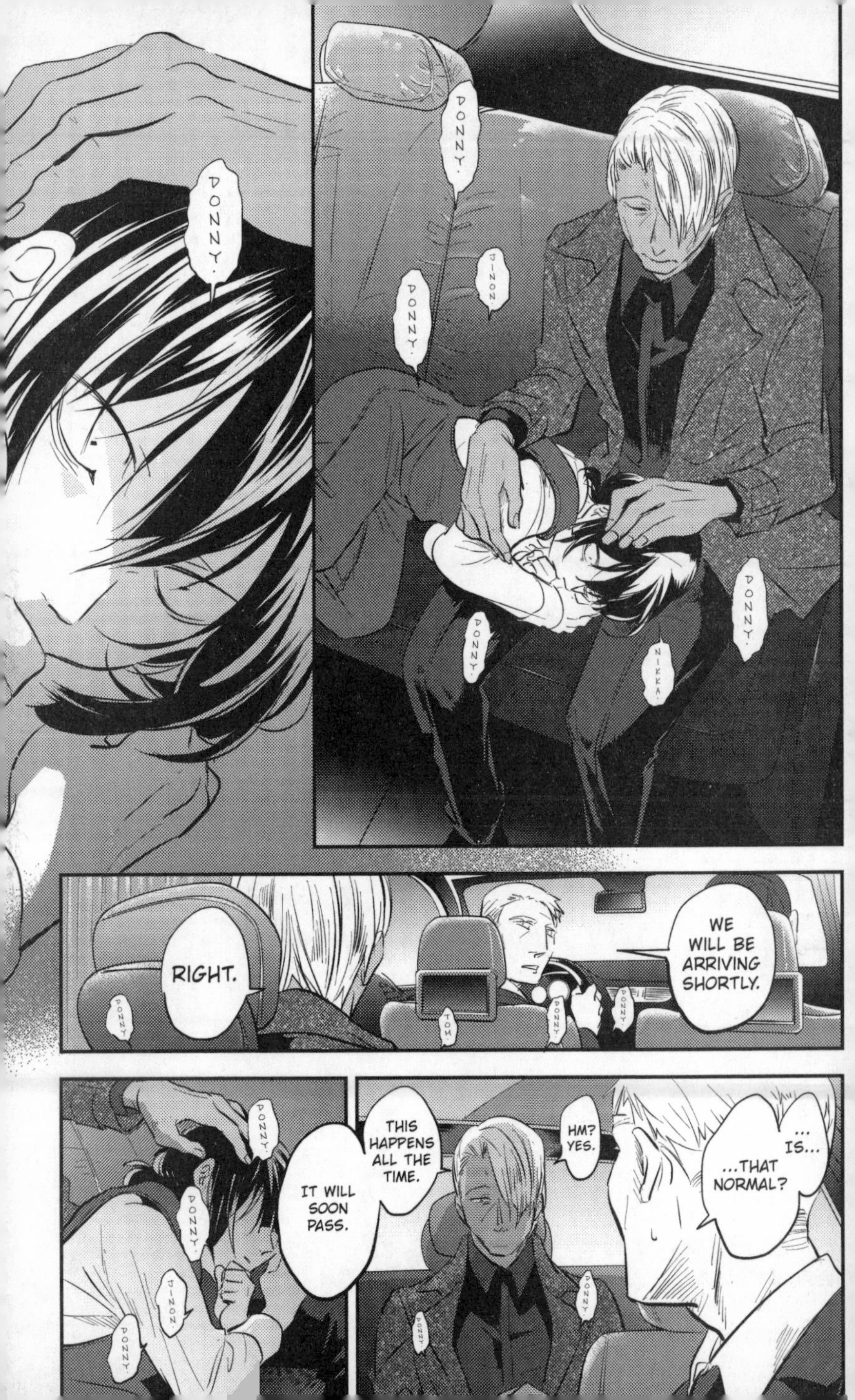
DONNY.
JINON.
DONNY.
DONNY.
NIKKA.
DONNY.
DONNY.
WE WILL BE ARRIVING SHORTLY.
DONNY.
DONNY.
TOM.
RIGHT.
DONNY
... IS...
...THAT NORMAL?
HM? YES.
THIS HAPPENS ALL THE TIME.
IT WILL SOON PASS.
DONNY.
DONNY.
DONNY.
DONNY.
JINON.
DONNY.

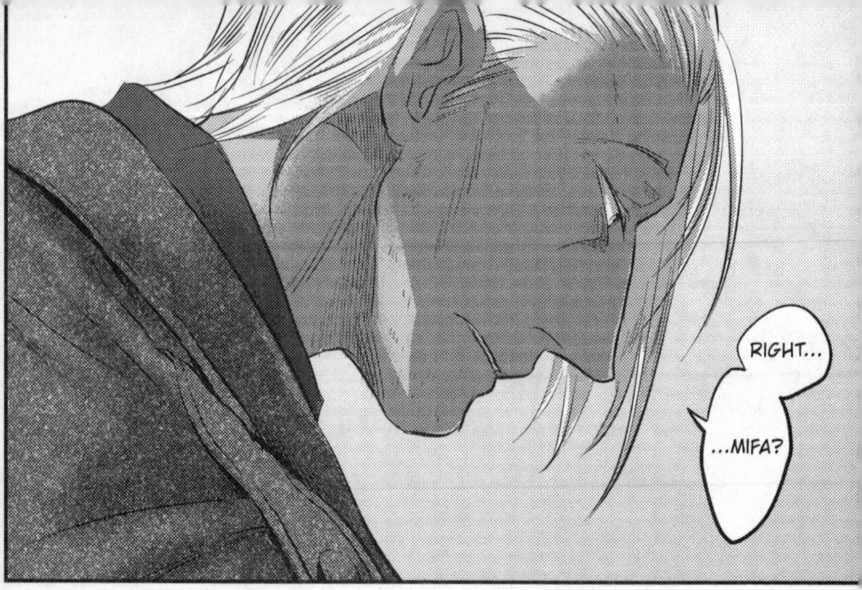
RIGHT...
...MIFA?

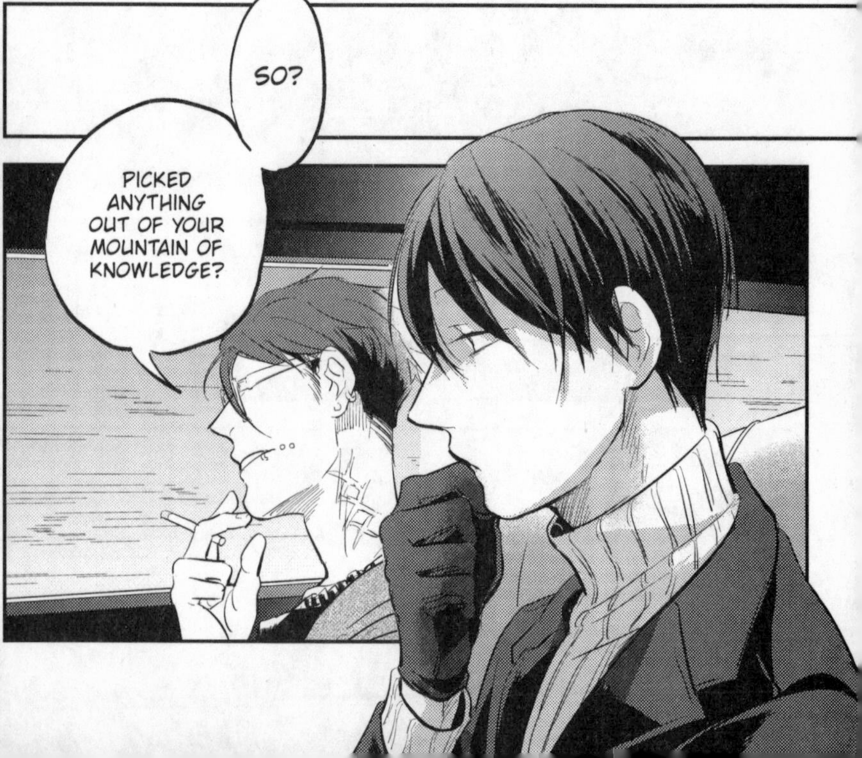
SO?
PICKED ANYTHING OUT OF YOUR MOUNTAIN OF KNOWLEDGE?

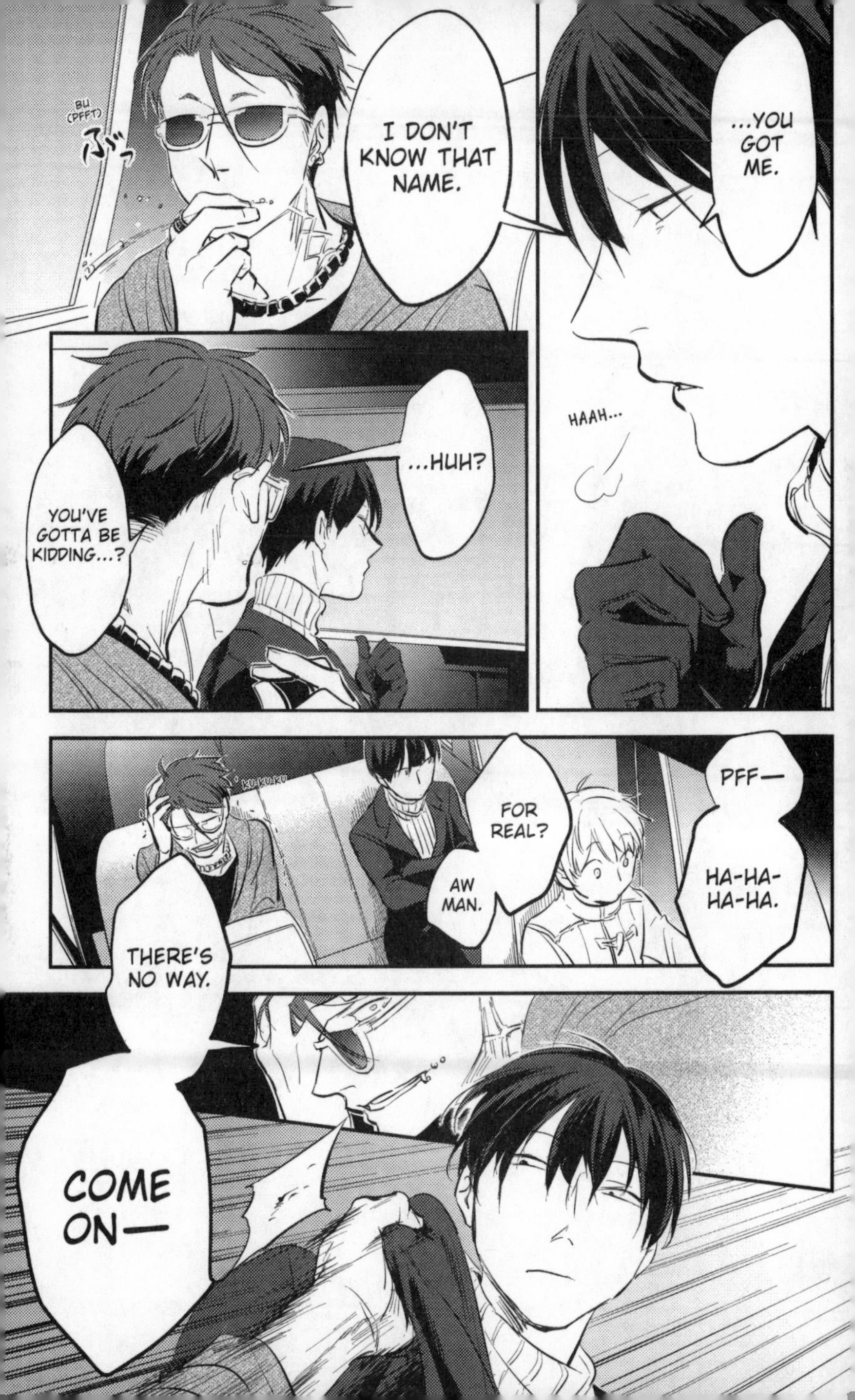
...YOU GOT ME.
HAAH...
I DON'T KNOW THAT NAME.
BU (PFFT)
ぶっ
...HUH?
YOU'VE GOTTA BE KIDDING...?
PFF—
HA-HA-HA-HA.
FOR REAL?
AW MAN.
KUKUKU
THERE'S NO WAY.
COME ON—

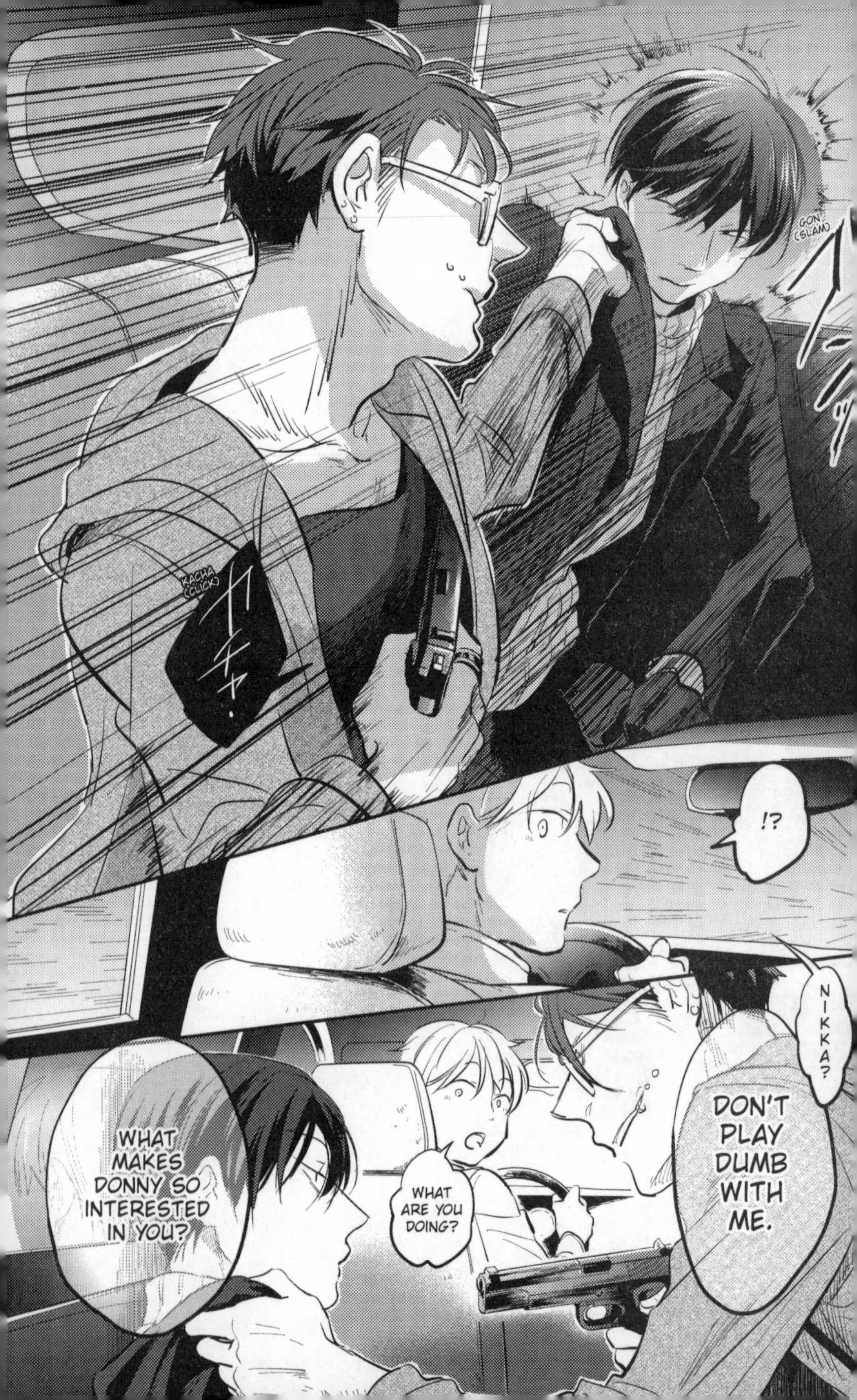
GON (SLAM)
KACHA (CLICK)
!?
NIKKA?
DON'T PLAY DUMB WITH ME.
WHAT ARE YOU DOING?
WHAT MAKES DONNY SO INTERESTED IN YOU?

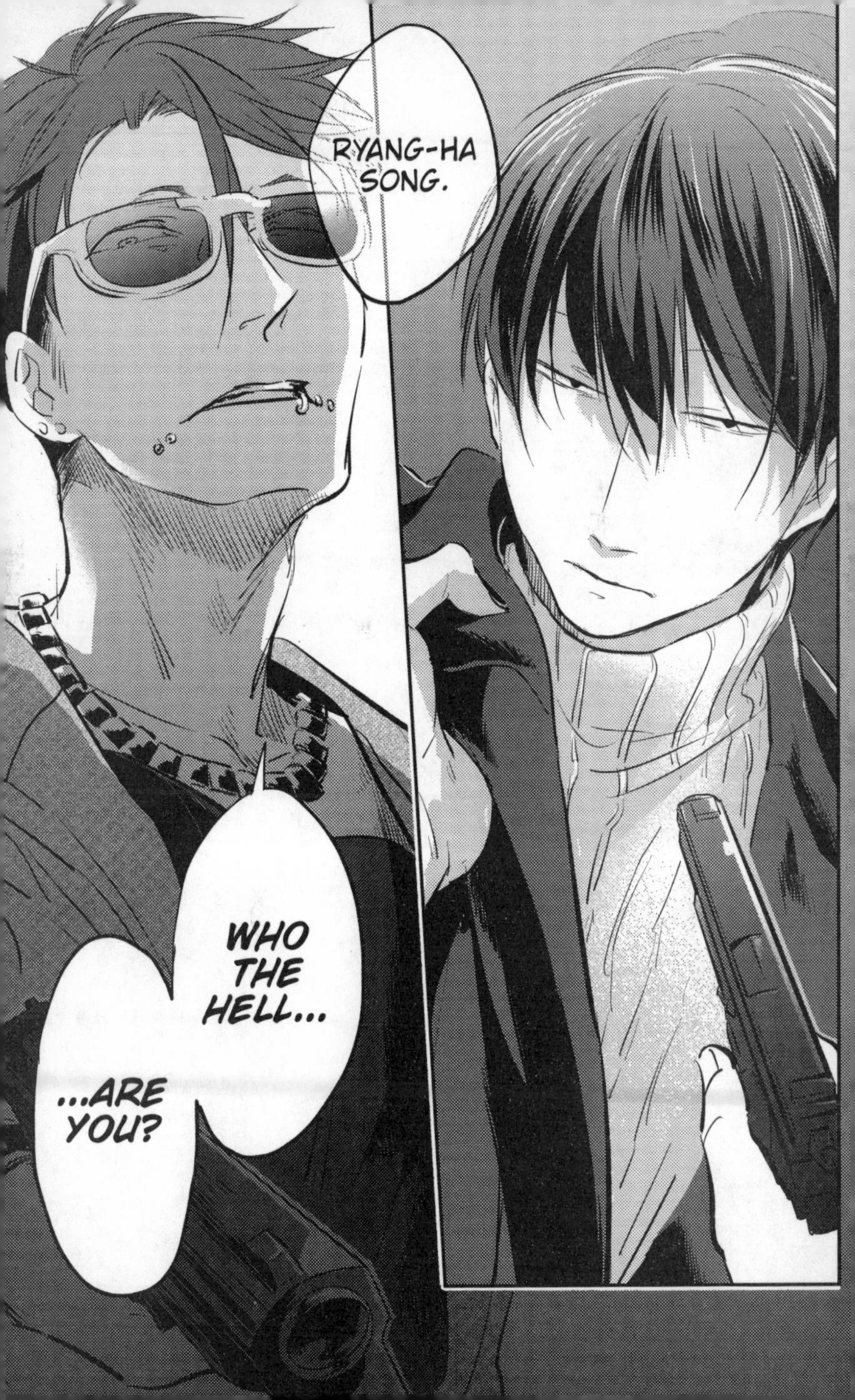
RYANG-HA SONG.
WHO THE HELL...
...ARE YOU?

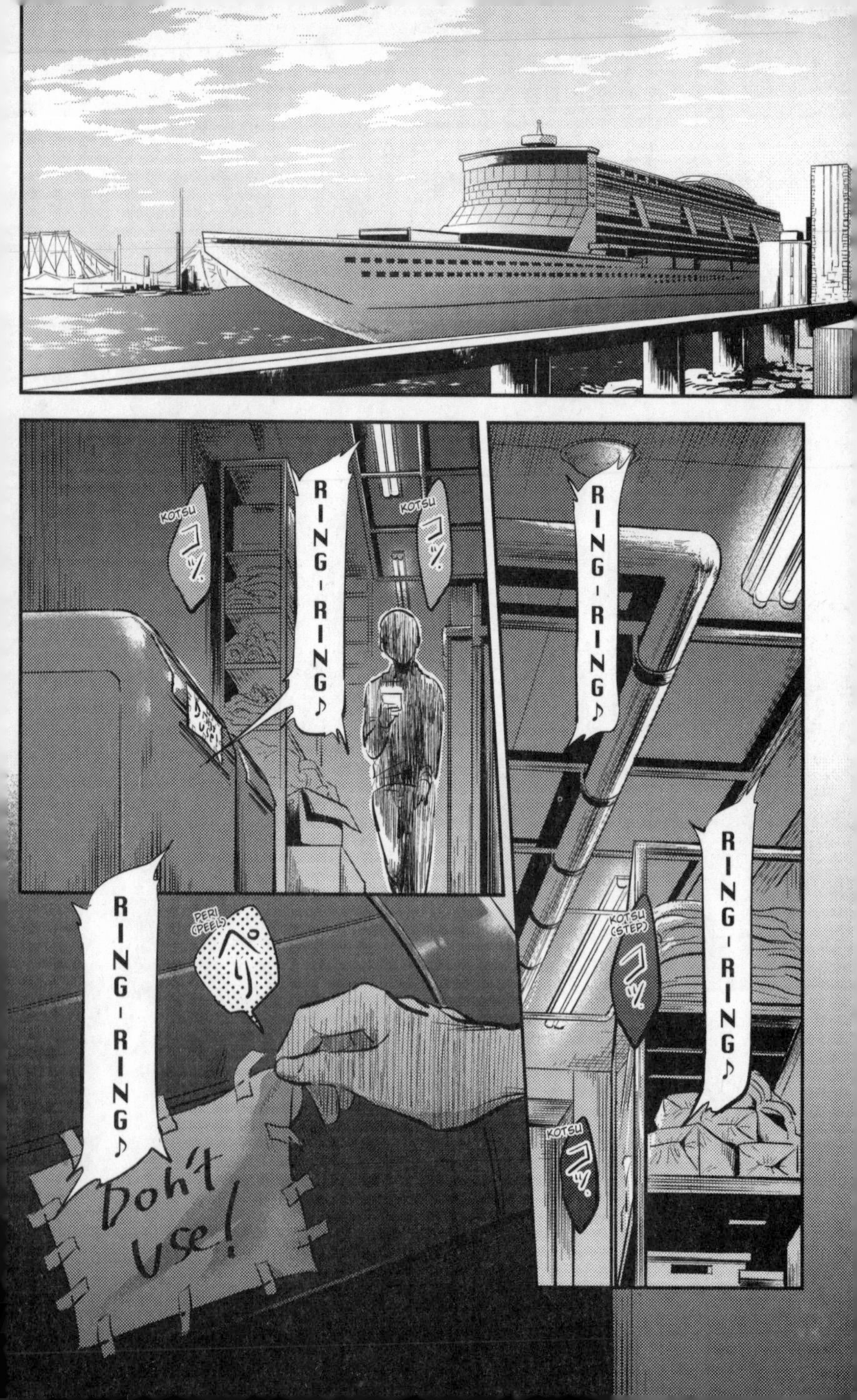
RING-RING♪
RING-RING♪
KOTSU (STEP)
コッ
KOTSU
コッ
KOTSU
コッ
RING-RING♪
KOTSU
コッ
RING-RING♪
PERI (PEEL)
ペり
Don't use!

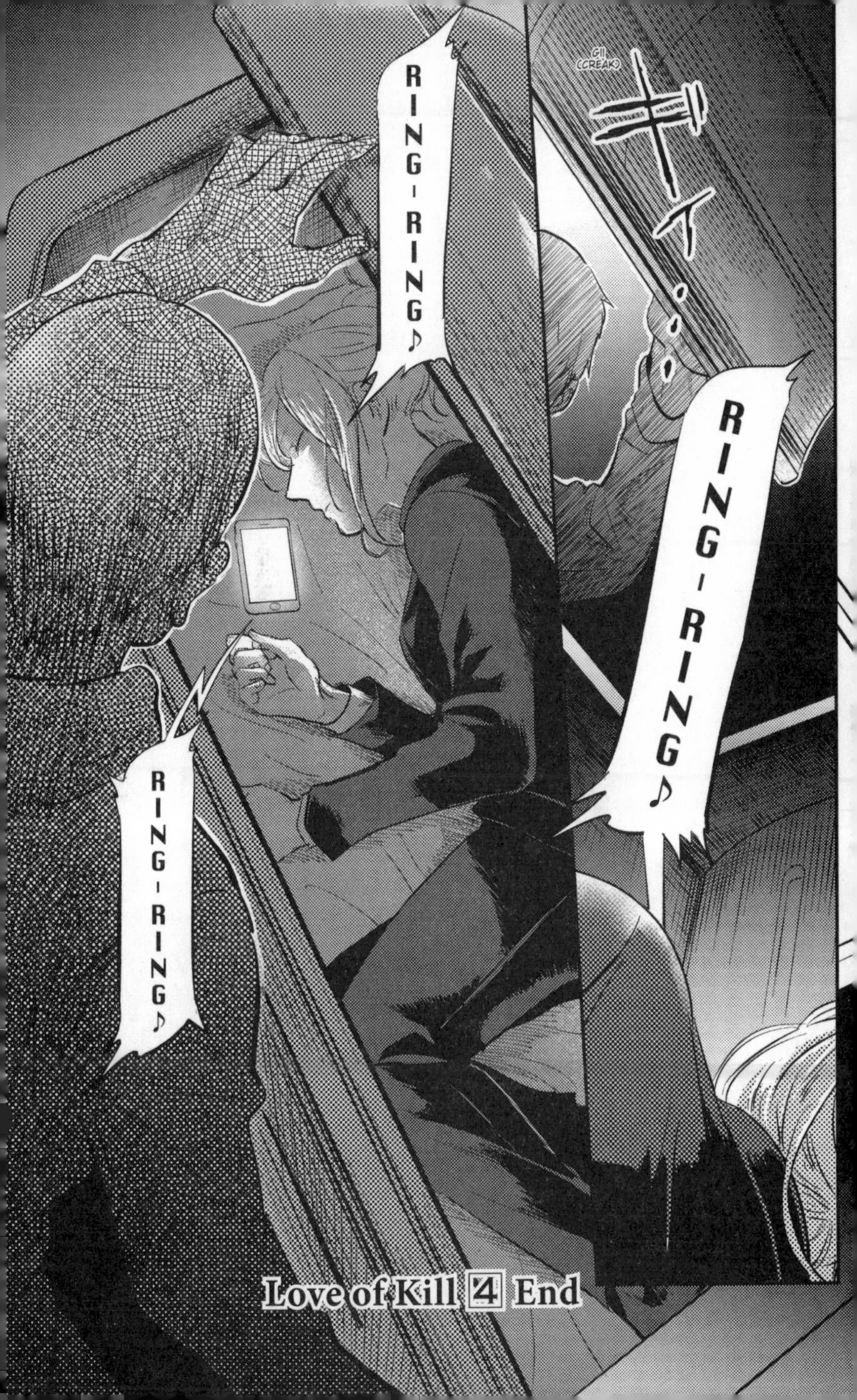
GII (CREAK)
RING-RING♪
RING-RING♪
RING-RING♪
Love of Kill 4 End

THE FOLLOWING IS A SPECIAL COMIC FOR THE COLLECTED VOLUME.

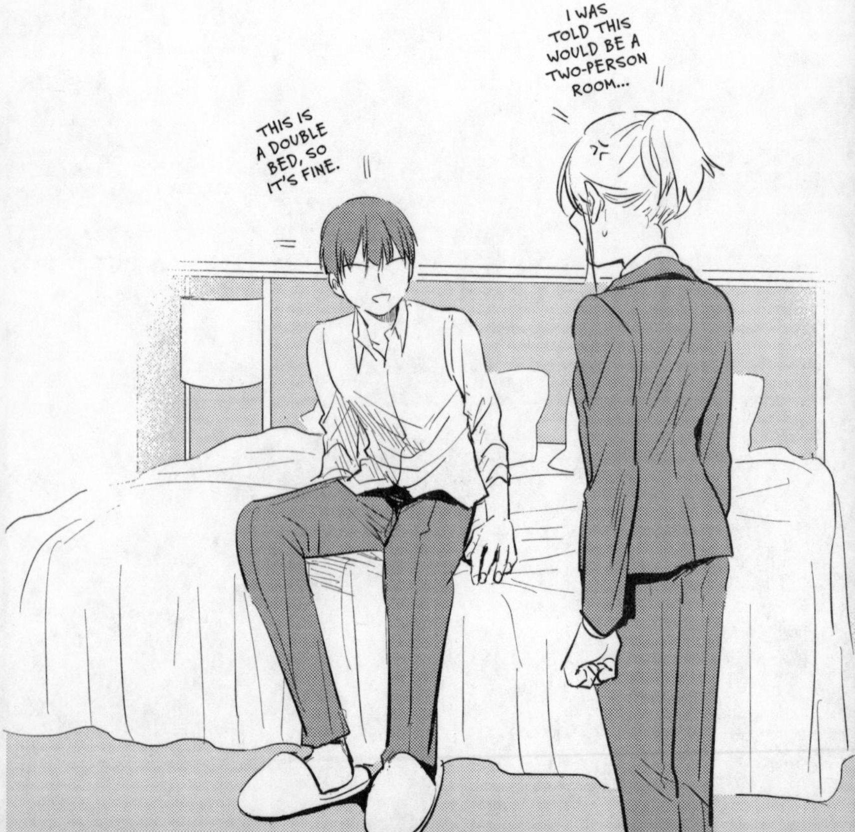
I WAS TOLD THIS WOULD BE A TWO-PERSON ROOM...
THIS IS A DOUBLE BED, SO IT'S FINE.

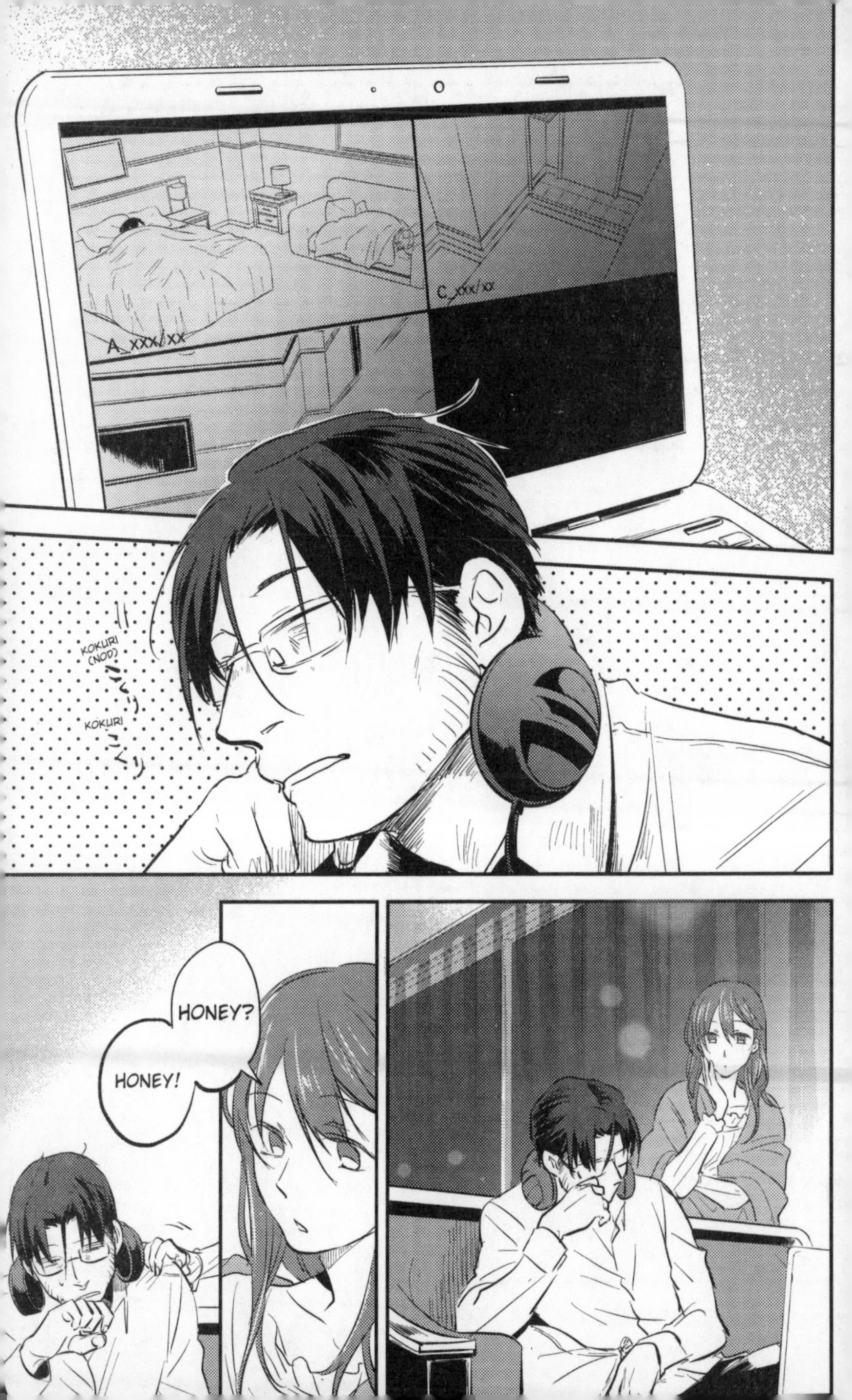
C_xxx/xx
A_xxx/xx
KOKURI (NOD)
KOKURI
HONEY?
HONEY!

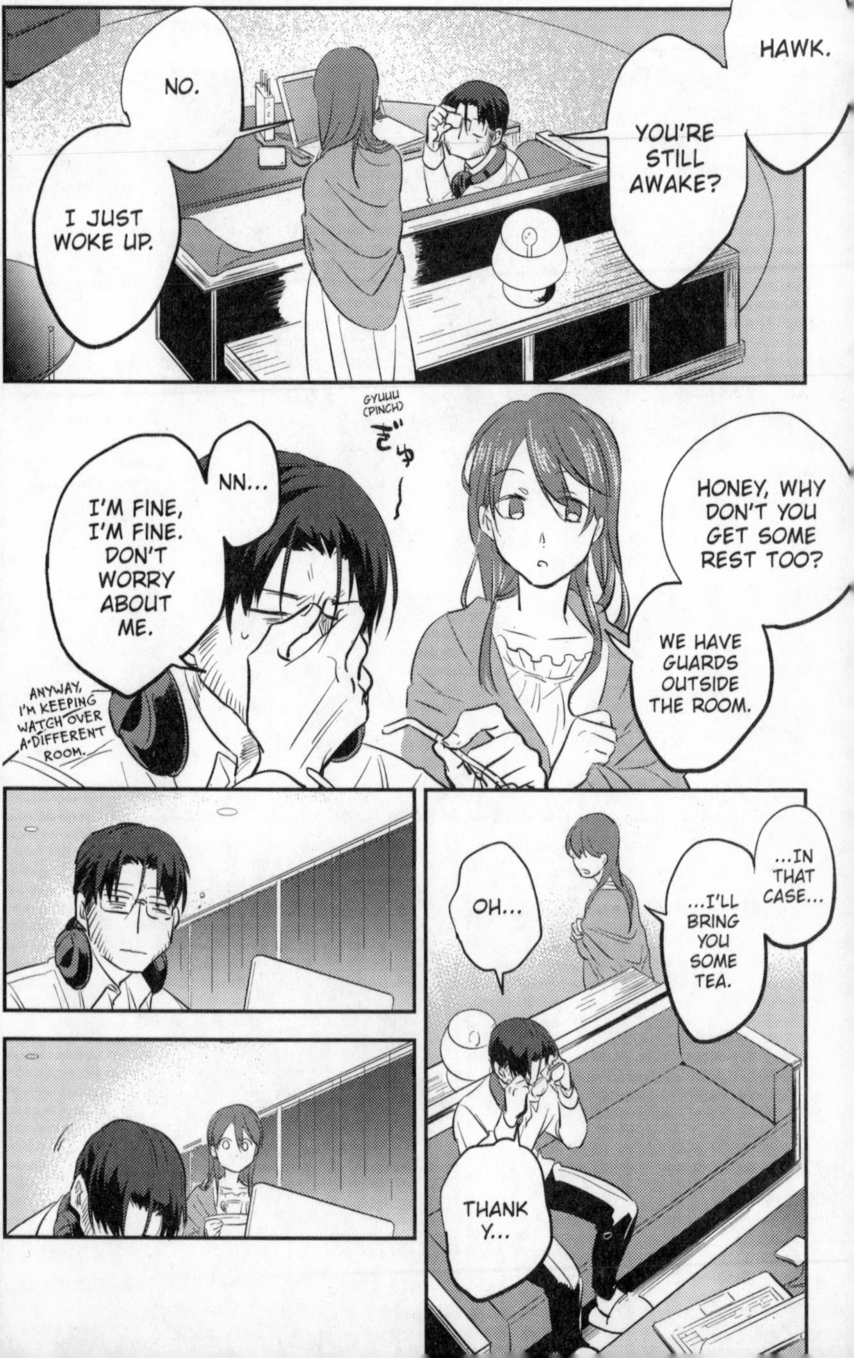
HAWK.
YOU'RE STILL AWAKE?
NO.
I JUST WOKE UP.
HONEY, WHY DON'T YOU GET SOME REST TOO?
WE HAVE GUARDS OUTSIDE THE ROOM.
GYUUU (PINCH)
NN...
I'M FINE, I'M FINE. DON'T WORRY ABOUT ME.
ANYWAY, I'M KEEPING WATCH OVER A DIFFERENT ROOM.
...IN THAT CASE...
...I'LL BRING YOU SOME TEA.
OH...
THANK Y...

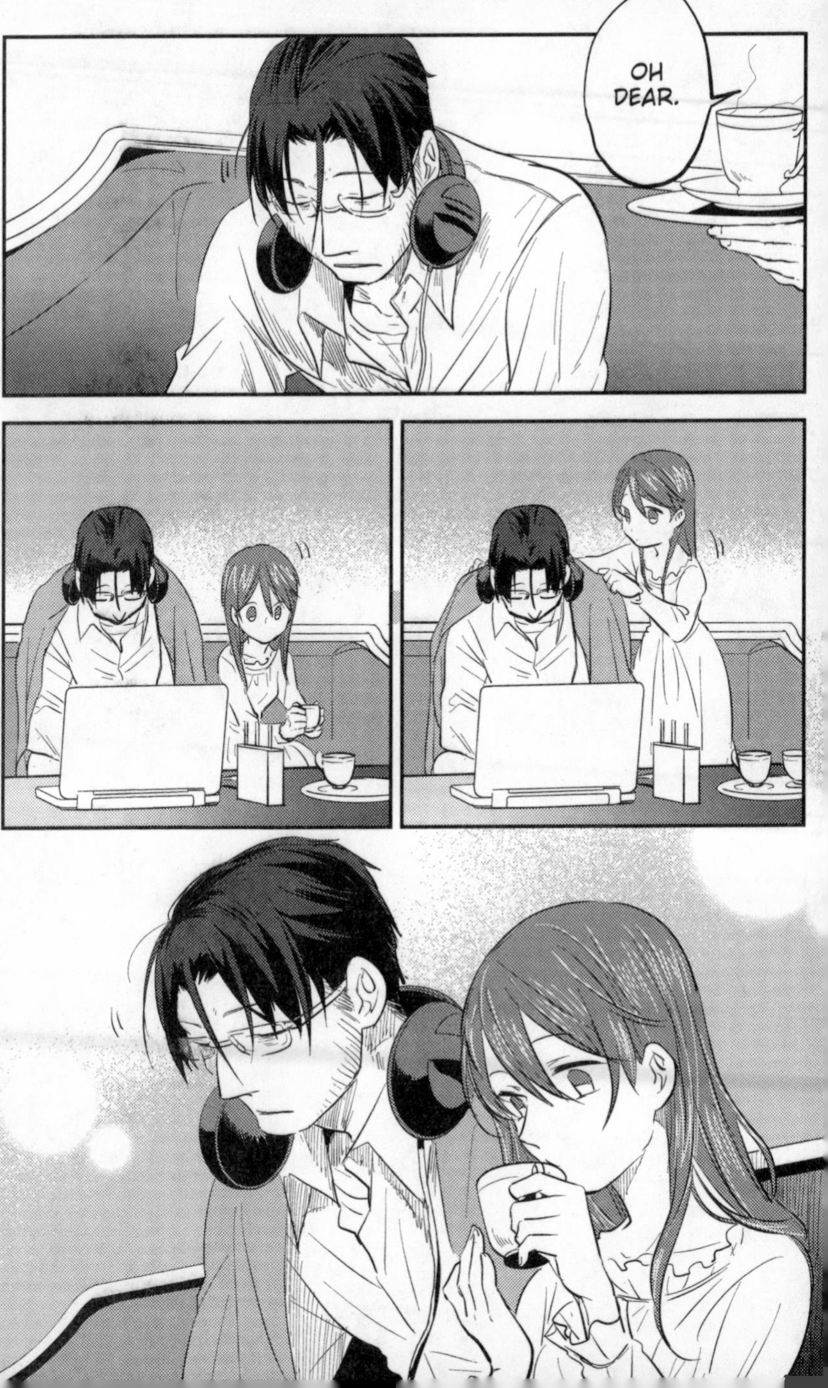
OH DEAR.

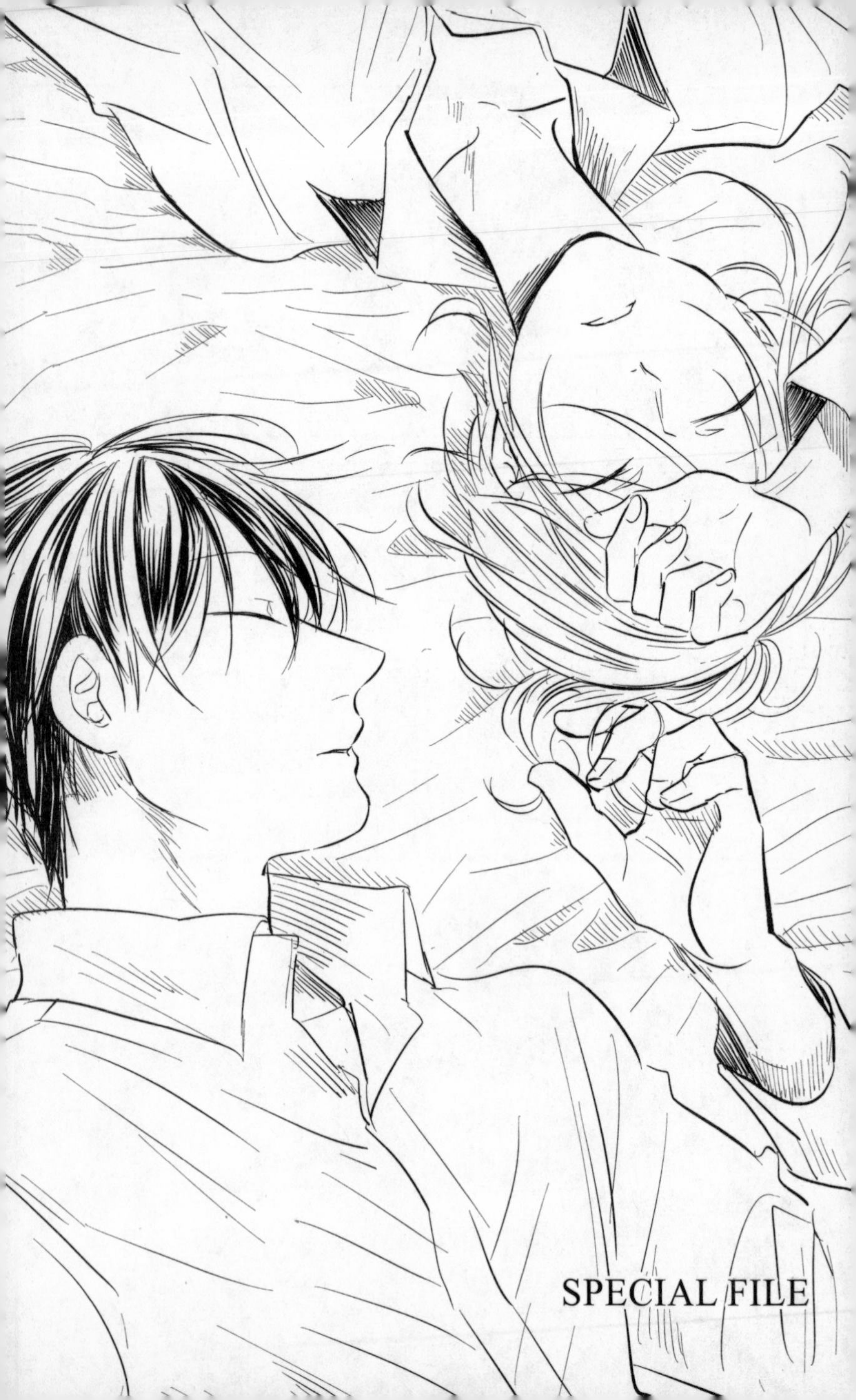
SPECIAL FILE

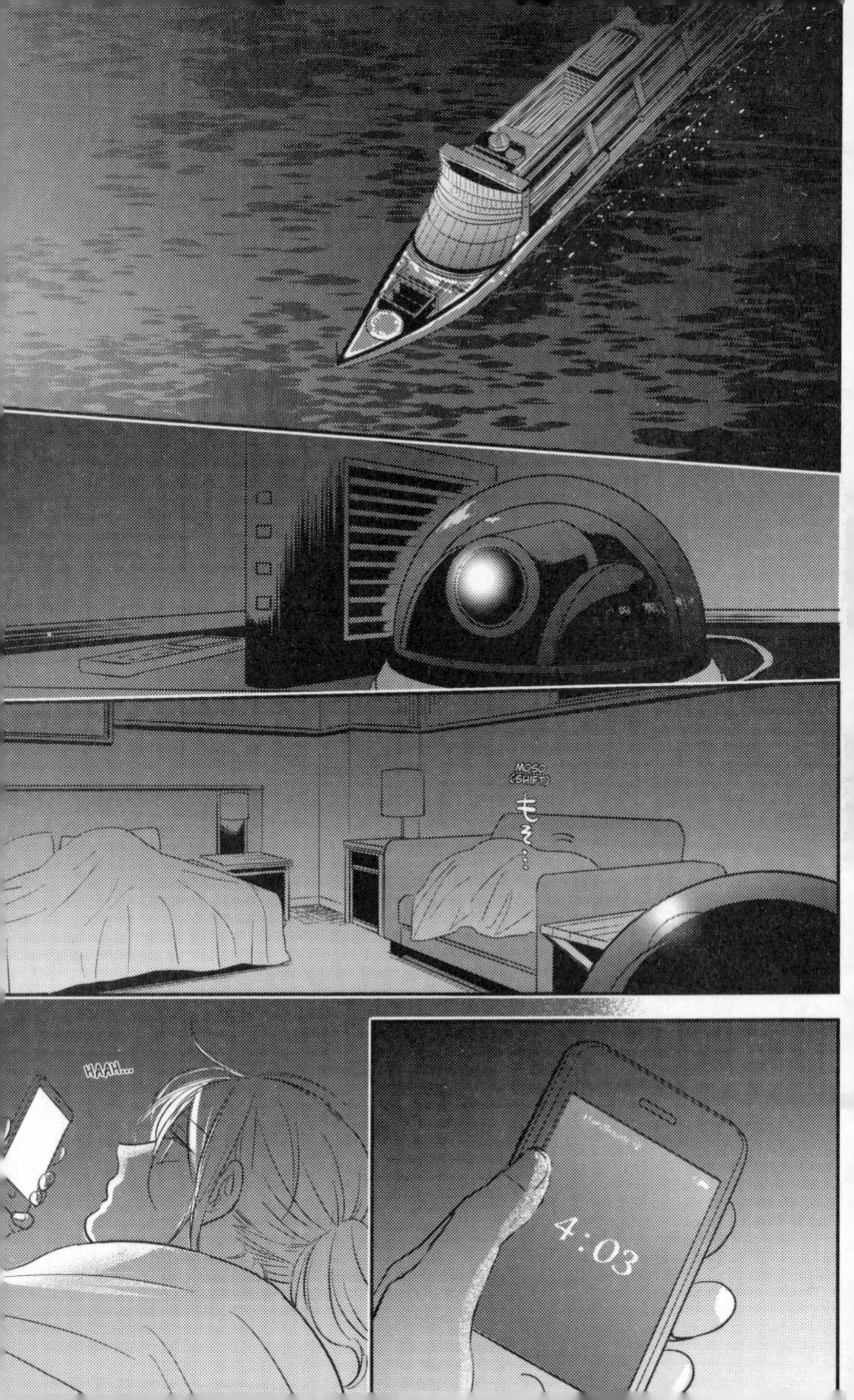
MOSO
(SHIFT)
もそ…
4:03
HAAH...

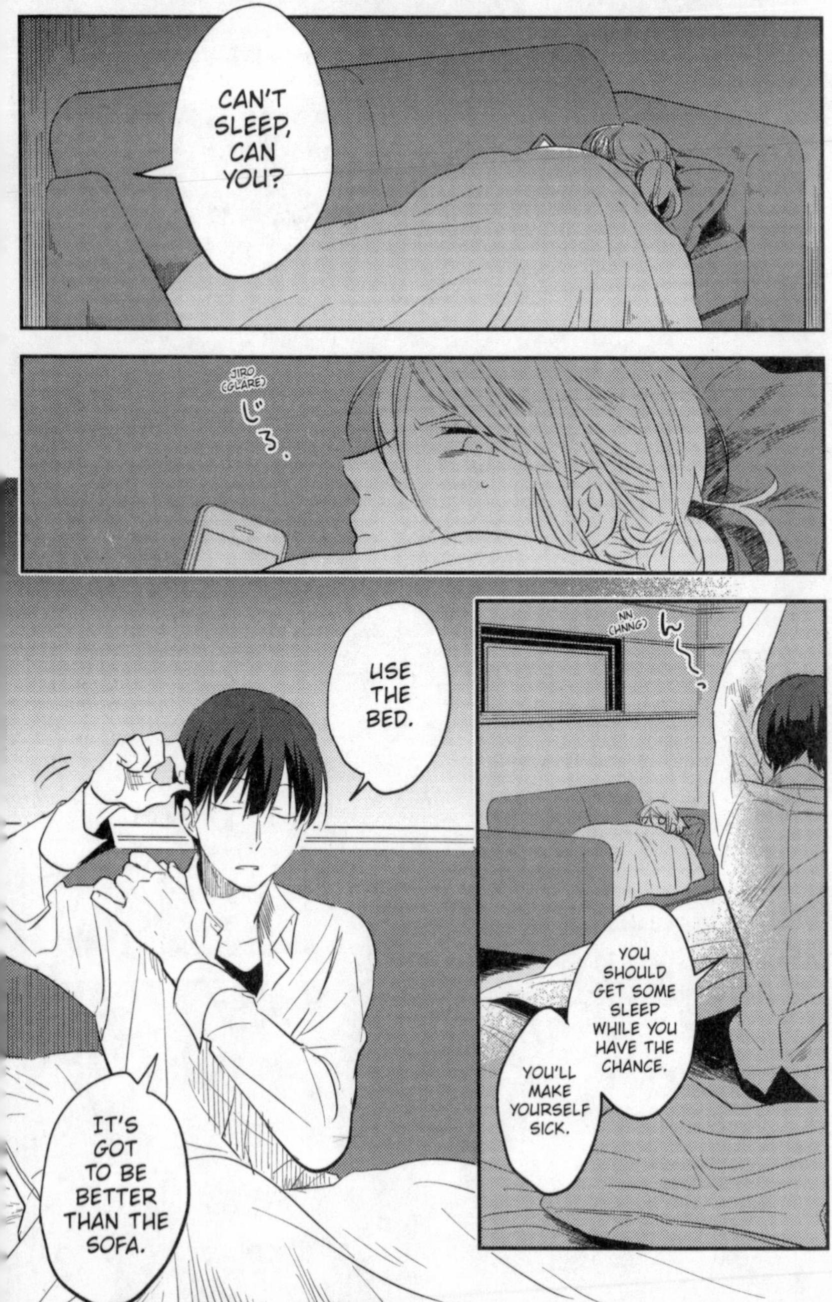
CAN'T SLEEP, CAN YOU?
JIRO (GLARE)
じろ。
NN (HNNG)
ん〜、
YOU SHOULD GET SOME SLEEP WHILE YOU HAVE THE CHANCE.
YOU'LL MAKE YOURSELF SICK.
USE THE BED.
IT'S GOT TO BE BETTER THAN THE SOFA.

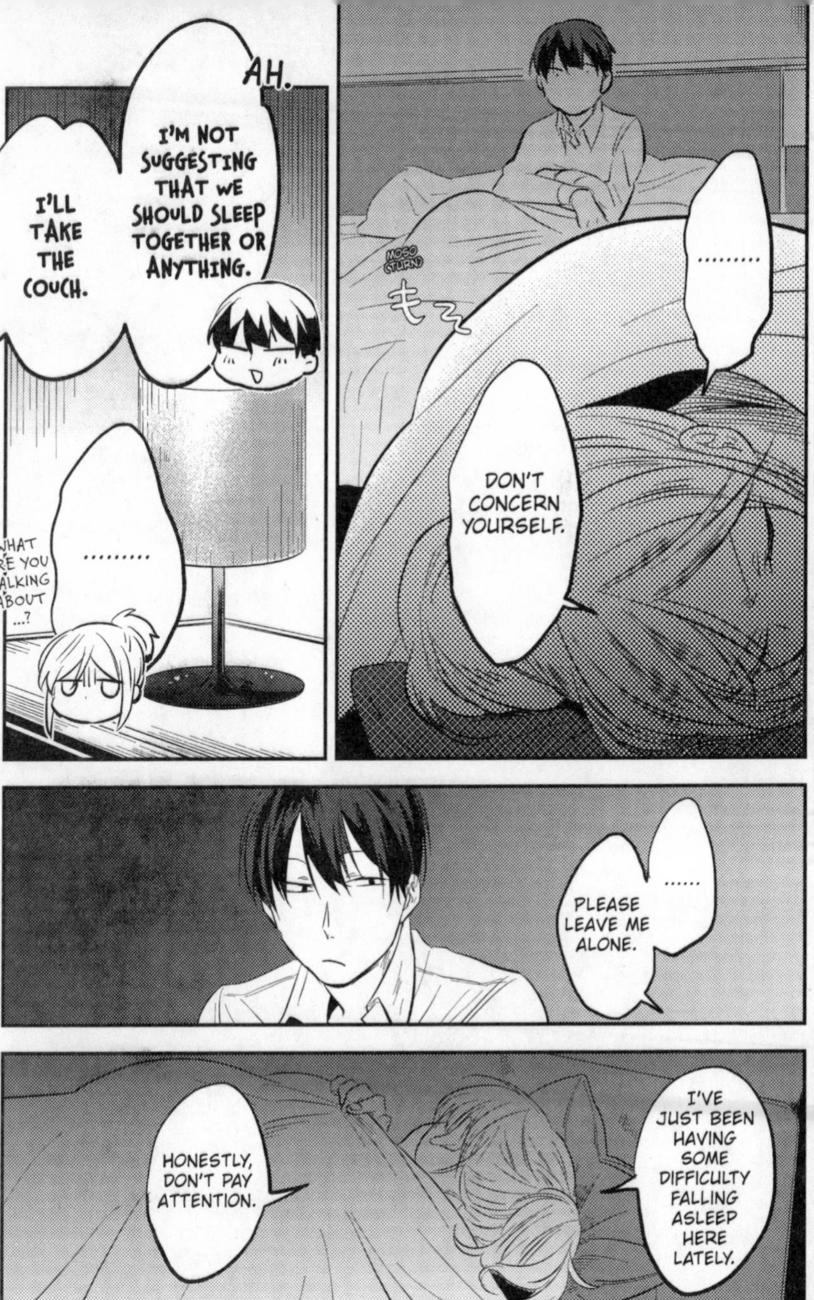
....
MOSO (TURN)
DON'T CONCERN YOURSELF.
AH.
I'M NOT SUGGESTING THAT WE SHOULD SLEEP TOGETHER OR ANYTHING.
I'LL TAKE THE COUCH.
....
WHAT ARE YOU TALKING ABOUT ...?
......
PLEASE LEAVE ME ALONE.
I'VE JUST BEEN HAVING SOME DIFFICULTY FALLING ASLEEP HERE LATELY.
HONESTLY, DON'T PAY ATTENTION.

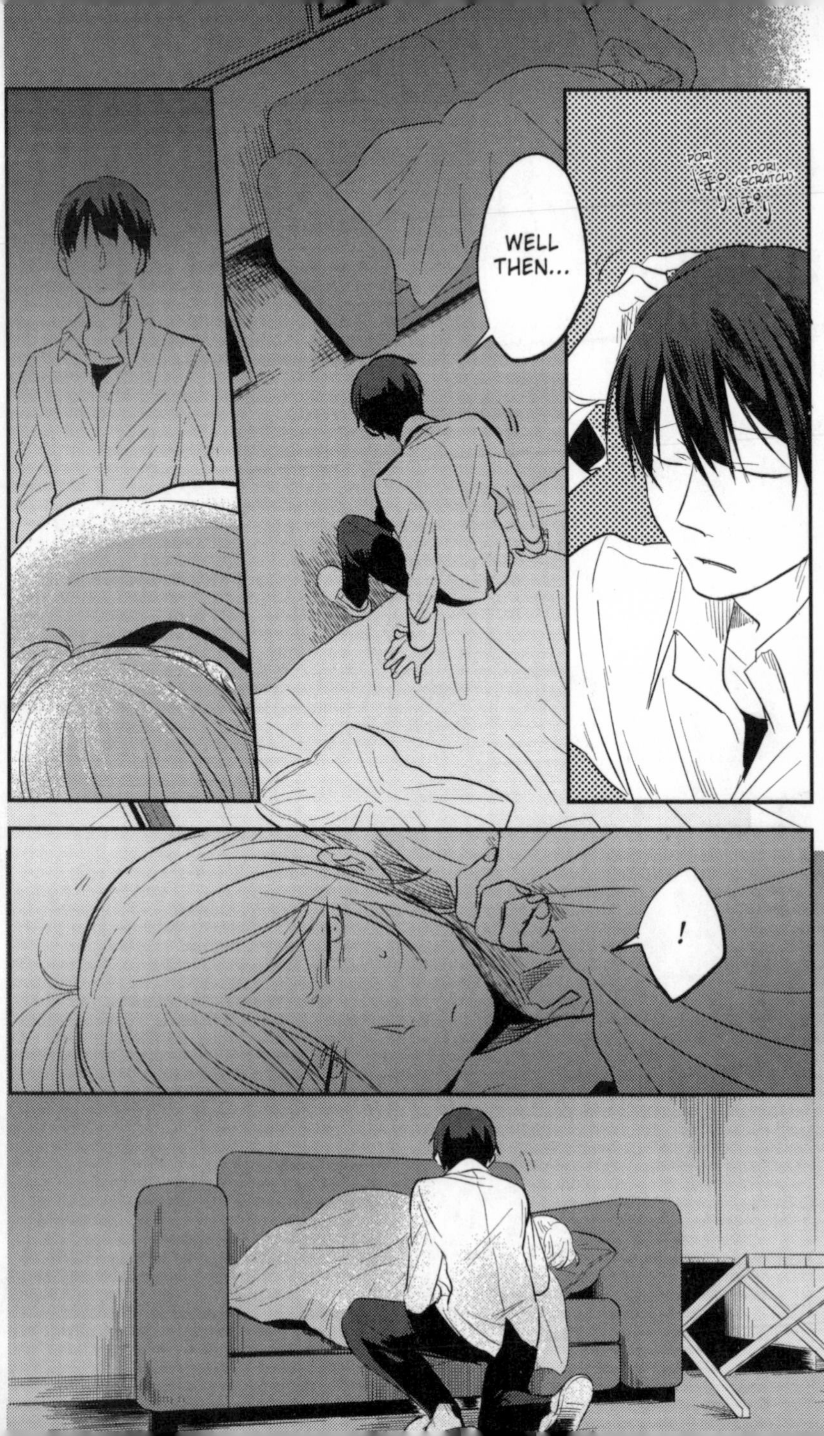
PORI PORI (SCRATCH)
ぽりぽり
WELL THEN...
!

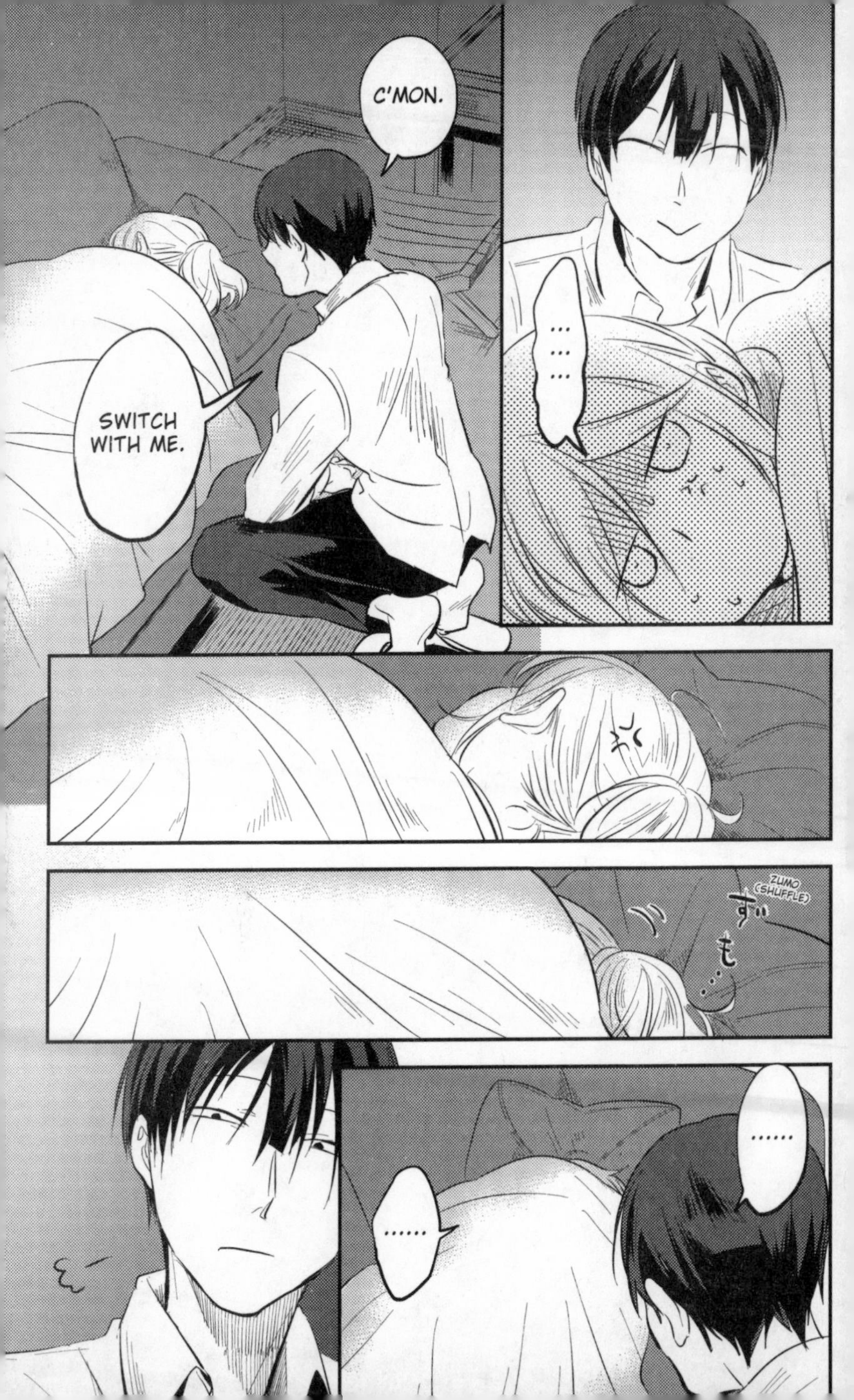
………
C'MON.
SWITCH WITH ME.
ZUMO (SHUFFLE)
……
……

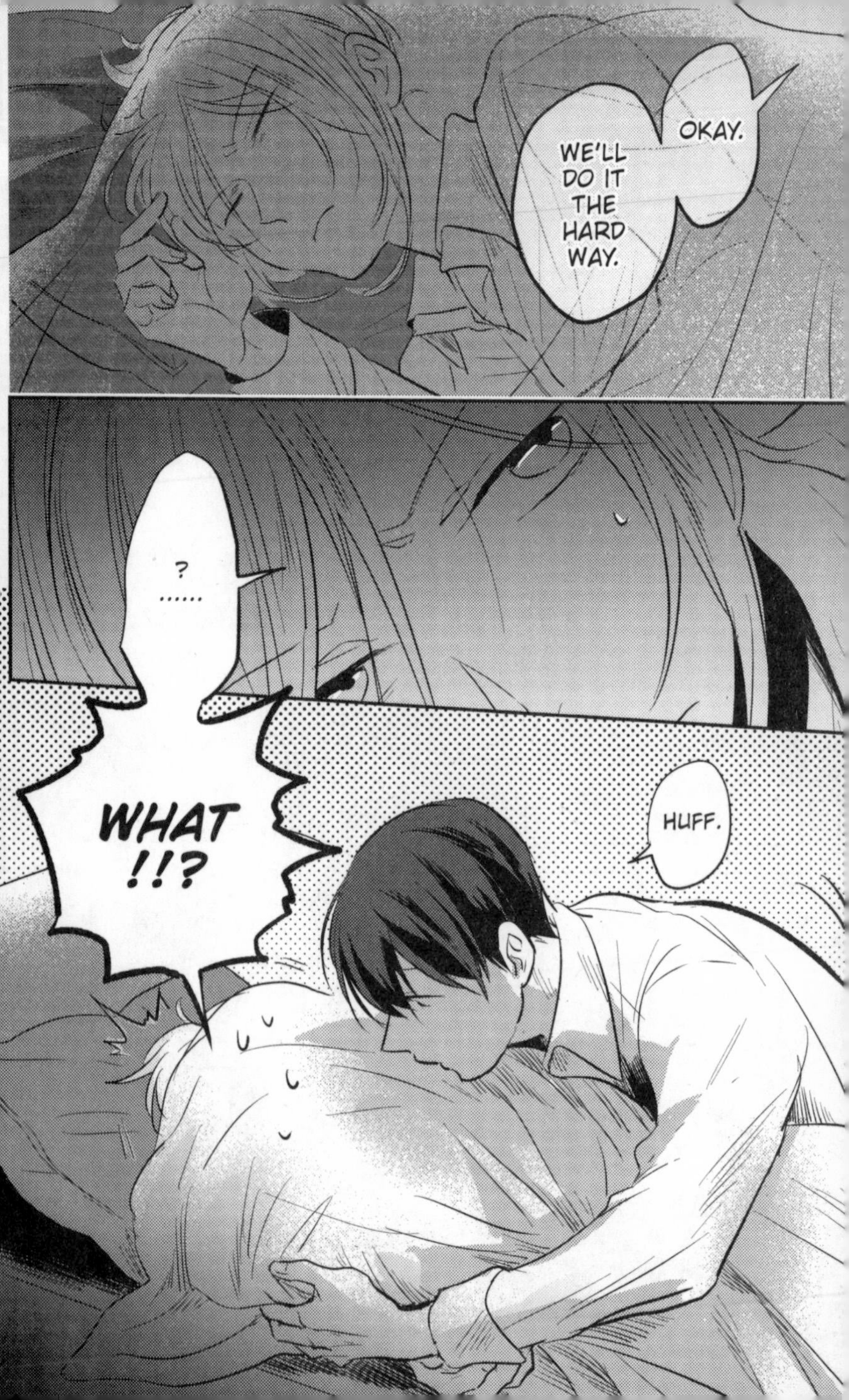
OKAY.
WE'LL DO IT THE HARD WAY.
?
......
HUFF.
WHAT!!?

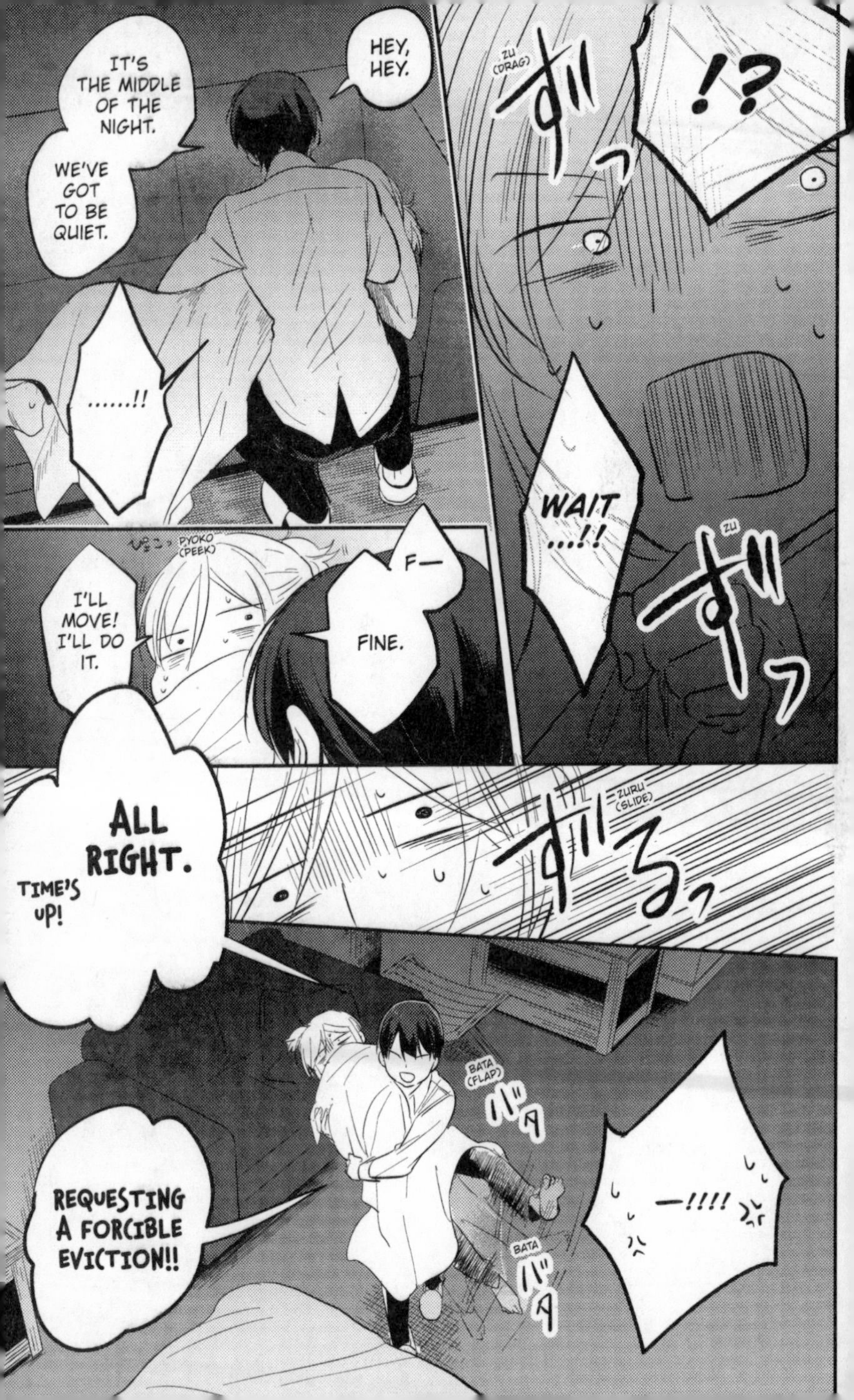
ZU (DRAG)
ずっ
!?
WAIT ...!!
ZU
ずっ
HEY, HEY.
IT'S THE MIDDLE OF THE NIGHT.
WE'VE GOT TO BE QUIET.
......!!
F—
FINE.
ぴょこっ PYOKO (PEEK)
I'LL MOVE! I'LL DO IT.
ZURU (SLIDE)
ずるっ
—!!!!
BATA (FLAP)
バタ
BATA
バタ
ALL RIGHT.
TIME'S UP!
REQUESTING A FORCIBLE EVICTION!!

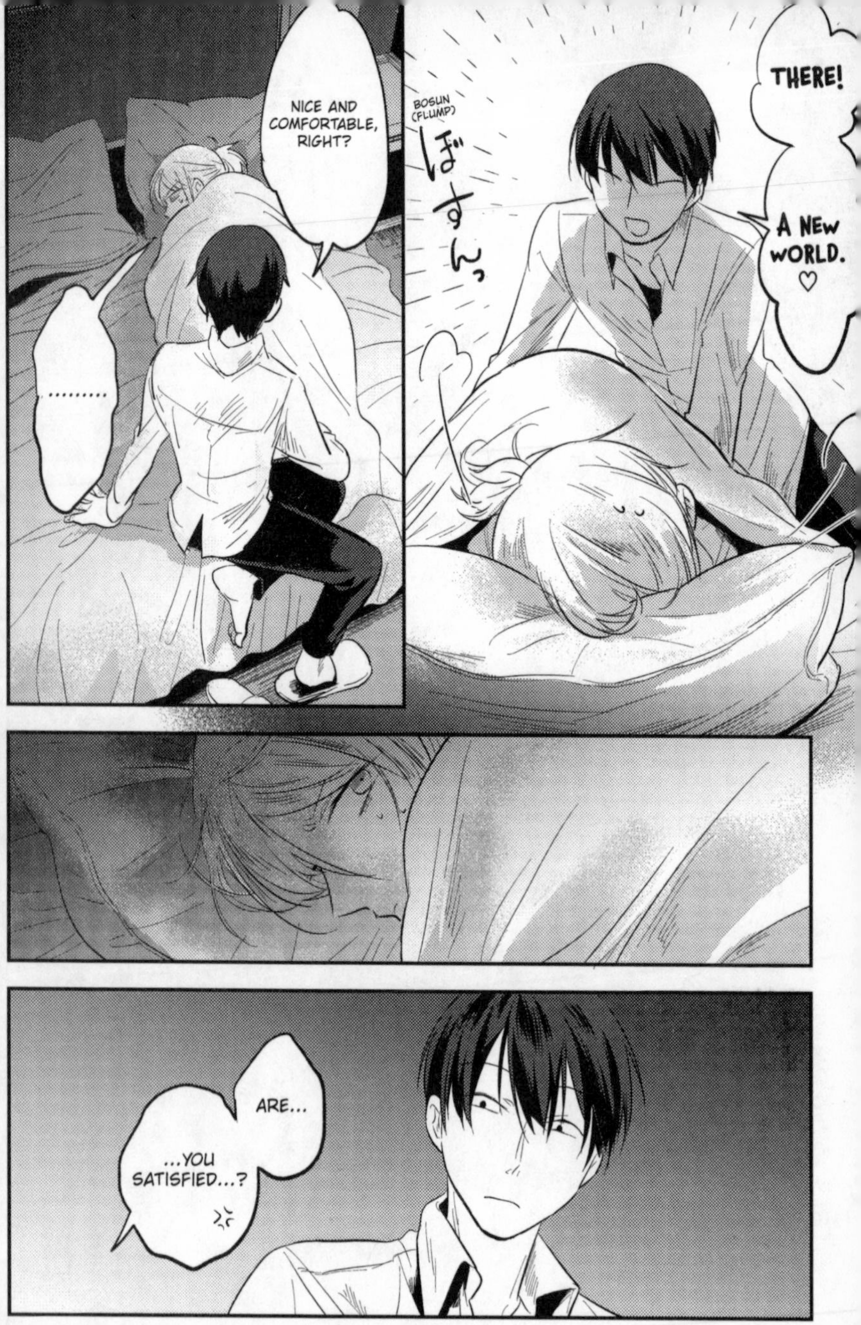
THERE!
A NEW WORLD. ♡
BOSUN (FLUMP)
ぼすんっ
NICE AND COMFORTABLE, RIGHT?
....
ARE...
...YOU SATISFIED...?

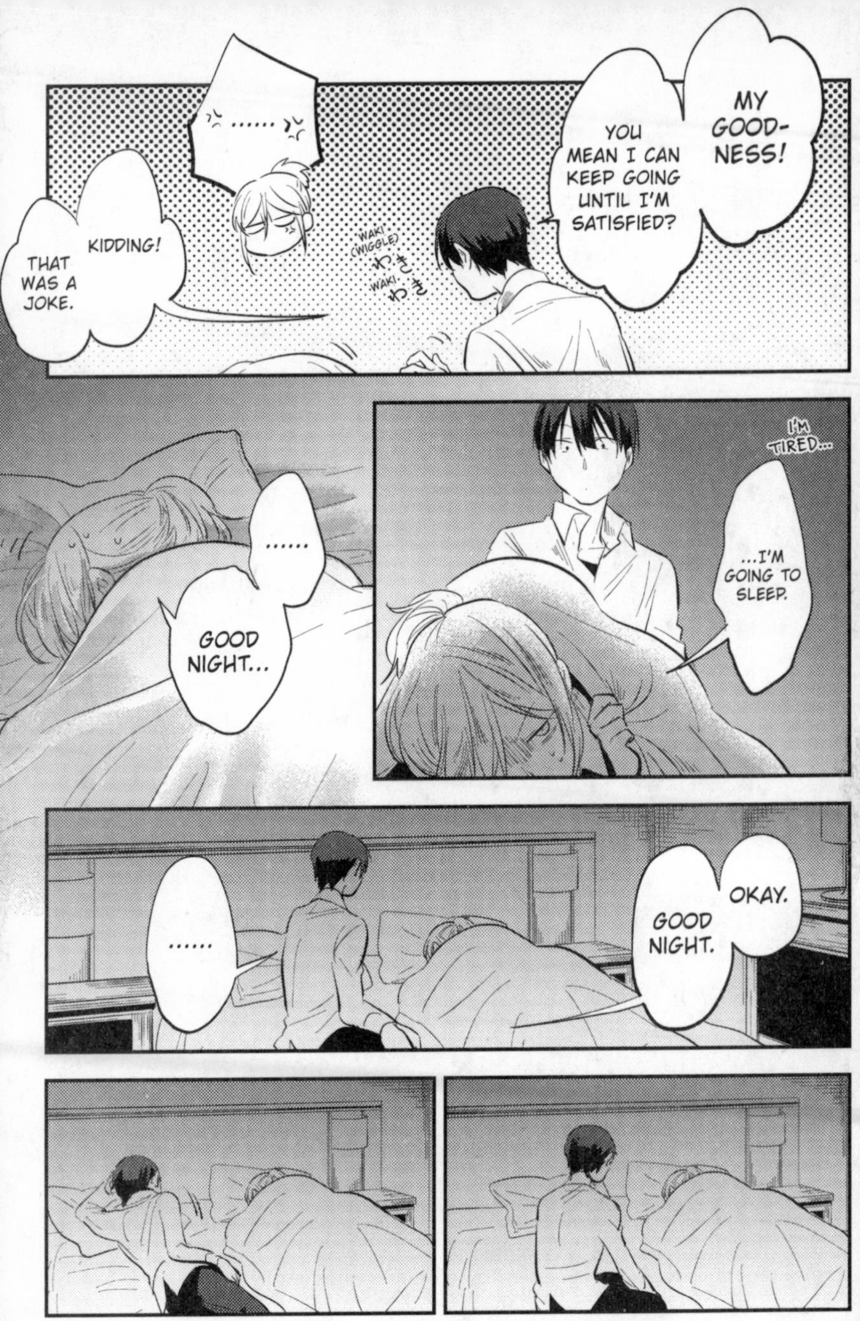
MY GOODNESS!
YOU MEAN I CAN KEEP GOING UNTIL I'M SATISFIED?
WAKI (WIGGLE) わき WAKI わき
......
KIDDING!
THAT WAS A JOKE.
I'M TIRED...
...I'M GOING TO SLEEP.
......
GOOD NIGHT...
OKAY.
GOOD NIGHT.
......

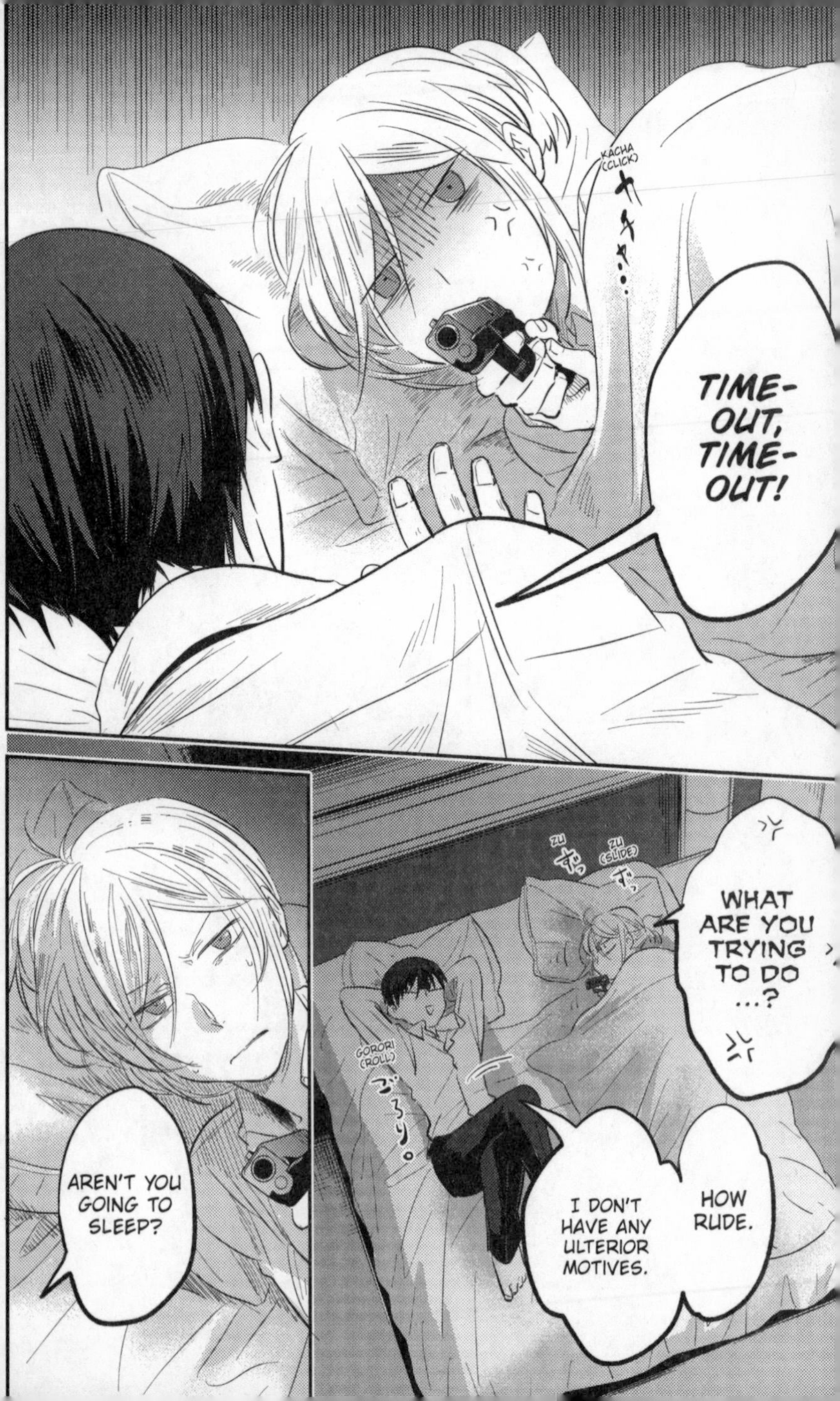
KACHA (CLICK)
TIME-OUT, TIME-OUT!
ZU ZU (SLIDE)
WHAT ARE YOU TRYING TO DO ...?
GORORI (ROLL)
HOW RUDE.
I DON'T HAVE ANY ULTERIOR MOTIVES.
AREN'T YOU GOING TO SLEEP?

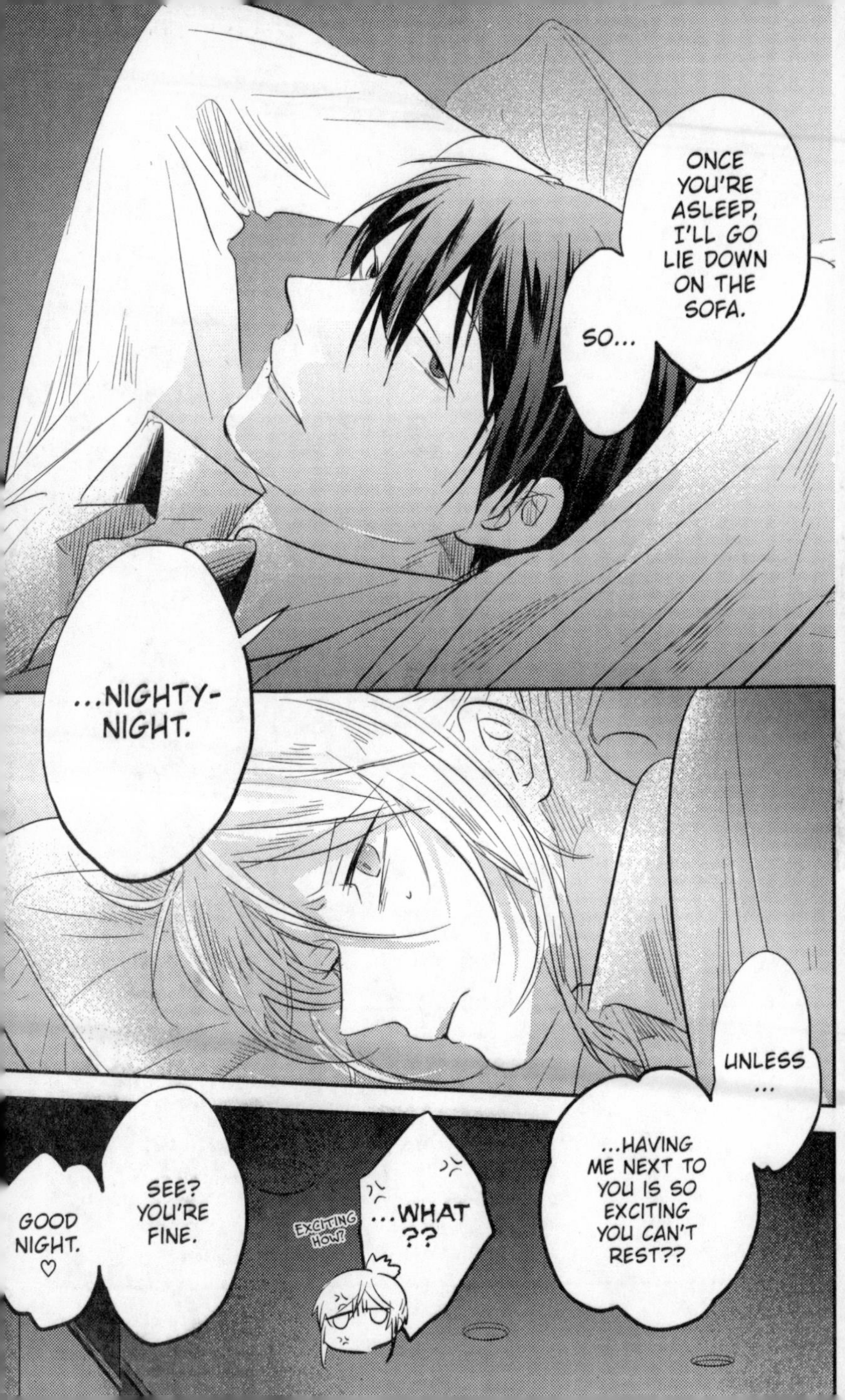
ONCE YOU'RE ASLEEP, I'LL GO LIE DOWN ON THE SOFA.
SO...
...NIGHTY-NIGHT.
UNLESS...
...HAVING ME NEXT TO YOU IS SO EXCITING YOU CAN'T REST??
...WHAT??
EXCITING HOW?
SEE? YOU'RE FINE.
GOOD NIGHT. ♡

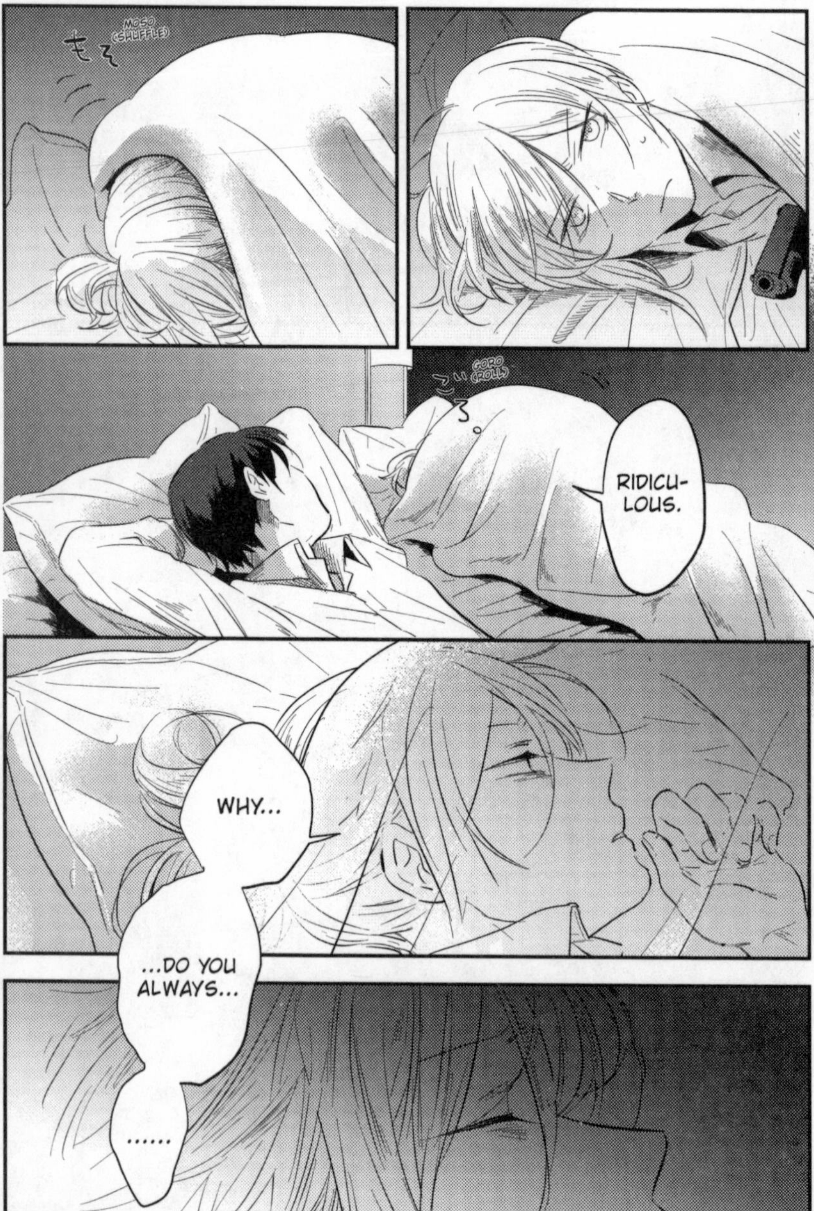
もそ
MOSO (SHUFFLE)
ごろ
GORO (ROLL)
RIDICU-LOUS.
WHY...
...DO YOU ALWAYS...
......

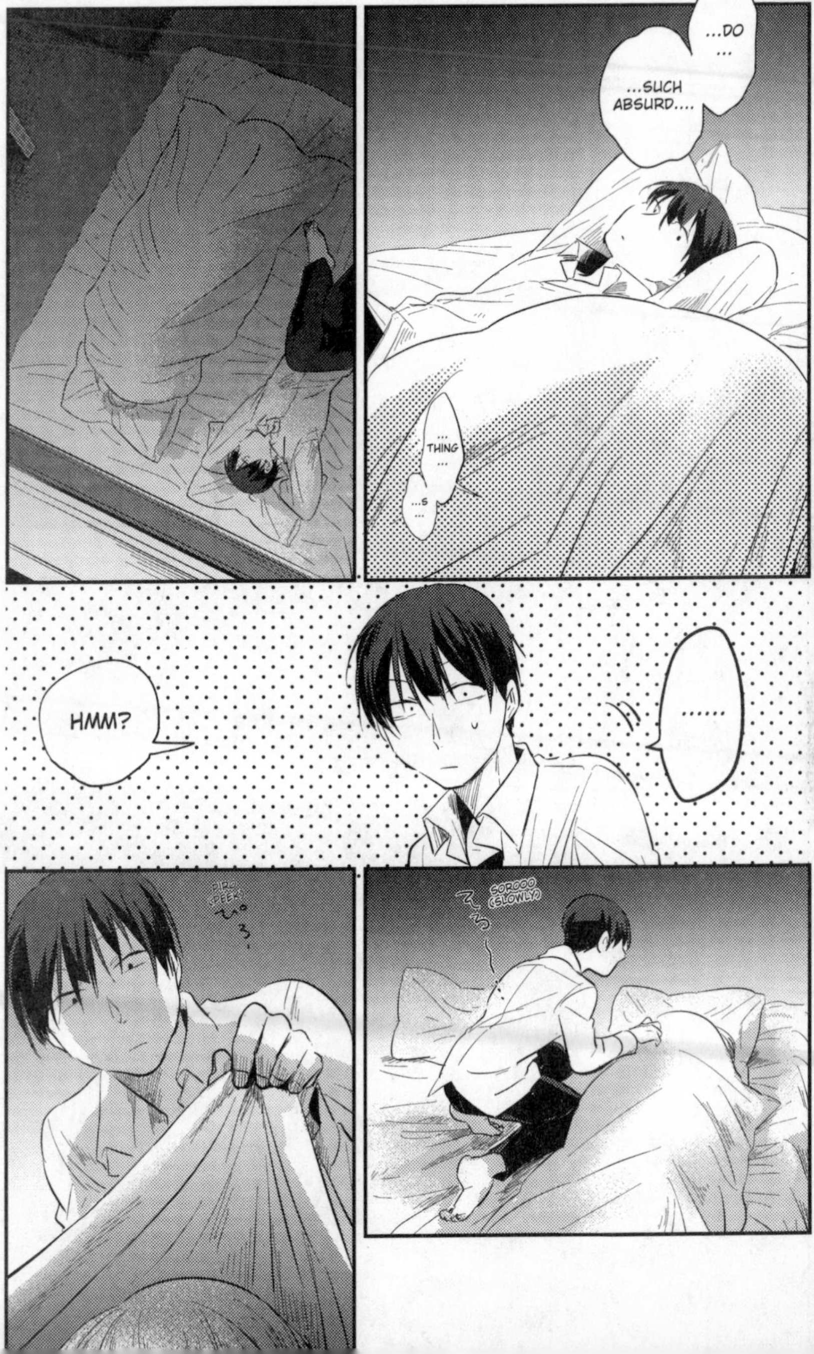
...DO ...
...SUCH ABSURD....
... THING ...
...S ...
......
HMM?
SOROOO (SLOWLY)
PIRO (PEEK)

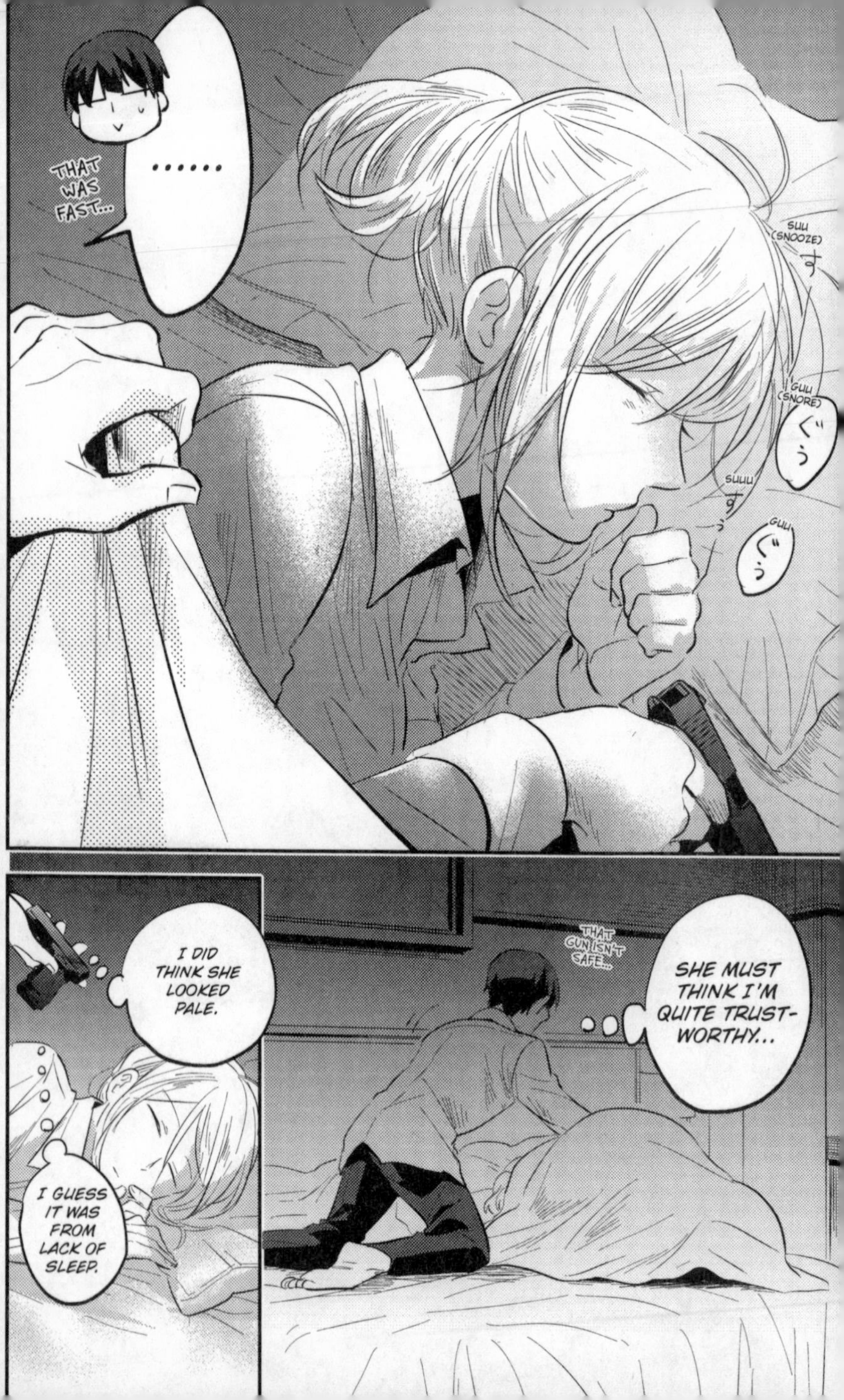
......
THAT WAS FAST...
SUU (SNOOZE) す
GUU (SNORE) ぐぅ
SUUU すぅ
GUU ぐぅ
SHE MUST THINK I'M QUITE TRUST-WORTHY...
THAT GUN ISN'T SAFE...
I DID THINK SHE LOOKED PALE.
I GUESS IT WAS FROM LACK OF SLEEP.

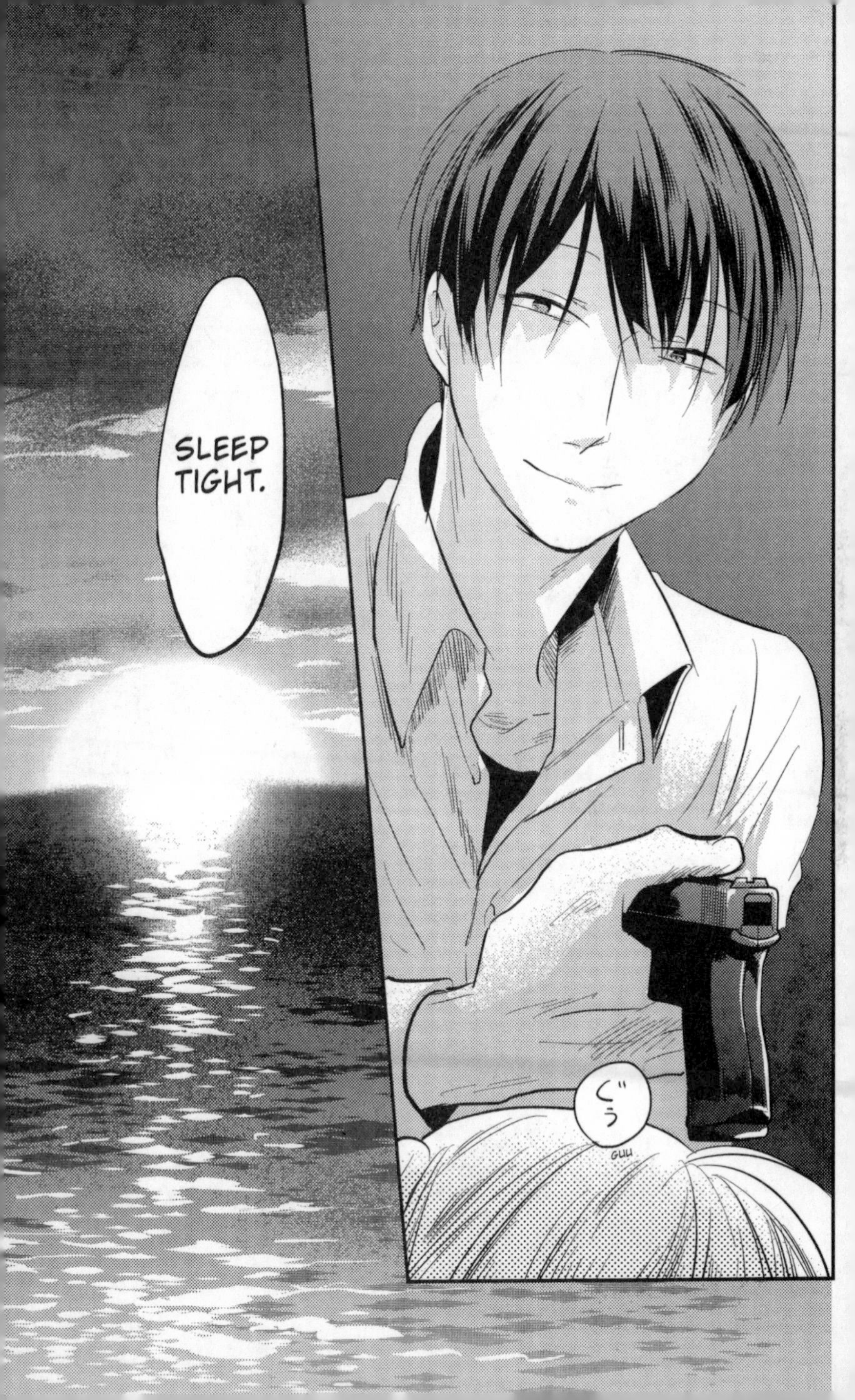
SLEEP TIGHT.
ぐぅ
GUU

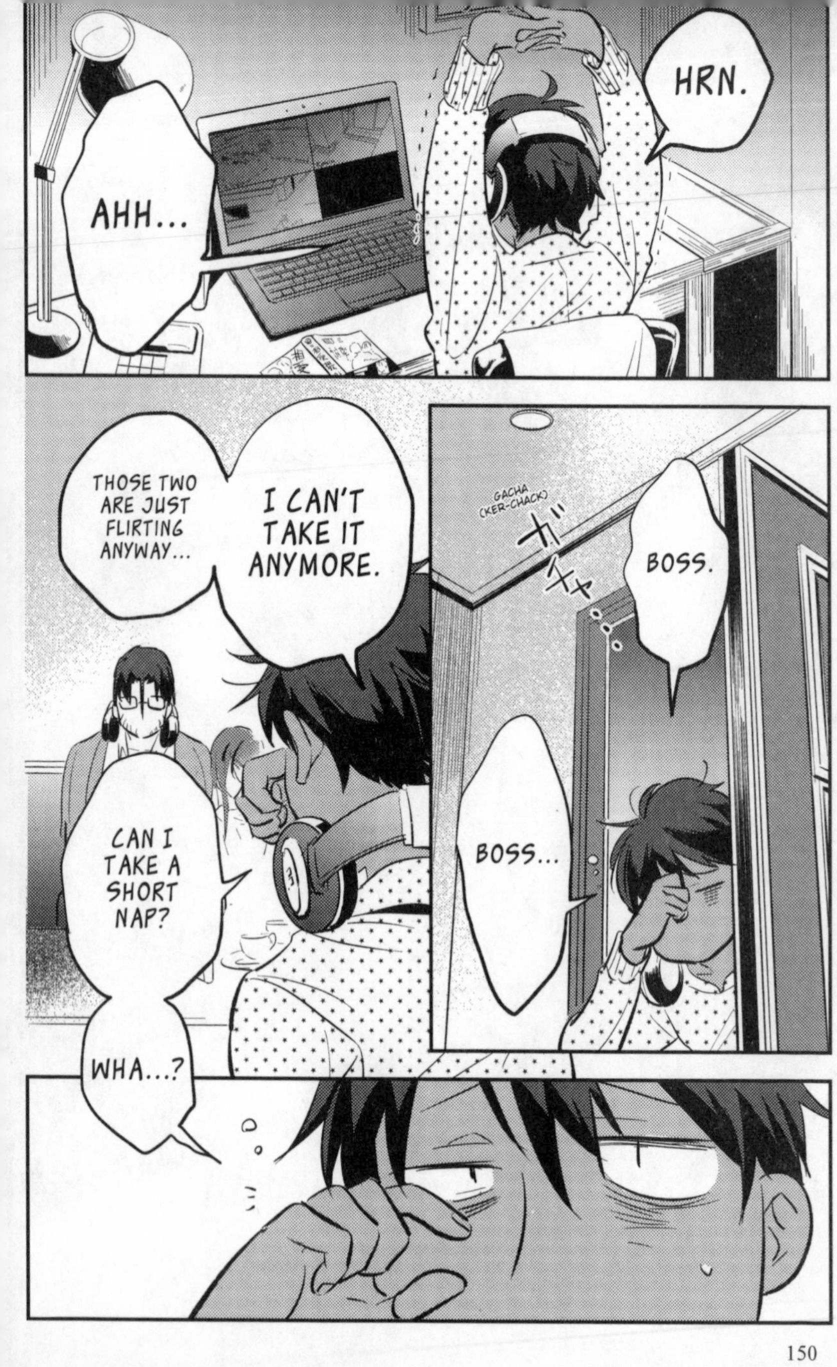
HRN.
AHH...
GACHA (KER-CHACK)
BOSS.
BOSS...
I CAN'T TAKE IT ANYMORE.
THOSE TWO ARE JUST FLIRTING ANYWAY...
CAN I TAKE A SHORT NAP?
WHA...?

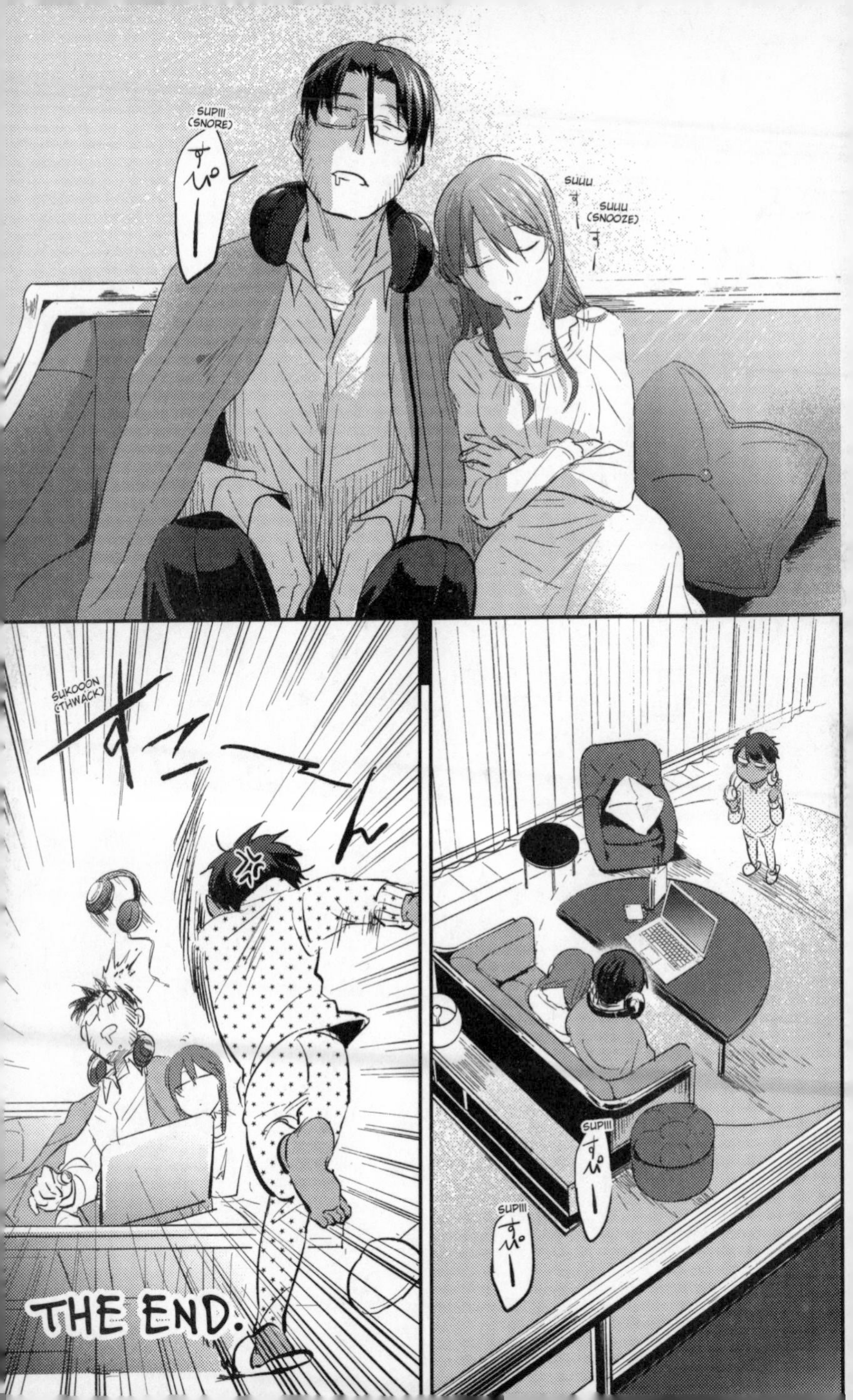
SUPIII (SNORE)
すぴー
SUUU
すー
SUUU (SNOOZE)
すー
SUPIII
すぴー
SUPIII
すぴー
SUKOOON (THWACK)
すこーん
THE END.

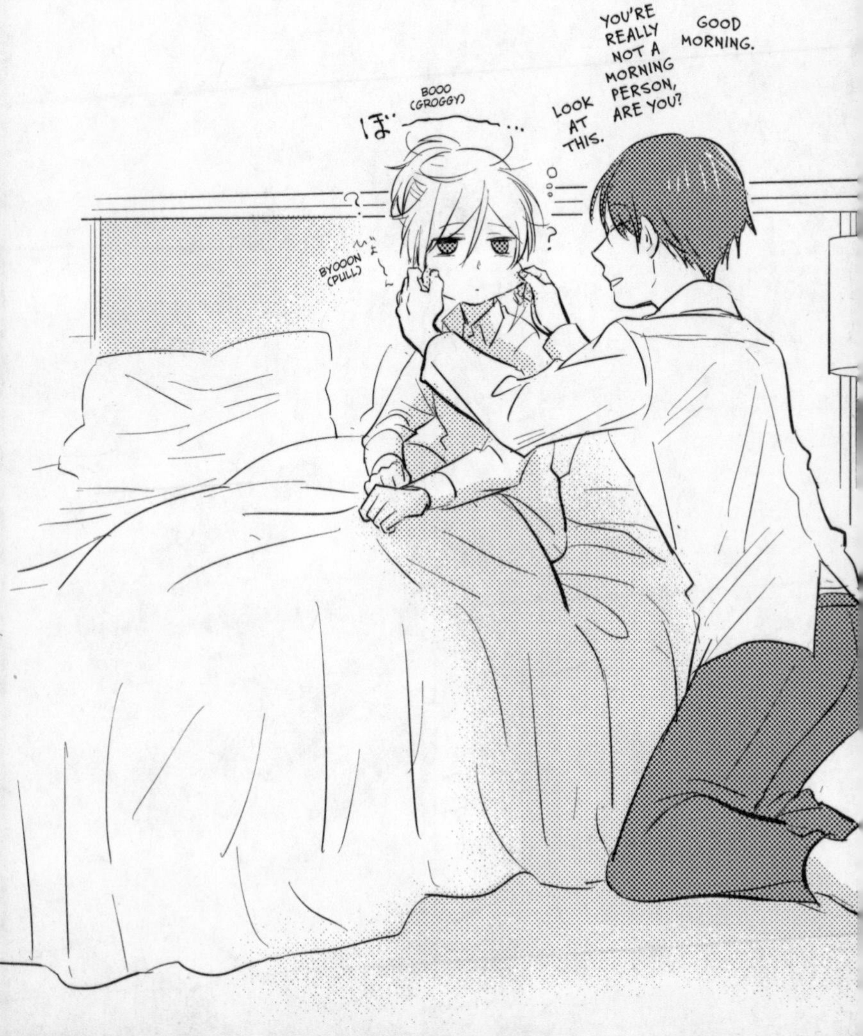
GOOD MORNING.
YOU'RE REALLY NOT A MORNING PERSON, ARE YOU?
LOOK AT THIS.
ぼー…
BOOO (GROGGY)
BYOOON (PULL)

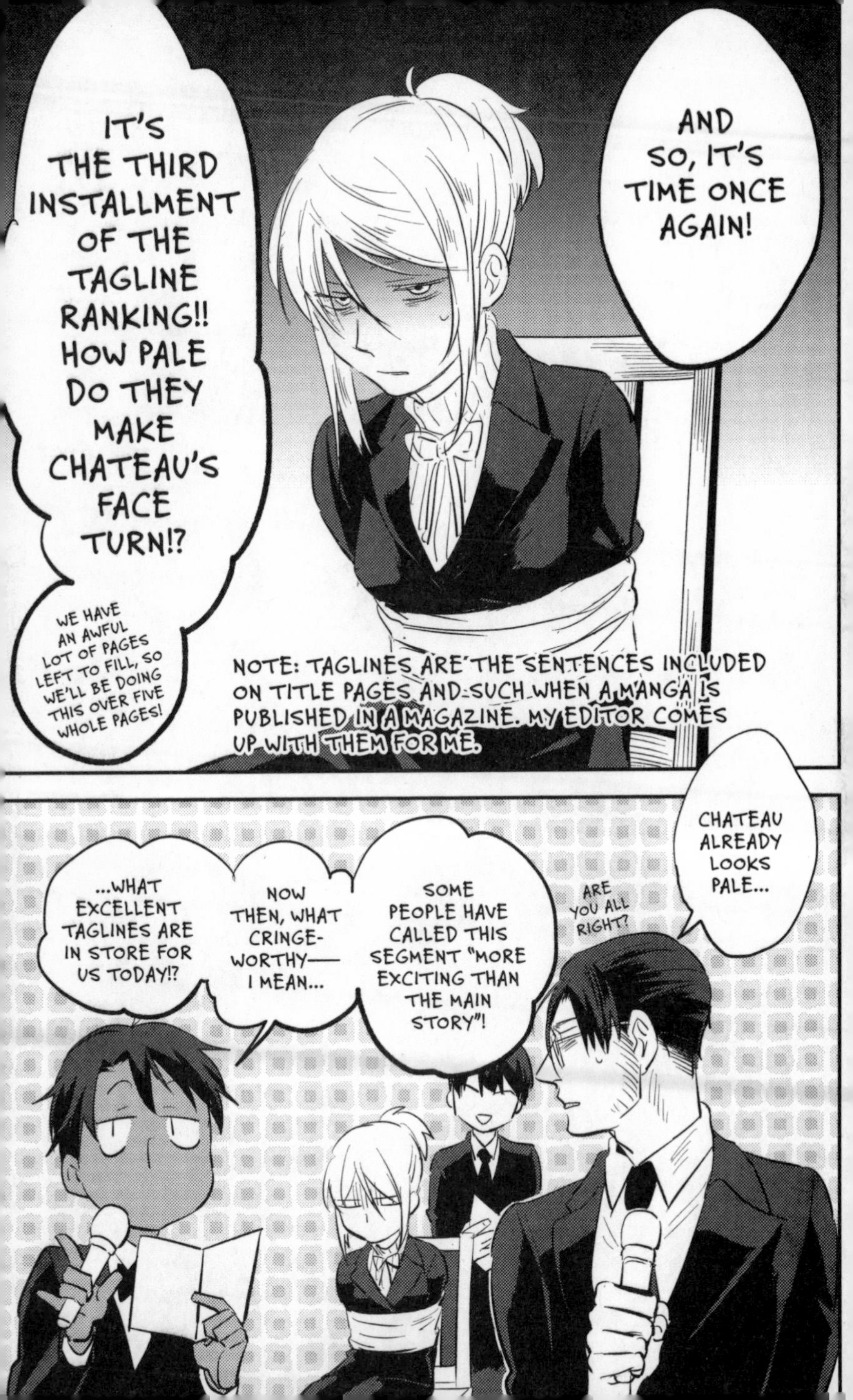
AND SO, IT'S TIME ONCE AGAIN!
IT'S THE THIRD INSTALLMENT OF THE TAGLINE RANKING!! HOW PALE DO THEY MAKE CHATEAU'S FACE TURN!?
WE HAVE AN AWFUL LOT OF PAGES LEFT TO FILL, SO WE'LL BE DOING THIS OVER FIVE WHOLE PAGES!
NOTE: TAGLINES ARE THE SENTENCES INCLUDED ON TITLE PAGES AND SUCH WHEN A MANGA IS PUBLISHED IN A MAGAZINE. MY EDITOR COMES UP WITH THEM FOR ME.
CHATEAU ALREADY LOOKS PALE...
ARE YOU ALL RIGHT?
SOME PEOPLE HAVE CALLED THIS SEGMENT "MORE EXCITING THAN THE MAIN STORY"!
NOW THEN, WHAT CRINGE-WORTHY— I MEAN...
...WHAT EXCELLENT TAGLINES ARE IN STORE FOR US TODAY!?

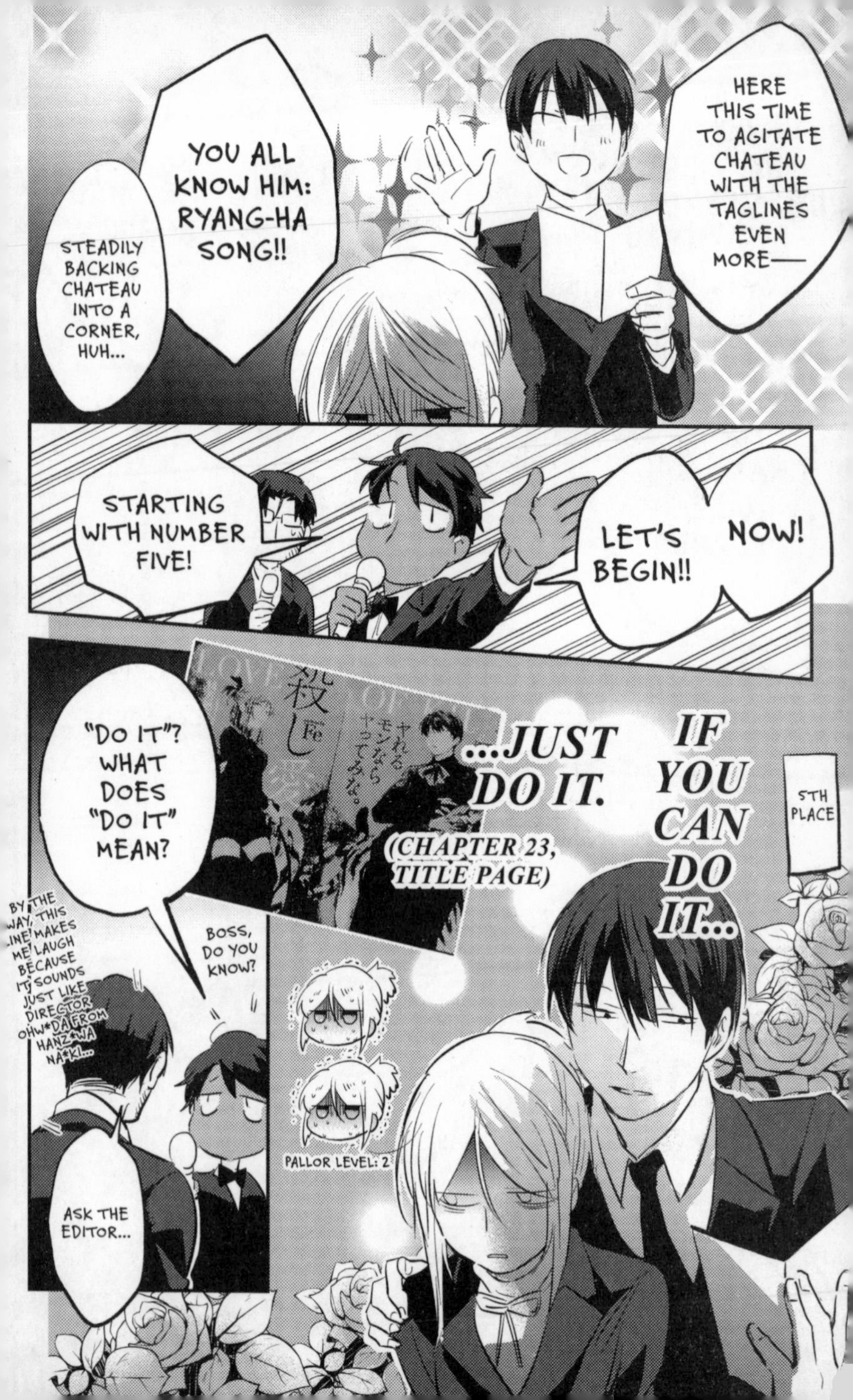
HERE THIS TIME TO AGITATE CHATEAU WITH THE TAGLINES EVEN MORE—
YOU ALL KNOW HIM: RYANG-HA SONG!!
STEADILY BACKING CHATEAU INTO A CORNER, HUH...
NOW!
LET'S BEGIN!!
STARTING WITH NUMBER FIVE!
5TH PLACE
IF YOU CAN DO IT...
...JUST DO IT.
(CHAPTER 23, TITLE PAGE)
やれるモンならやってみな。
PALLOR LEVEL: 2
"DO IT"? WHAT DOES "DO IT" MEAN?
BOSS, DO YOU KNOW?
ASK THE EDITOR...
BY THE WAY, THIS LINE MAKES ME LAUGH BECAUSE IT SOUNDS JUST LIKE DIRECTOR OHW*DA FROM HANZ*WA NA*KI...

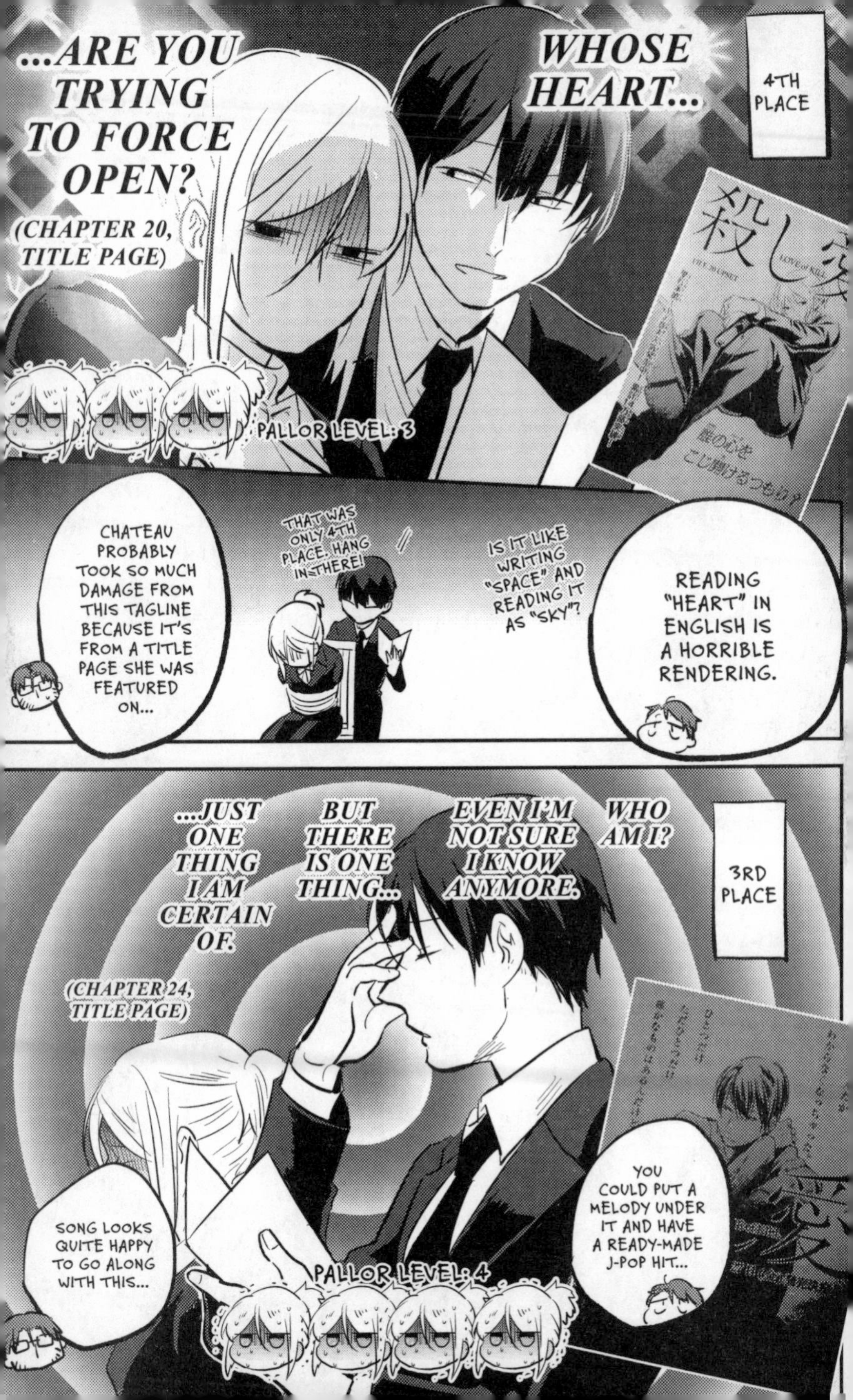
4TH PLACE
WHOSE HEART...
...ARE YOU TRYING TO FORCE OPEN?
(CHAPTER 20, TITLE PAGE)
PALLOR LEVEL: 3
READING "HEART" IN ENGLISH IS A HORRIBLE RENDERING.
IS IT LIKE WRITING "SPACE" AND READING IT AS "SKY"?
THAT WAS ONLY 4TH PLACE, HANG IN THERE!
CHATEAU PROBABLY TOOK SO MUCH DAMAGE FROM THIS TAGLINE BECAUSE IT'S FROM A TITLE PAGE SHE WAS FEATURED ON...
3RD PLACE
WHO AM I?
EVEN I'M NOT SURE I KNOW ANYMORE.
BUT THERE IS ONE THING...
...JUST ONE THING I AM CERTAIN OF.
(CHAPTER 24, TITLE PAGE)
YOU COULD PUT A MELODY UNDER IT AND HAVE A READY-MADE J-POP HIT...
PALLOR LEVEL: 4
SONG LOOKS QUITE HAPPY TO GO ALONG WITH THIS...

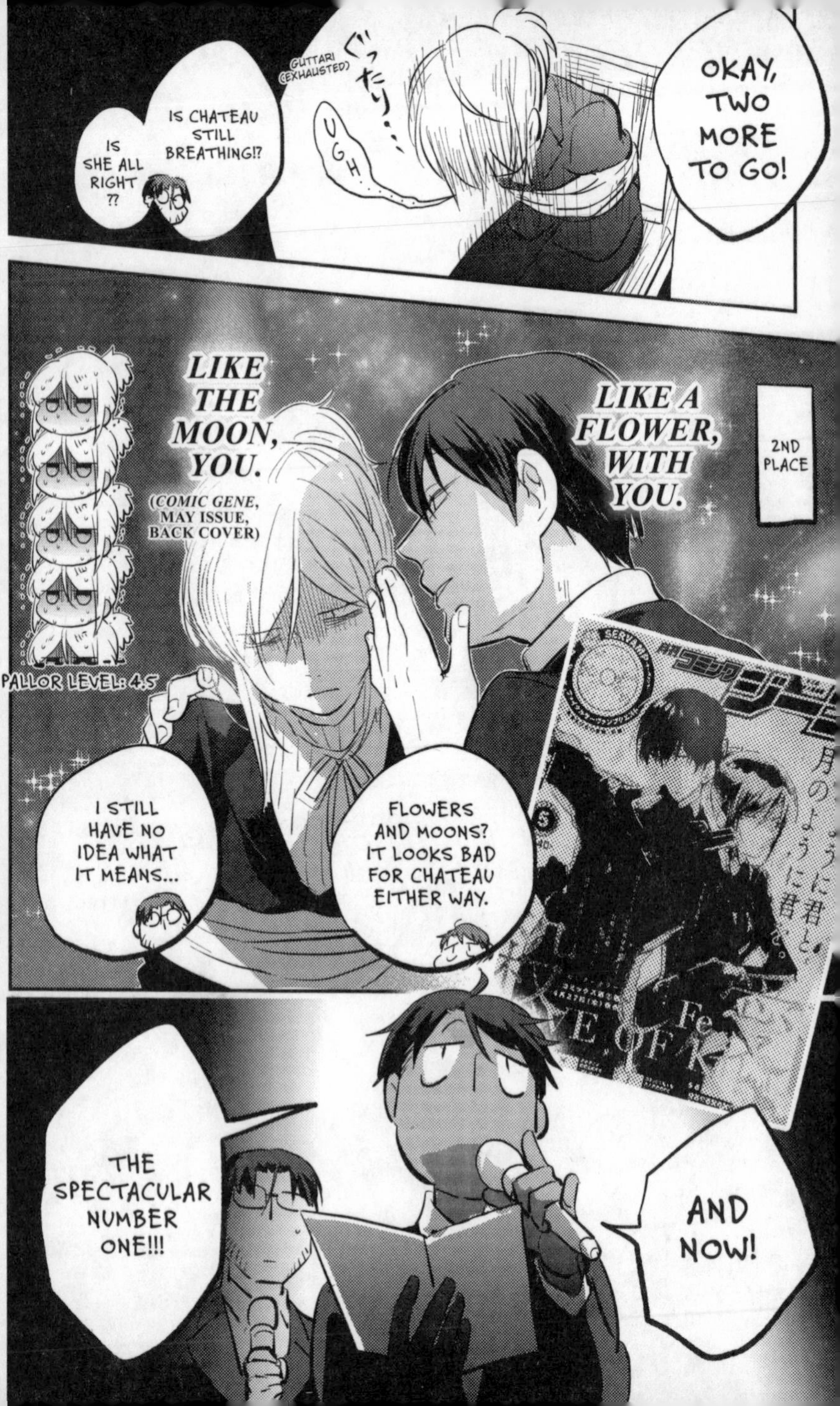
OKAY, TWO MORE TO GO!
UGH...
ぐったり・・・
GUTTARI (EXHAUSTED)
IS CHATEAU STILL BREATHING!?
IS SHE ALL RIGHT ??
2ND PLACE
LIKE A FLOWER, WITH YOU.
LIKE THE MOON, YOU.
(COMIC GENE, MAY ISSUE, BACK COVER)
月のように君と
PALLOR LEVEL: 4.5
FLOWERS AND MOONS? IT LOOKS BAD FOR CHATEAU EITHER WAY.
I STILL HAVE NO IDEA WHAT IT MEANS...
AND NOW!
THE SPECTACULAR NUMBER ONE!!!

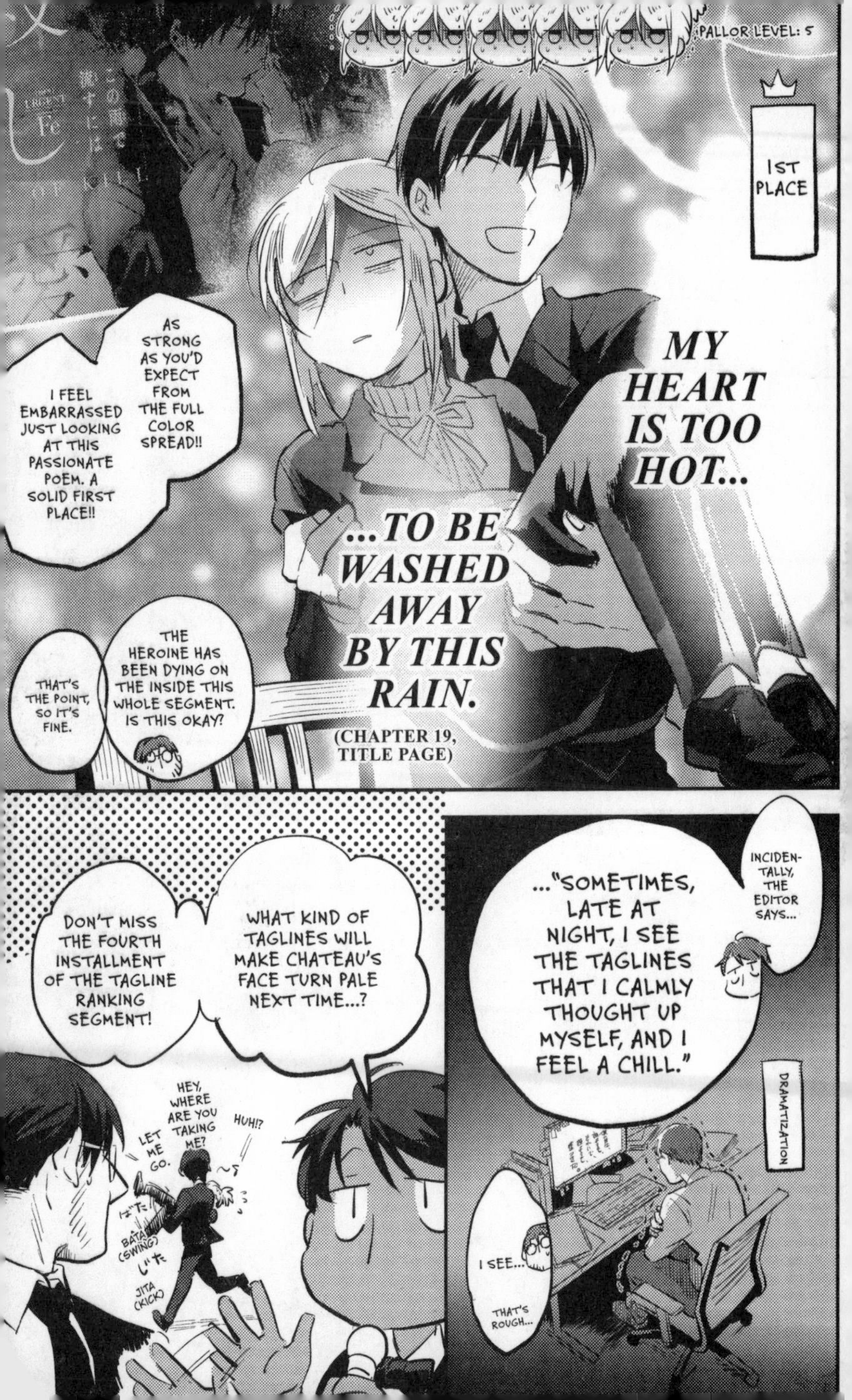
PALLOR LEVEL: 5
1ST PLACE
MY HEART IS TOO HOT...
...TO BE WASHED AWAY BY THIS RAIN.
(CHAPTER 19, TITLE PAGE)
AS STRONG AS YOU'D EXPECT FROM THE FULL COLOR SPREAD!!
I FEEL EMBARRASSED JUST LOOKING AT THIS PASSIONATE POEM. A SOLID FIRST PLACE!!
THE HEROINE HAS BEEN DYING ON THE INSIDE THIS WHOLE SEGMENT. IS THIS OKAY?
THAT'S THE POINT, SO IT'S FINE.
INCIDENTALLY, THE EDITOR SAYS...
..."SOMETIMES, LATE AT NIGHT, I SEE THE TAGLINES THAT I CALMLY THOUGHT UP MYSELF, AND I FEEL A CHILL."
DRAMATIZATION
I SEE...
THAT'S ROUGH...
WHAT KIND OF TAGLINES WILL MAKE CHATEAU'S FACE TURN PALE NEXT TIME...?
DON'T MISS THE FOURTH INSTALLMENT OF THE TAGLINE RANKING SEGMENT!
HUH!?
HEY, WHERE ARE YOU TAKING ME?
LET ME GO.
ばた
BATA (SWING)
じた
JITA (KICK)

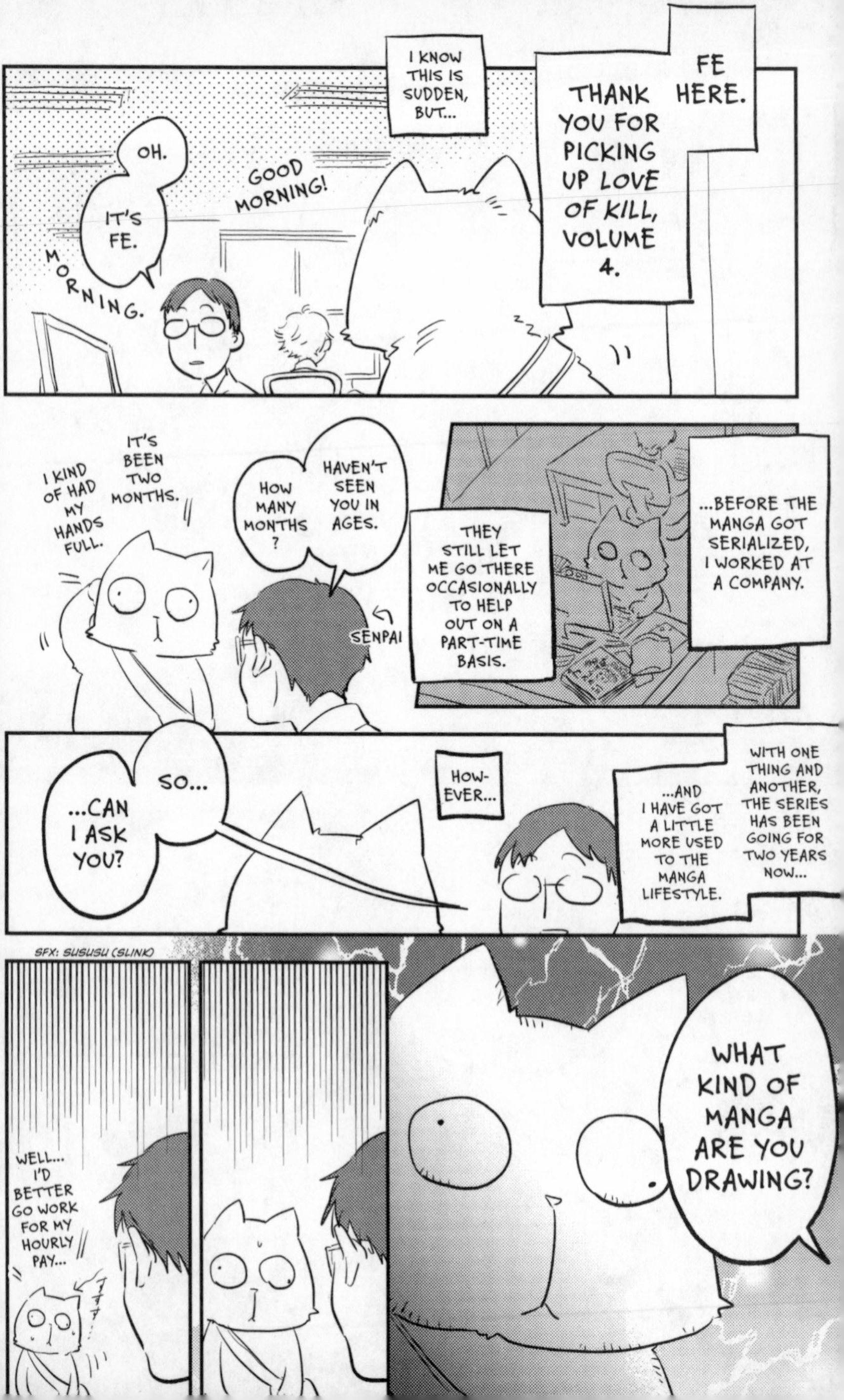
FE HERE.
THANK YOU FOR PICKING UP LOVE OF KILL, VOLUME 4.
I KNOW THIS IS SUDDEN, BUT...
GOOD MORNING!
OH.
IT'S FE.
MORNING.
...BEFORE THE MANGA GOT SERIALIZED, I WORKED AT A COMPANY.
THEY STILL LET ME GO THERE OCCASIONALLY TO HELP OUT ON A PART-TIME BASIS.
HAVEN'T SEEN YOU IN AGES.
HOW MANY MONTHS?
SENPAI
IT'S BEEN TWO MONTHS.
I KIND OF HAD MY HANDS FULL.
WITH ONE THING AND ANOTHER, THE SERIES HAS BEEN GOING FOR TWO YEARS NOW...
...AND I HAVE GOT A LITTLE MORE USED TO THE MANGA LIFESTYLE.
HOW-EVER...
SO...
...CAN I ASK YOU?
WHAT KIND OF MANGA ARE YOU DRAWING?
SFX: SUSUSU (SLINK)
WELL... I'D BETTER GO WORK FOR MY HOURLY PAY...

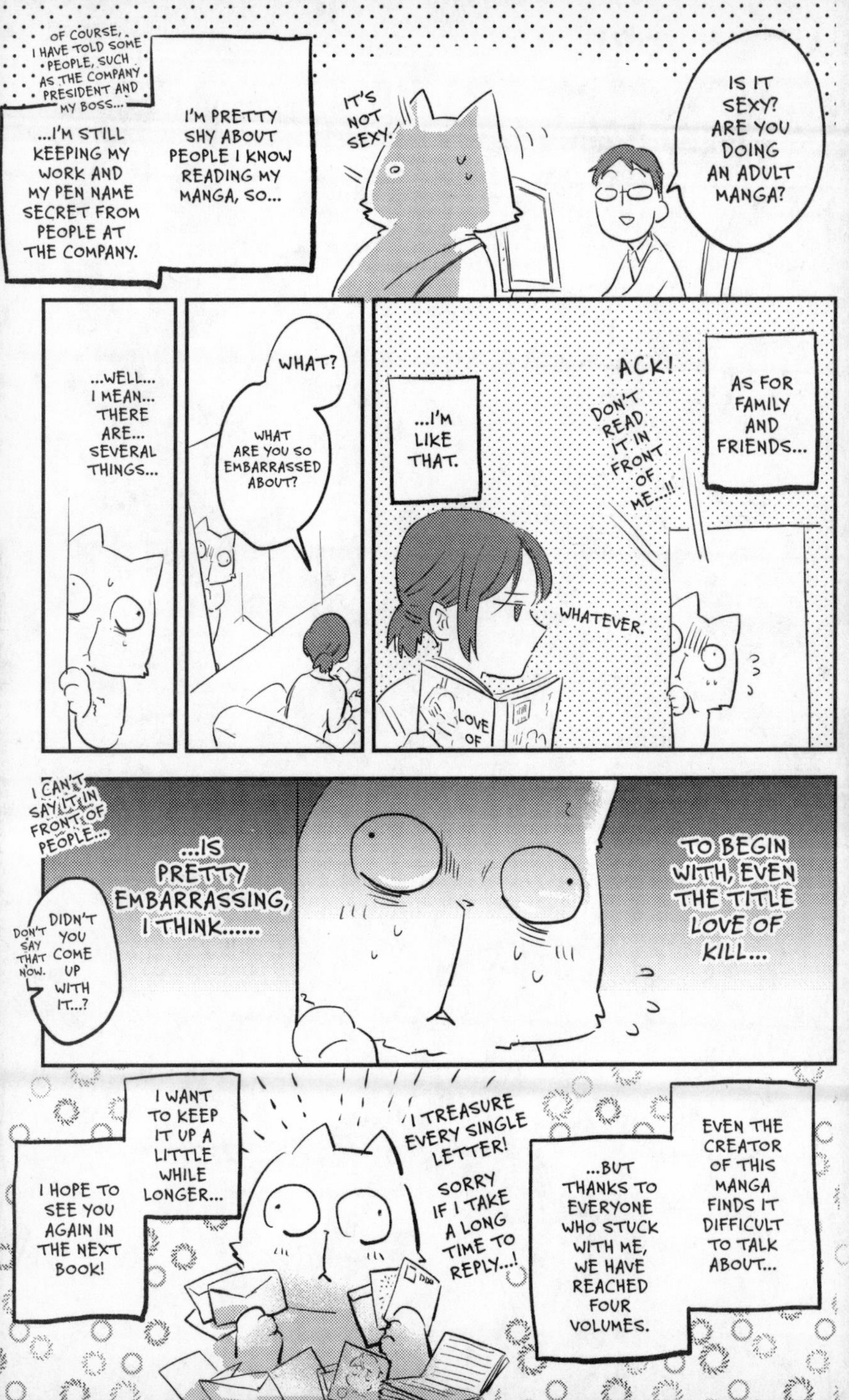
IS IT SEXY? ARE YOU DOING AN ADULT MANGA?
IT'S NOT SEXY.
I'M PRETTY SHY ABOUT PEOPLE I KNOW READING MY MANGA, SO...
OF COURSE, I HAVE TOLD SOME PEOPLE, SUCH AS THE COMPANY PRESIDENT AND MY BOSS...
...I'M STILL KEEPING MY WORK AND MY PEN NAME SECRET FROM PEOPLE AT THE COMPANY.
AS FOR FAMILY AND FRIENDS...
ACK!
DON'T READ IT IN FRONT OF ME...!!
...I'M LIKE THAT.
WHATEVER.
LOVE OF
WHAT?
WHAT ARE YOU SO EMBARRASSED ABOUT?
...WELL... I MEAN... THERE ARE... SEVERAL THINGS...
TO BEGIN WITH, EVEN THE TITLE LOVE OF KILL...
...IS PRETTY EMBARRASSING, I THINK......
I CAN'T SAY IT IN FRONT OF PEOPLE...
DIDN'T YOU COME UP WITH IT...?
DON'T SAY THAT NOW.
EVEN THE CREATOR OF THIS MANGA FINDS IT DIFFICULT TO TALK ABOUT...
...BUT THANKS TO EVERYONE WHO STUCK WITH ME, WE HAVE REACHED FOUR VOLUMES.
I TREASURE EVERY SINGLE LETTER!
SORRY IF I TAKE A LONG TIME TO REPLY...!
I WANT TO KEEP IT UP A LITTLE WHILE LONGER...
I HOPE TO SEE YOU AGAIN IN THE NEXT BOOK!

AFTERWORD

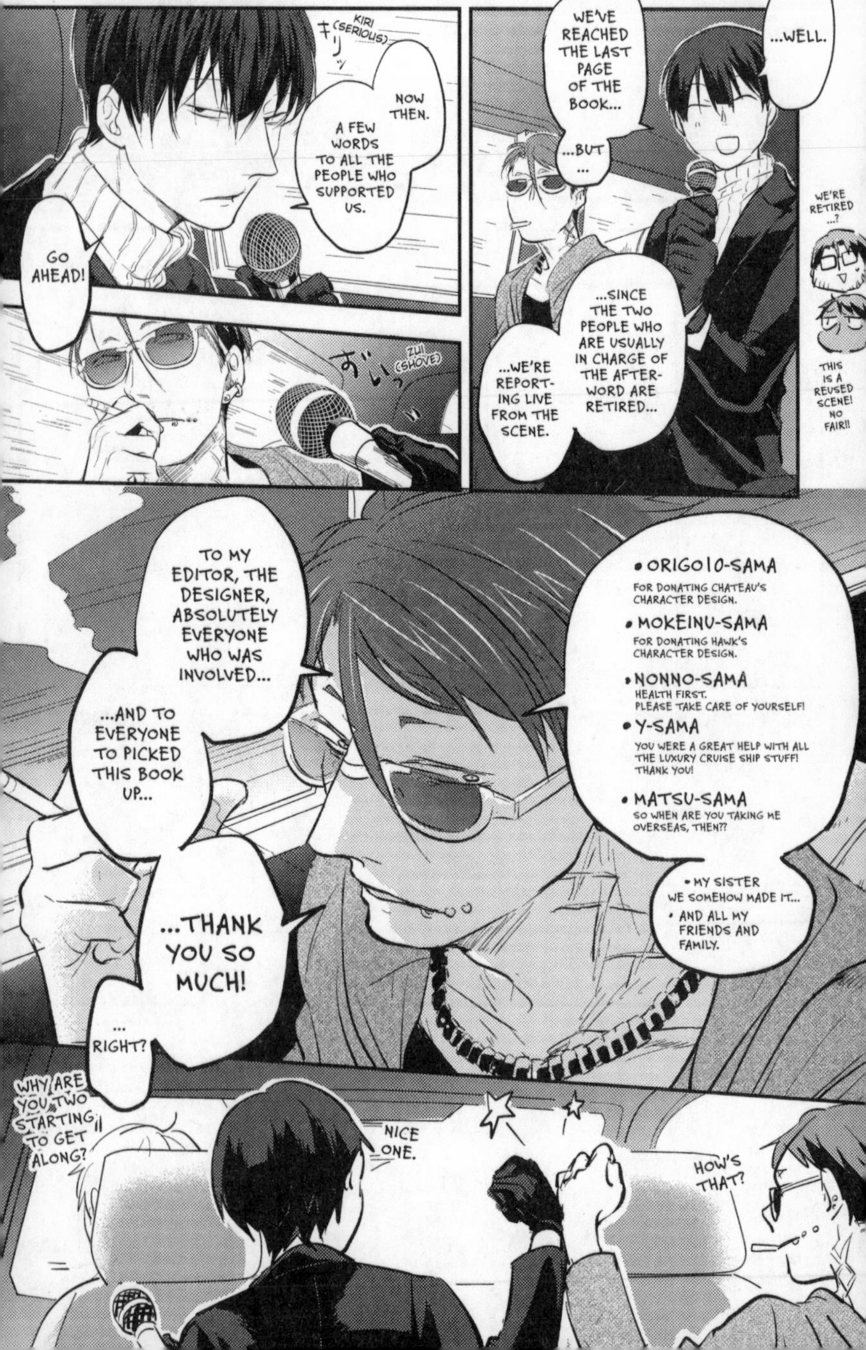
WE'RE RETIRED ...?
THIS IS A REUSED SCENE! NO FAIR!!
...WELL.
WE'VE REACHED THE LAST PAGE OF THE BOOK...
...BUT ...
...SINCE THE TWO PEOPLE WHO ARE USUALLY IN CHARGE OF THE AFTER-WORD ARE RETIRED...
...WE'RE REPORT-ING LIVE FROM THE SCENE.
KIRI (SERIOUS)
NOW THEN.
A FEW WORDS TO ALL THE PEOPLE WHO SUPPORTED US.
GO AHEAD!
ZUI (SHOVE)
• ORIGO10-SAMA
FOR DONATING CHATEAU'S CHARACTER DESIGN.
• MOKEINU-SAMA
FOR DONATING HAWK'S CHARACTER DESIGN.
• NONNO-SAMA
HEALTH FIRST. PLEASE TAKE CARE OF YOURSELF!
• Y-SAMA
YOU WERE A GREAT HELP WITH ALL THE LUXURY CRUISE SHIP STUFF! THANK YOU!
• MATSU-SAMA
SO WHEN ARE YOU TAKING ME OVERSEAS, THEN??
• MY SISTER
WE SOMEHOW MADE IT...
• AND ALL MY FRIENDS AND FAMILY.
TO MY EDITOR, THE DESIGNER, ABSOLUTELY EVERYONE WHO WAS INVOLVED...
...AND TO EVERYONE TO PICKED THIS BOOK UP...
...THANK YOU SO MUCH!
... RIGHT?
HOW'S THAT?
NICE ONE.
WHY ARE YOU TWO STARTING TO GET ALONG?

TRANSLATION NOTES

PAGE 154
Director Owada, from the Japanese TV series *Hanzawa Naoki*, in a famous scene, forces the titular character to prostrate himself in apology while shounting the now famous line: "Do it! Hanzawa! I'm telling you to bow down!"

PAGE 155
The word for "heart" is normally pronounced *kokoro* in Japanese, but in the tagline, it is actually read as "heart," the English pronunciation of the word.

Indian Guy compares changing the pronunciation of "heart" with reading the word for "space" (pronounced *uchuu*) as *sora*, which is also the word for "sky."

PAGE 158
Senpai refers to one's senior at school or in the workplace: In this case, a more experienced coworker at the author's part-time job.

INSIDE COVER
Take away the *W*s from "window" and you're left with "indo," which means "India." It's also a big part of Indian Guy's nickname in Japanese: *Indo-kun*.

LOVE -OF- KILL 04

Fe

Translation: Eleanor Ruth Summers   **Lettering: Chiho Christie**

KOROSHIAI Vol. 4
© Fe 2017
First published in Japan in 2017 by KADOKAWA CORPORATION, Tokyo.
English translation rights arranged with KADOKAWA CORPORATION, Tokyo, through Tuttle-Mori Agency, Inc., Tokyo.

English translation © 2021 by Yen Press, LLC

Yen Press
150 West 30th Street, 19th Floor
New York, NY 10001

Visit us at yenpress.com
facebook.com/yenpress
twitter.com/yenpress
yenpress.tumblr.com
instagram.com/yenpress

First Yen Press Edition: September 2021

Yen Press is an imprint of Yen Press, LLC.
The Yen Press name and logo are trademarks of Yen Press, LLC.

The publisher is not responsible for websites (or their content) that are not owned by the publisher.

Library of Congress Control Number: 2020951788

ISBNs: 978-1-9753-2545-9 (paperback)
        978-1-9753-2546-6 (ebook)

10 9 8 7 6 5 4 3 2 1

WOR

Printed in the United States of America